SLAVES FOR PEANUTS

SLAVES FOR PEANUTS

A STORY OF CONQUEST, LIBERATION, AND A CROP THAT CHANGED HISTORY

Jori Lewis

THE
NEW
PRESS

NEW YORK
LONDON

Requests for permission to reproduce selections from this book should be made
through our website: https://thenewpress.com/contact.

Published in the United States by The New Press, New York, 2022
Distributed by Two Rivers Distribution

ISBN 978-1-62097-156-7 (hc)
ISBN 978-1-62097-157-4 (ebook)
CIP data is available

The New Press publishes books that promote and enrich public discussion and
understanding of the issues vital to our democracy and to a more equitable world.
These books are made possible by the enthusiasm of our readers; the support of a
committed group of donors, large and small; the collaboration of our many partners in
the independent media and the not-for-profit sector; booksellers, who often hand-sell
New Press books; librarians; and above all by our authors.

www.thenewpress.com

Composition by dix!
This book was set in Palatino Linotype

Printed in the United States of America

10 9 8 7 6 5 4 3 2 1

Contents

Part VIII

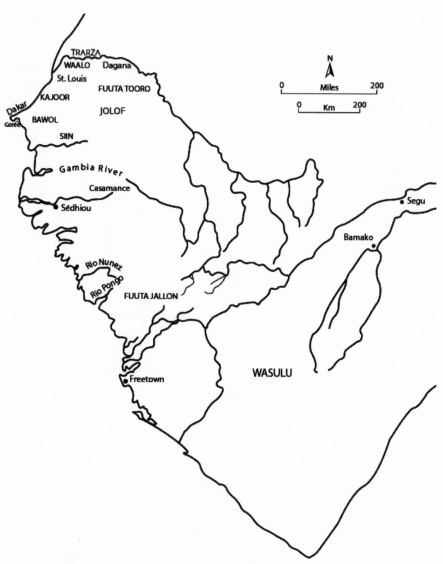

TRARZA
WAALO   Dagana
St. Louis
                FUUTA TOORO
Dakar   KAJOOR
Gorée   JOLOF
        BAWOL
            SIIN
        Gambia River
            Casamance
        Sédhiou
            Rio Nunez
            Rio Pongo
                FUUTA JALLON
            Freetown

Segu
Bamako

WASULU

N

0   Miles   200
0   Km   200

Western Africa

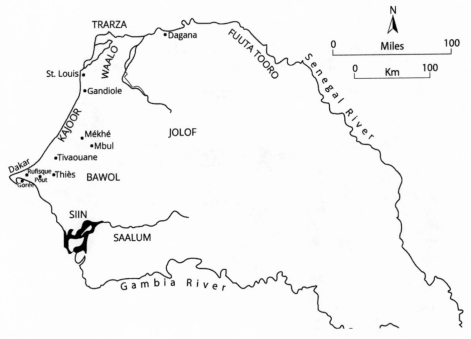

Senegambia

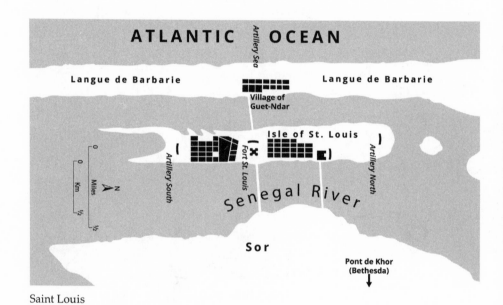

ATLANTIC OCEAN

Langue de Barbarie

Langue de Barbarie

Village of
Guet-Ndar

Isle of St. Louis

Fort St. Louis

Artillery Sea

Artillery South

Artillery North

Senegal River

Sor

Pont de Khor
(Bethesda)

N

Miles

Km

0

0

½

½

Saint Louis

Preface

I had never seen a peanut grow until I went to Senegal. I'm told that Papa Lewis, my great-grandfather, had grown peanuts on his Arkansas farm, along with okra and corn, soybeans and cotton, but he died long before I was born. His son, my grandfather's elder brother, must have predicted what was coming for American agriculture early on, and pulled out his mixed cropping system to focus on soy and cattle alone.

I still associate peanuts with that Arkansas family, though, because I remember always coming back from our vacations there with bags of freshly roasted peanuts nestled in their tan shells, but I guess we bought them at someone else's farm stand. Peanut snacking was a regular occupation as we drove the seven or eight hours back to Illinois, cracking open the shells to pop the peanuts into our mouths. Sometimes I would suck on the shell for extra salt while I stared out the window, watching the topography change: from the rice fields that sat low along the rivers; to the spiky hills of the Ozarks, half forest and half rock; and finally back to the flat landscapes I knew best, a glance at the horizon yielding unvarying glimpses of lonely farm houses in the middle of fields of corn whose stalks had grown twice as tall as any man.

Those flat vistas from my childhood always flash through my mind on my trips through Senegal's main agricultural zones, where plots of millet and peanuts occupy a procession of fields broken up only by a tree here or there, or a parade of wandering cows. It was in one such field that I first espied the peanut's tiny flowers, the color of sunshine and so similar in shade and size, if not in form, to the buttercups I used to pick in our yard as a child. Nothing else was familiar, though:

not the horse-drawn plows, not the sight of people bending to harvest peanuts by hand, not the work songs of the men who came from
Guinea-Bissau to separate the stems and leaves from the shells, not the
great mound of peanuts outside the peanut oil factory—piled so high it
could block out the sun.

I had been interested in how something as humble as the peanut
had acted as the motor of the Senegalese economy for so long; for more
than a century this small country had been one of the top producers of
the oily legume in the world. It was only an offhand comment by a future ex-boyfriend, an agronomist, that pushed me down a slightly different path. One day, he was telling me about one of the villages where
he worked, where the farmers were organizing a collective. They had
decided to exclude a smart and capable man from a leadership position, a man I had met on trips to the region, who was the person ob-
jectively most qualified for the job. They had excluded him because he
was known to be descended from people who had once been enslaved.
I flinched when I heard this. As a descendant of the enslaved myself, I
found it both painful to hear about this discrimination and difficult to
understand.

In trying to make sense of this, in trying to understand the reasons
and justifications, I started to search for other descendants of slavery, both in those peanut lands and in regions farther afield: in mud
houses in the village, in reed-lined fields that hugged the river, and in
high-rise apartments in Dakar. Eventually, my search and attempt to
find out more led me to a series of historical records.

I would have liked to say that I was able to resurrect the voices
of those who had been enslaved. But writing a historical narrative
about the enslaved is complicated because there are multiple layers
of silences. There is the fundamental silencing of Indigenous voices
in the colonial archives, which privilege those of European officials.
And many of the available epic poems or oral histories that have been
passed from generation to generation often tell the stories of society's
elites—the kings, nobles, warriors, and important religious leaders.
Women rarely feature, and the enslaved almost never; they are muted,

and the distance of a century reveals only flickering, spectral forms. How do we tell the stories of people that history forgets and the present avoids?

I have tried here to uncover a handful of stories about a handful of people. I wish I could have done more.

Part I

1

A Shelter for Runaway Slaves

On May 27, 1879, the official weekly newspaper of the colony of Senegal noted that a certain Moussa Sidibé had claimed his freedom at the age of twenty-five. *Le Moniteur du Sénégal et Dépendances* regularly revealed the names of the formerly enslaved men, women, and children who had been given their freedom papers in the past month. It was official business of the court, nestled between colonial decrees, bankruptcy announcements, weather tables, and ads for ferruginous lemonade and quinine elixirs. The newspaper listed them by date of liberation and included their ages, the name of the person who had registered them, and their destination. In the case of minors—for many of the newly freed were children—the destination was a person; a child would be entrusted to a mother, a father, or a guardian. For an adult former captive, though, the destination was figurative.

For Moussa Sidibé on May 27, 1879, the newspaper listed him as "delivered to himself."

There were at least two other Moussa Sidibés listed as claiming their freedom in 1879: a forty-year-old who had been liberated on January 3 and a thirty-year-old on August 12. But were any of these Moussa Sidibés the one who was a younger man, just twenty-one, when he fled to the colonial capital of Saint Louis, looking for his freedom?

That Moussa Sidibé had come from the neighboring kingdom of Kajoor, where, he said, he had been enslaved for the past five years. "I was obliged to serve an excessively harsh master," he later said, "who made every effort to make my life bitter."

France first abolished slavery in some of its colonies in 1794. It was a move borne more out of desperation than of conscience; the Jacobin government was goaded into it by an ongoing uprising of enslaved people who were seizing their freedom in Saint-Domingue, and a subsequent civil war in that colony, the "pearl of the Antilles." Saint-Domingue was one of the richest and most productive colonies in the Americas, and it exported more sugar and, hence, more wealth than most of its neighbors combined. It was a prize to be coveted; so when the rebellion broke out, the Spanish and British saw their chance to claim it for themselves. In response, the French decided to mobilize the enslaved to their side by issuing a general emancipation—a move Abraham Lincoln would copy some seventy years later. The Black army, led by a man who had himself been born a slave, Toussaint Louverture, succeeded in pushing back the British and Spanish so that France could regain a loose hold on the colony. Toussaint drafted a new constitution that codified this emancipation as a right on Saint-Domingue. It said: "Here all men are born, live, and die free and French."

When Napoleon Bonaparte came to power in France, though, he disagreed; he wanted Saint-Domingue to be French, of course, but he did not want everyone to be free. Starting in 1802, a series of laws and decrees would re-establish slavery across the French Empire. But the people of Saint-Domingue refused, resisting with all their might, even after Napoleon's forces captured and deported Toussaint Louverture to France, where he later died. The war hemorrhaged men and money until the French were forced to concede, and the colony formerly known as Saint-Domingue was born anew as the Republic of Haiti.

This Haitian Revolution called the long-established institution of slavery into question and inspired, through admiration and fear, discussions about emancipation across the Atlantic world. Memories of the slave rebellion in Haiti must have haunted legislators and parliamentarians in the United States and Great Britain and influenced them as they banned the trans-Atlantic slave trade for their ships and citizens in the years that followed.

France issued a second and more definitive emancipation decree in

1848. It was a hasty document, pushed through the assembly at a time when its opponents were weak and fewer people were paying attention. In 1848, a wave of political revolutions swept across Europe, and in France the people overthrew the monarchy, not for the first time or the last, and formed the short-lived Second Republic.

In its early days, the provisional republican government was full of zeal and fervor for reforms; it wanted to make France live up to the promise of the French Revolution, and outlined a broad egalitarian vision for society, enshrining the motto that would become the country's touchstone: *Liberté, Egalité, Fraternité.* The abolitionist movement, after a century of churning along on the fringes, espoused by misfits, outcasts, and wide-eyed idealists, managed to get everything it wanted in the space of a few months. The new order was as swift as it was direct. It started with this stark statement: "Slavery can no longer exist on French land."

Abolition was mostly for the benefit of the faraway colonies in the Caribbean, since France's holdings in Africa were limited to a handful of trading outposts in coastal cities, more a hodgepodge of settlements than a cohesive colony, with an ever-rotating population of temporary agents for trading companies. These settlements were administered through the French navy, and both manpower and money were in too short supply to imagine any grander goal than the facilitation of commerce with the people of the interior. They waited at coastal perches situated at points between the Senegal River's mouth to Grand Bassam to Gabon. More expansive ambitions would come later, but for the moment this limited approach suited both French politicians and the treasury.

Still, if any places in sub-Saharan Africa could be called "French land" in 1848, they were Gorée, an island just off the coast of Senegal, and Saint Louis, a series of islands near the mouth of the Senegal River. Saint Louis was the residence of the colonial governor, the base of the French military in West Africa, and the headquarters of most European and mixed-race merchants who had, for centuries, traded slaves, gum arabic, hides, and ivory along the river and the Atlantic coast.

In 1848, the good people of Saint Louis may not have been trading slaves across the ocean anymore, but they still had plenty of slaves at home, cleaning their houses, working on their ships, and tending to their fields and gardens. Those enslaved people would have to receive their freedom.

Losing their own local slaves was one thing, but the 1848 abolition law included a provision that made merchants and administrators in Saint Louis shake with rage and fear: the measure said not only that slavery should be banned from French land, but also that "the principle that French soil frees the slave who touches it, is put into practice in the colonies and the Republic."

The merchants and bureaucrats were afraid because just outside of Saint Louis there was a whole continent—one where the French were guests, not hosts—where the social reality of enslavement was as entrenched as it was uncontroversial for the traditional kings, aristocrats, and religious leaders who controlled the area. The people of Saint Louis depended on the largesse of those leaders to conduct their business. It was in the interest of these merchants and administrators to maintain the equilibrium that had long reigned and to not involve themselves in the domestic matters of their foreign friends.

But wherever in the world slavery has existed, no matter its form, there has always been some resistance to it. And the discontented enslaved outside of Saint Louis, as elsewhere, often expressed that discontent in the most basic of ways.

They ran.

Saint Louis was to be a free city where no slaves would exist and where slaves could also find their liberty. It was to become a refuge.

Moussa Sidibé was just a boy when he was captured and sold into slavery in the early 1870s. It was a turbulent time in the forested region called the Wasulu where he was born, an area that stretches across modern-day southern Mali, eastern Guinea, and northern Côte d'Ivoire. Young Moussa said the cause of his enslavement was war. "One day our king received a message from a powerful chief telling him to prepare to host him," he wrote. "This is the way a king speaks when he wants to declare war on another. Although our king recognized that his enemy was superior, he would not make any offers to keep the peace as his subjects advised him."

Of course, their king lost. "Despite the courage of his valiant war-riors, the country was taken by the enemy," said Moussa. "Our king, unwilling to be delivered alive to the invaders, gathered his wives and children in a hut that he filled with gunpowder, which he then blew up; after making sure that all of them had perished, he killed himself."

The inhabitants of Moussa Sidibé's village fled into the forest. "While I was trying to escape, I was caught, it is sad to say, by people of my own nation who sold me to the Moors." The Wasulu was a prime zone for the exportation of enslaved people in the region during the second half of the nineteenth century, and a nearby town had an active slave mar-ket. Young Moussa was sold there, and then sold again, and eventually ended up in Kajoor, a kingdom not far from Saint Louis where captives were in demand to toil on farms growing millet and peanuts for trade.

Some years into his captivity, Moussa started to hear that there was a place called Saint Louis where the enslaved might become free. But, child that he was, he was easily scared off by his master's lurid tales of the town and of the evil white beings who lived there. "He told me that if I went there, the whites would catch me, fatten me with bread and sugar and then put me on a ship that would take me to a country where they would eat me roasted," wrote Moussa.

Still, one day he grew bold enough to risk it and set out on what he thought was the way to Saint Louis. It would not have been more than a few days of walking, over dunes and through forests of thorny trees, with tawny gazelles and tourmaline birds as company, and finally over the many arms of the river to reach the city.

Saint Louis is part of a riverine archipelago that sits just where the mouth of the Senegal River should meet the Atlantic Ocean. But, thou-sands of years ago, by a quirk of geology and ocean currents, the orig-inal mouth silted up and a sand spit formed parallel to the coast. It blocked the river from its final destination and redirected the mouth to parts south. For hundreds of years, the sand spit's width has been approximately what it is now, less than a mile across, but it did get lon-ger, stretching a bit farther south every year.

The sand spit walled the islands of the archipelago away from the

ocean, too, so the river flowed around them and, during the rainy season, sometimes over a few of them. That was the fate of the area where
the French first settled in 1638 on the island of Bocos, not far from the
turbulent mouth of the river and its infamous bar—an area dotted
with shifting shoals where the force of the river's flow and the ocean's
waves slam together. The bar made navigation dangerous for visitors,
which was a strategic advantage for the French, for it meant that they
could easily control access to the river and defend themselves from invaders from the sea.

Bocos flooded all too often for the French merchants who set up
comptoirs there to trade in slaves and goods with the people from up
the river or across the dunes. After about twenty years, they decided to
move to another island a bit upriver that flooded less often. The people
who ceded the island to the French merchant company called it Ndar,
but the colonists wanted to put their own stamp on it, as they so often
did; they called it Saint Louis for the French king.

Saint Louis prospered despite all the odds. It went from a sandy island with a small, fortified post to a proper city as traders and dealers
imported stone from the Canary Islands to build houses, and people
from the kingdoms up the river or across the dunes staked their tents
or built houses of mud and reeds. Eventually, the city filled the whole
island and had to expand; to the west, people established villages on
the sand spit that was the bulwark against the ocean, while to the east,
they settled on a swampy island called Sor that was surrounded by a
thick forest of mangrove trees whose branches crawled in the brackish
water like spider legs.

Soon, bridges from island to island were built, to link the major
points of the archipelago and provide for communication and commerce with the people up the river and across the dunes. Still, going to
Saint Louis took fortitude and determination.

Moussa was determined, but soon ran into trouble. "Scarcely had I
walked for a few days than I was met by some Wolofs . . . who asked
me where I was going. Not wanting them to suspect me of escaping,
I told them that my master's horses were lost." Maybe they did not

believe him? Maybe they saw in him an opportunity for themselves? "After having examined me closely, they chained my feet, repeating to me that I was not telling the truth, and that I was only a slave trying to get away from my master," Moussa later said.

The men forced Moussa in a different direction, maybe not back to his master, but not to Saint Louis.

That night, one of the men slept close to Moussa, putting his leg over the young man's body to make sure he would not slip away in the night. The other man must not have known that he was a deep sleeper, because Moussa somehow managed to escape while his captors slept.

He finally made it to Saint Louis and put his name on the list to be freed, only to be informed that he would have to wait for some three months to claim his freedom.

The status of Saint Louis as a free city was one that the colonial government preferred to downplay, and often ignore. By 1879, the colonial administration had long embraced a policy that did not make it easy for runaway slaves to obtain their freedom in Saint Louis. It was clear that the reality of life on a few islands situated on the edge of Africa did not, could not, or would not live up to the lofty principle of being a land of freedom. It was, in a way, a false promised land.

Instead, the colonial government in Saint Louis established a legal dance full of missteps and pitfalls. Runaway slaves could only get freedom papers after establishing a place of residence in Saint Louis for three months. And if, by chance, their owners should find them before those three months were up, well, that was not the problem of the colonial government.

"It was then that I heard for the first time the name of Mr. Taylor, the protector of the poor slaves," Moussa said. "I went to his house and explained to him my state; he received me."

Mr. Taylor was, in fact, the Reverend Walter Samuel Taylor, the principal pastor of the Paris Evangelical Missionary Society's outpost in Senegal and the director of an extraordinary outreach program—the Shelter for Runaway Slaves.

The mission had started helping these runaways a few years before. When Taylor later took over as leader of the mission, he expanded this outreach, seeing it as an opportunity to grow their church, as well as a moral obligation. Taylor was himself the son of enslaved people who had been freed from the hold of a slave ship, just as it was headed across the wide Atlantic Ocean to an uncertain future. "Woe unto me, a child of former slaves who were freed," Taylor wrote, "if I do not move heaven and earth to do good to the bodies and souls of the runaway slaves of Senegal!"

Taylor would hide the young man in his own home for the required ninety-day waiting period until Moussa could receive his certificate of freedom. It was just a piece of paper, a fragile document with his name, approximate age, birthplace, and the names of his parents. It said that the person described in this document had the right to be free and to "possess his own self."

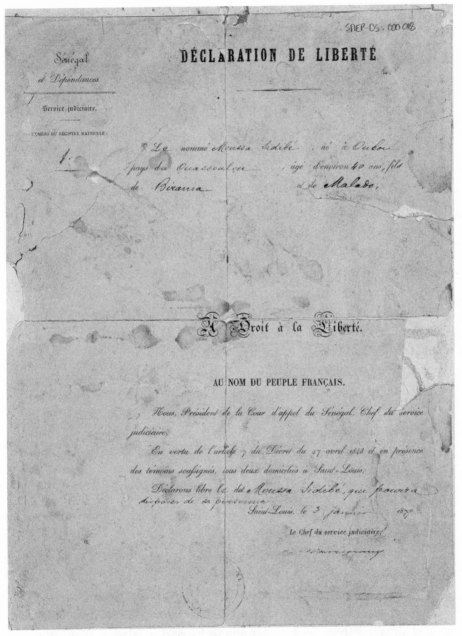

DÉCLARATION DE LIBERTÉ

Sénégal
et Dépendances.

Service judiciaire.

NUMÉRO DU REGISTRE MATRICULE :

1.

Le nommé Moussa Sidibé, né à Oulou pays du Ouassoulou, âgé d'environ 40 ans, fils de Birama et de Maledo,

A Droit à la Liberté.

AU NOM DU PEUPLE FRANÇAIS.

Nous, Président de la Cour d'appel du Sénégal, Chef du service judiciaire;

En vertu de l'article 7 du Décret du 27 avril 1848 et en présence des témoins soussignés, tous deux domiciliés à Saint-Louis;

Déclarons libre le dit Moussa Sidibé, qui pourra disposer de sa personne.

Saint-Louis, le 3 janvier 1877

Le Chef du service judiciaire,

Freedom papers for a Moussa Sidibé. *Courtesy of Defap*

2

A Crossroads

Walter Taylor's path to Saint Louis started in the 1860s, when he settled in an outpost on the Gambia River. That river, unlike the Senegal River to the north, is a true crossroads, an ecotone where the arid grasslands meet the humid forest. For generations, people came together along that river, bringing their best from lands far away—salt from the coast, kola from the forests, and cotton from the plains. The white men who came from the oceans, however, would start a process that would alter their trade and change everything.

Sailors backed by the Portuguese crown were the first Europeans to come to the Gambia River in the mid-fifteenth century. They had tried first to test out the Senegal River, but its turbulent waters scared them off from much immediate investigation. The Gambia River, however, opened its mouth several miles wide and welcomed ships into Africa's interior.

The sailors steered their lightweight caravels into the river on a search for gold and for traces of the mythical Prester John, a Christian prince who was rumored to live in the depths of Africa, an island of Christian virtue in what was, reputedly, a sea of infidels and pagans. They didn't find Prester John, or much gold either, at least not on the first trip. On previous voyages along the African coast they had found another kind of treasure; farther north, they had kidnapped people and dragged them back to Europe to be sold as slaves. Word must have gotten out about the ships of kidnappers, and by the time the first ship arrived in the Gambia River, the people there fought back. They attacked the sailors with spears, swords, and poisoned darts, and attempted to take over the ship. The Europeans soon changed their strategy; instead of kidnapping Africans, they would buy them.

The British came to the Gambia almost a century later—still looking for Prester John and still looking for gold. Richard Jobson sailed up the Gambia River in 1620 in search of gold. He didn't find any, but heard wild rumors that farther up the river, "the houses whereof are covered onely [sic] with gold." That led him to lobby the British royal family for more support.

When an African merchant called Buckor Sano offered Jobson and his crew some slaves, though, Jobson refused. "We were a people, who did not deale [sic] in any such commodities, neither did we buy or sell one another, or any that had our owne [sic] shapes," he wrote. Sano was amazed. "He seemed to marvel much at it, and told us, it [slaves] was the only merchandise they carried down into the country, where they fetch all their salt, and that they were sold there to white men, who earnestly desired them, especially such young women, as he had brought for us," wrote Jobson. Soon enough, Jobson's refusals would seem quaint as the British quest for gold was supplanted by the search for slaves. By the end of the seventeenth century, the British were exporting thousands of slaves from the Gambia River each year.

The trans-Atlantic slave trade on the Gambia and Senegal Rivers never reached the dizzying heights of the Bight of Benin, so well frequented by slavers that they called it the Slave Coast, or of West Central Africa (including Congo, Angola, and St. Helena), which alone provided close to half of all slaves who were ever transported to the Americas. Great Britain and Portugal were, by far, the biggest slavers, although French traders tried to keep up.

But in 1807, Great Britain did what had been unimaginable only a few decades before: it banned the trans-Atlantic slave trade for its citizens. The reasons why the British government abolished a trade that had been so good to its merchants are, like so many things, multiple. It could have been the larger social discourse about freedom via the French and American Revolutions, or the skillful anti-slavery lobby in London, or an attempt to stem off an increasingly restive Caribbean population that had instigated successive and sometimes successful slave revolts as in Haiti.

Some intellectuals also believed, as students of Adam Smith and the free market, that the future of the colonies would be better served with free labor since the enslaved had no incentive to work any more than they were compelled. The market forces could provide free men with better enticements such as money and goods, which would help them work harder. This theory about the free market, free trade, and capitalism sometimes—although not always—found points in common with the abolitionist movement.

Colonial administrator, writer, editor, statistician, and booster of the empire Robert Montgomery Martin was a proponent of the free-trade philosophy and an abolitionist. The abolition of slavery as an institution in the British Empire in 1833 aligned with his free-trade values. If slavery and the slave trade were to stop not just in the British holdings but everywhere, he wrote, it would benefit the economy. "The products of a vast and fertile territory, abounding in gold, ivory, timber, corn, and oil; in cotton and in silk, in spices and in fruits, in gums, drugs, and dyes, would be abundantly poured forth in exchange for the manipulations and exercise of British skill and capital."

Sometime in 1834, just as Martin was finalizing the Africa volume of his five-volume opus on *The History of the British Colonies,* he received a letter and a parcel from someone who might have had an answer for the woes of industrialists, abolitionists, and capitalists. "It may add some interest to your chapter on our African settlements if you notice the probable discoveries that may yet be made in the products of that quarter of the world, which, till very lately, was seldom visited for any more legitimate article of produce than human flesh," said the note.

Inside the parcel sat a bottle of oil, "pure golden coloured oil, with a pleasant flavour, free from the frequent rancidity of olive oil," wrote Martin.

The letter was signed by one Matthew Forster, the principal partner of a London trading house, Forster & Smith, that had substantial holdings in the British outpost on the Gambia River in West Africa, from whence this product hailed.

Forster wrote to Martin that he had great hopes that the people of Africa, instead of producing human flesh for sale, would produce another precious commodity: vegetable oils made from plants found in the tropics, like the seeds of palm trees and, like the sample in the package, something he called the ground nut.

3

A Spark, a Solution,
the Industrial Revolution

Robert Montgomery Martin would have been all the more excited by the possibilities of the unassuming bottle of oil he got in the post because nineteenth-century Europe was starving for oils and searching for them wherever they could. Traders imported tallow from the outer reaches of Russia and from as far as Australia. They killed scores of whales for the animals' fatty blubber. European traders scoured the Levant for sesame seeds and olives.

Oil, any kind of oil, was in demand because European economies were growing and oil had more uses than ever before. Over the centuries of the trans-Atlantic slave trade, European slave traders had made grand fortunes, and many more businesses had benefited from the economy that sprung up around that trade: from shipbuilders and carpenters to insurers and bankers to sugar wholesalers and coffeehouse owners. By the end of the eighteenth century, that circle of businesses had expanded to include the keystones of the Industrial Revolution.

In Britain, for example, work that was once done by animals or men was being done by machines; the spinning jenny replaced the time-intensive hand labor of whole cotton-spinning villages; threshing machines separated the wheat from the chaff instead of scores of farm laborers doing so; and steam engines powered machines in cotton mills that replaced human force. Great urban centers emerged where before there were just market towns and agricultural estates. Money that was generated by the slave trade opened cotton mills in Manchester and ironworks in Scotland; it built new steam-powered ships for the high seas and laid down railway tracks across the country; and it invested in coal mines to fuel all those mills, factories, ships, and railways.

One thing that all these machines needed—whether steam-powered engines, the wheels of a train, or the levers and pulleys in a foundry—was a little grease to help them run. The British railway system of the 1860s needed 13,000 tons of grease annually. Lards and tallows were possibilities, but they did not last long as lubricants since long exposures to heat and moisture caused them to oxidize and disintegrate.

By this time, the buyers for oil in the industrial sector had to compete with buyers for an ancient product enjoying a new flush of popularity around the same time: soap.

The first European explorers to West Africa marveled at the cultural practices of the people they found there. British gold prospector Richard Jobson praised the clean habits of the Fulbe milkmaids that he met and the milk they brought him. But we know that, as a creature of his time, Jobson was probably not so clean himself. That's because Europe in the sixteenth and seventeenth centuries, just as it was tentatively exploring the outside world, held tight to certain beliefs, notably about hygiene. And soap, which archaeologists say has been around since ancient Mesopotamians mixed leftover animal fat with ash, had by then fallen into disuse in Europe.

One provocation for its decline was the bubonic plague or the Black Death, which started decimating Europe in the fourteenth century. Some historians think that the initial epidemic may have killed between 30 percent and 60 percent of Europe's population. Outbreaks of the plague reoccurred throughout the following centuries with deadly regularity. From 1665 to 1666, an outbreak of the plague killed nearly 80,000 people in London. And in the 1720s, nearly half of the population of Marseille, France, succumbed to the disease.

The theory of disease that prevailed at the time held that miasmas—or noxious odors, mists, and vapors—may have caused these dangerous outbreaks. In 1568, the surgeon to the French king wrote explicitly about this idea, an idea translated for a British audience decades later: "Steam-baths and bath-houses should be forbidden, because when one emerges, the flesh and the whole disposition of the body are softened and the pores open, and as a result, pestiferous vapor can rapidly enter the body and cause sudden death, as has frequently been observed."

Medical professionals told people that the key to good health and the best method to resist the plague and other infections like the new "pox," syphilis, was to make one's pores invulnerable and their bodies impervious to anything that could disrupt the body's humors.

England's Elizabeth I was rumored to bathe only once a month, and her successor, James I, apparently did not bathe at all, except the occasional washing of his fingers. In seventeenth-century France, the child who would become Louis XIII did not have his first full bath until he was almost seven years old. During the Spanish Inquisition, bathing too often was a sign of heresy. Anyone charged with being "known to bathe" might be a secret Jew or Muslim, since both groups perform ritual washing.

These were societies that had little use, or at least little regular use, for soap.

In the mid-eighteenth century this started to change. The rapid pace of urbanization and industrialization exacerbated the squalid living conditions of the urban poor. More and more, the upper classes started to equate the uncleanliness of the poor with sickness, including with the spread of certain fevers and diseases. The result was an explosion of demand for soap both for personal hygiene and for industries like textile production, which required soap to remove natural greases from wool and cotton.

In 1785, soap-boilers all over Great Britain produced just over 17,000 tons of soap. But by 1814, the national production of soap had more than doubled.

Soap is made from fat or oil and an alkaline element, usually lye. When boiled together, the two elements blend to become soap. Soap-makers could use whatever they had handy to make their soap—using lye from wood ash or kelp or mined potash, depending on their environment. In terms of oils, most Northern Europeans used waste fats like beef or sheep tallow. In the Middle East, soap-makers used olive oil, sesame oil, and the oil from cypress trees.

In order to scale up production at the beginning of the hygiene revolution and the Industrial Revolution, soap-makers suddenly needed to look to areas far beyond their borders to get their source materials. Soap industrialists had to import wood ash from North America or mine potash in continental Europe, all of which was costly. A scientific breakthrough brought them some relief at the end of the eighteenth century, though, when a French inventor developed an industrial process to produce soda ash from readily available salt, which brought down the price of one raw material. All that was left was to bring down the cost of the other main raw material: oil.

Whale fat was too expensive; tallow rendered from beef or mutton was hard to produce in sufficient quantities; and olive oil from Southern Europe and the Levant was prone to supply interruptions because of frost or war.

One of the first solutions that presented itself was palm oil. Palm oil, an orange-tinted oil made from the fruit of the *Elaeis guineensis*, a palm tree native to West Africa, was produced in African villages and exported to Europe throughout the time of the slave trade, although never in large quantities. It was not the best-quality oil for soap-making purposes, but it was cheap and abundant, so suddenly there was an explosion of demand for it.

In the same letter that Matthew Forster wrote to Martin about the peanut, he also described the rapid growth of the palm oil market. "The first importation of palm oil is within the recollection of persons *now alive*, and when the slave trade was abolished in 1808, the quantity imported annually did not exceed one or two hundred tons. The annual importations now exceed twelve thousand tons!"

Former slave ship captains who were clever enough to adapt to the changing regulatory environment conducted a good part of this trade. It is not surprising that slavers transitioned so smoothly. Europeans who traded in slaves on the coasts of Africa often traded in other goods as well: animal skins, spices, ivory, palm oil, gold, beeswax, and gum arabic, to name a few.

Abolitionists of the day believed that the suppression of the slave trade, and the development of the new trade commodities, what they called "legitimate commerce," should go hand in hand.

Abolition campaigner Thomas Clarkson, who traveled across Great Britain drumming up grassroots support for the abolitionist cause, propagated the images of the slave trade that we know so well today: the plans of how to pack hundreds of slaves into a slave ship like so many human sardines; the illustrations of chains, collars, shackles, and the whips. And Clarkson, too, was a proponent of the idea of legitimate commerce. In his speeches, whether before Parliament, to a sympathetic church group, or on the docks of Liverpool, Clarkson often made the economic case for ending the slave trade and carried with him a box of the other products that Africa might have to offer: samples of wood, a bit of indigo, bags of spices, and tufts of cotton that he said grew there spontaneously. "It would be much more to our interest to deal in these, than in slaves," wrote Clarkson.

Soon enough, these ideas were becoming widespread as a commercial logic grew up around them. One company that used palm oil in its candle production harnessed the prevailing anti-slavery sentiment as a marketing tool. It put out advertisements for its "distilled palm oil candles" that ran alongside snippets of testimonies to the Select Committee on the West Coast of Africa: "What policy would you recommend, from your observation and experience on the coast, as best calculated to promote civilisation in Africa, and put down the Slave Trade?—Captain Bailey: It would be best to increase the legitimate trade in Palm Oil." The link was clear: by buying these candles an ordinary housewife would be helping to end the slave trade.

But while the British went wild for palm oil, hailing it as the solution to their woes, the French soap-makers hesitated. Not all oils had the same properties, and not all soaps were made equal. There was soft soap and hard soap, white soap, mottled soap, and yellow soap. Some soaps lasted longer or lathered more or had smoother textures. Others dissolved like sugar in a cup of tea because they were made, mostly, of water. The British soap-makers produced lower-quality soap in the largest quantities—yellow soap that got its color from palm oil. A

London soap-boiler in 1835 noted, "Liverpool is the great market now for the export of soap and there is the great consumption of palm oil and almost all soap for exportation is made from palm oil exclusively."

French soap-makers in Marseille had long been renowned for their craft, producing a durable hard soap, their *savon de Marseille*, made entirely from olive oil. The port of Marseille imported olive oil for its soap factories from Crete, the Peloponnese, Italy, Spain, and North Africa. Exports were often affected by wars or disastrous frosts. In the eighteenth century alone, frost hit the olive groves of southern France nine times, each time killing off a substantial portion of the region's olive trees. Farmers replanted, of course, but olive trees could take several years to bear fruit. So the French, too, were looking for reliable oil substitutes.

French industrialists knew they needed to figure something out. They tried palm oil, but found that they could not move the product in France. French consumers were used to white soap and refused to buy the yellow kind, even though it was cheaper. In the Paris of 1840, you would have had to shell out 170 francs for 100 kilograms of the pure savon de Marseille made with olive oil, but only 60–65 francs for the same quantity of palm oil soap.

So Marseille soap-makers started to try other oils. They tested cottonseed, flaxseed, and carnation, but nothing quite measured up. Finally, in the 1840s, they tried peanuts, and found it could be mixed with olive oil at certain proportions without changing the color, texture, or quality of the traditional soap. Peanuts became the default solution to a problem that had plagued the industry for a generation. All they had to do was find a constant supply.

4

From Here to There and Back Again

Arachis hypogaea, from Köhler's Medizinal-Pflanzen.

"All the travelers who have roamed throughout Africa, and who have directed their observations towards agriculture and natural history, mention peanuts," wrote French aristocrat and naturalist Charles-Nicolas-Sigisbert Sonnini de Manoncourt in the early 1800s. Sonnini never made it south of the Sahara himself, but spoke with all the authority of a partially informed man who had read a lot of books.

Sonnini collected these secondhand observations and his own experiences with the species in the South American colony of French Guiana in a book about the peanut that was published in 1808. He remarked, "Peanut agriculture, which has been generally adopted by African Negroes, shows, in my opinion, that this plant is native to their country."

His logic, predictably, was racist. "As long as we have known the character and tastes of Negroes who, in spite of their very old acquaintance with civilized nations, are far from trying new experiments and innovations, not only in agriculture but in any other subject . . . we can no longer be tempted to suppose that those same Negroes, so constant in their customs and in their mode of life, very near to a savage state, have taken from America the fruits of the peanut, or have gone to fetch them there."

Sonnini's contributions were part of a vigorous debate spanning the better part of a couple of centuries. Botanists and scholars did not know where the peanut came from, because by the time anyone started paying attention it was turning up in almost every remote corner of the known world. In the early sixteenth century, Fujianese farmers in China were growing "lo-hua-sheng," which literally means the seeds "born from flowers fallen to the ground." Also in the sixteenth century, Garcilaso de la Vega, the son of an Inca woman and a Spanish conqueror in what is now Peru, wrote about a "fruit that grows underground which the Indians call inchic. . . . The inchic is very like almonds in consistency and taste. . . . With honey it makes an excellent marzipan." In the seventeenth century, a botanist noticed Jamaican slaves growing what they called either "pindalls" [pindars] or "gubgubs" [goobers] in their kitchen gardens. And as Sonnini wrote, "This plant is cultivated in the country of Bambouk [eastern Senegal] . . . and on the excellent soil of Sierra Leone."

In the 1930s, French tropical agronomist Auguste Chevalier opined, "The question [problem] of the peanut's origin has made streams of ink flow." He identified two schools of thought: the botanists who believed that the peanut had originated in Africa and the others who believed it had originated in the Americas. And one botanist, Count Ficalho, split the difference, according to Chevalier, by elaborating "an interpretation that would agree with everyone: Peanuts would have existed in the wild in both Africa and America and its cultivation would have originated on both continents at once."

In the early twentieth century, after the slow accumulation of physical evidence pointing in one direction, botanists started to form something like a consensus about the peanut's origin. And it took the twenty-first-century study of the peanut's genome to definitively determine its birthplace.

The peanut we know and love today, *Arachis hypogaea*, was born more than 10,000 years ago on a flat, hard-baked scrap of earth in Bolivia's Gran Chaco, an area of hot and arid savannas in lowlands that emerge just east of the Andes' continental spine. It is descended from the product of two different species that were from different areas hundreds of miles away from each other. Some travelers brought one of the species into the region where other species grew; they met and were mixed together by a pollinating insect in what one scientist said "may have been only a single hybridization event,"—that is to say, a one-night stand.

The fruit of this union was different from either of its parents; it developed four sets of chromosomes instead of the two sets of chromosomes its progenitors had. That meant it was cut off from them; it couldn't mix itself back in with most of its cousins. So *Arachis hypogaea* continued to evolve by itself.

With the help of humans who recognized its worth, *Arachis hypogaea* spread. It climbed the Andes, trudged through the Atacama Desert, navigated the length of the Paraguay River, and crossed the Amazon rainforest. It went by road and boat, by pack animal and by human strength, spreading throughout the continent.

After Christopher Columbus, the white men came in relentless waves to triumph over and plunder the new world. The conquerors were the vanguard; then came the clergy. The first were to subdue the people and the second were to study them and maybe even change them, doing double duty as both naturalists and evangelists. Both parties needed to show their kings or queens in Europe what possibilities there were on the other side of the world for material or spiritual expansion.

Once there, whatever the conquerors could get their hands on, they took: plants, rocks, animals, and people, too. On Columbus's first voyage, he speculated about the value of local crops after he made landfall on the island we now know as Cuba: "The people have plenty of mames which are like carrots and have the flavor of chestnuts; and they have faxones and beans of kinds very different from ours. They also have much cotton, which they do not sow, as it is wild in the mountains, and I believe they collect it throughout the year, because I saw pods empty, others full, and flowers all on one tree. There are a thousand other kinds of fruits, which it is impossible for me to write about, and all must be profitable."

On one of those early trips, someone, no one knows who, must have seen the peanut. It was something the Europeans had never seen before and he—for the clergy and the conquerors were always men—took it. Maybe it was being sold at the market? Or maybe he saw it being harvested? Maybe his Indigenous guides or slaves brought some to munch on during a foray into the interior?

It is possible that a white man first saw the peanut even on that first trip in 1492; maybe it was one of those strange beans Columbus saw in Cuba. Maybe it was on the island called Quizqueia or Haiti by its own people, but that Columbus renamed as La Isla Española or Hispaniola—the Spanish island. There, the Taíno people called this food *mani*, according to Bartolomé de las Casas, a settler and slave owner turned Dominican friar who came to the island in 1502. He described it in his *Historias de las Indias*, writing, "They had another fruit which was sown and grew beneath the soil; which were not roots but which resembled the meat of the filbert nut. . . . These had thin shells in which they grew."

On the tropical coast that bulged out into the southern Atlantic Ocean, in a land that would one day be known as Brazil, the

Indigenous group there, the Tupi, had the same crop, but they called it
manobi, according to a Calvinist missionary in the 1550s. "They grow
in the soil like truffles connected one to the other by fine filaments.
The pod has a seed the size of a hazelnut and similar taste; it is grey
brown and the hull is the hardness of the pea."

And around the same time, when Hernán Cortés invaded Tenoch-
titlan and eventually destroyed the Aztec Empire, Friar Bernardino
de Sahagún indexed all the useful plants and medicines to be found
among the Aztecs. He referenced the peanut there; it was being used
as a medicine that the Nahuatl called *tlacacauatl*, literally "earth
cacao."

Someone, one of these conquerors or religious naturalists, pocketed
a few peanuts, and so it went off to explore new pastures in Africa,
Asia, and the South Seas. It would go everywhere and install itself in
kitchen gardens, wide-open fields, and in arid grasslands not so different from the place where it was born.

Just as we don't know who took peanuts from Hispaniola or coastal
Brazil, so, too, we don't know who brought them to Africa or when.
The why, though, we can intuit; they were tasty little things and were
easy to transport as seeds.

The peanut sowers were most likely Spanish or Portuguese. In the
early fifteenth century, almost as soon as navigators learned to steer
their lightweight caravels to points due south, they made their way
down the African coast to tentatively explore the mysteries of the unknown, search for a Christian king, and—the real goal—undercut the
Moors in the spice, gold, and people trades.

What European sailors did in Hispaniola and across the New World
was a pattern they had first established in Africa: they took without
asking.

When one of Henry the Navigator's captains first sailed farther
south than any white man had before, he passed the river that divided
the Moors from the Blacks—the Senegal River. Since Europeans had
only a rudimentary understanding of African geography, they thought
it was the Nile. The captain "fell in with some almadias or canoes, one

of which he captured, with four natives. . . . [He] returned with his captives to Portugal, where he met with a flattering reception."

Soon after that, the Portuguese started to settle on islands: islands in the middle of oceans, islands in the middle of rivers all across the belly of the Atlantic. They would bring together opportunistic explorers, heretics and Jews who had been expelled from the Iberian Peninsula, and Africans, some willing but many more unwilling—prisoners of war, convicts, and the unlucky who were pressed into servitude by an arbitrary spin of fortune's wheel.

On continental Africa, the Portuguese explorers, raiders, and merchants traded with the Mande people, who were linked to a state far in the interior whose power and wealth were the stuff of legend—the Mali Empire. The Portuguese were keen to move inland to see the great cities of that empire, made famous in the medieval world by its reported wealth and its Mandimansa, or emperor, who, more than one hundred years before, had made the pilgrimage to Mecca with, some say, a procession of five hundred slaves, each carrying a staff made of solid gold. On at least two occasions in the 1480s and 1490s, the Portuguese even sent delegations to visit the Mandimansa, sailing up the Gambia River and crossing hills and savannas to reach the walled city that was its capital, Niani.

Maybe it was all they were permitted or maybe it was all they wanted, but Portuguese traders only set up coastal posts on the swampy lower rivers of Guinea. There, they sometimes married local chiefs' daughters and settled in these outposts, integrating into the community as insider-outsiders who could tap into family trading networks and facilitate exchanges of goods, money, language, and culture. These traders and opportunistic settlers often brought useful plants to grow in the kitchen gardens surrounding their forts or settlements. The plants had many purposes: feeding the settlers in desolate places, provisioning ships, and establishing more products for trade. Maybe the peanut found a niche for all of these purposes?

The people along the Senegambian coast, and, for that matter, all across Africa, may have been able to adopt the peanut so easily because they already had a similar crop, *Vigna subterranea*, in their repertoire.

Vigna subterranea grows with the same biological imperative as *Arachis hypogaea* as it buries itself in the ground to grow. Its leaves look similar, and it also grows in a shell. But there are differences; its flowers bloom a delicate lilac instead of orange-yellow, its flavor is more like a bean even when roasted, and it is not rich in oil. African farmers could have become peanut masters so fast because they already had a good idea about the secrets of its cultivation.

In coastal Guinea, *Vigna subterranea* was called *mancarra*, but, little by little, the peanut adopted this name for itself. The Mandinka also named this new crop *tiga* after the old one. In other places, though, the words for each crop were distinct. The Wolof of Senegambia called the peanut *gerte*, but *Vigna subterranea* was *gadianga*. And the Fulbe, who lived in all of these places, called the groundnut *deppu*, but the peanut was *mbiriiwu*.

This mix of interchangeable names causes confusion in the historical record.

When French explorer Rene Caillié set out from the Rio Nunez in 1827 to try to make it to Timbuktu, he talked constantly about encountering what the French called the *pistache de terre*—the ground pistachio. He says he bought them in markets, saw them in fields, and bought them from passing herders. Sometimes they were grilled and salted, sometimes they were made into a kind of cake. "Several Foulah [Fulbe] shepherds who were tending their flocks in the neighborhood came to see us and sold us what they called *cagnan*. This is a sort of small loaves or roles [*sic*], made of pistachio nuts, baked and pounded then mixed with maize and sweetened with honey. These loaves form a portion of their provision when traveling." In other words, it was a nineteenth-century energy bar.

Some ethnobotanists who have studied Caillié's journey suggest this pistachio was, in fact, *Vigna subterranea*, and that he must have been mixing up the two crops. It is possible. But before leaving on this trip, Caillié had already done a tour of the region, from Mauritania to Freetown. In 1825, Caillié took a job as an overseer in a colonial experimental garden on the Senegal River, where a respected botanist was testing out useful plants to see if they might be grown in Senegal.

Caillié felt the work was beneath him: "I felt that I possessed energy enough for something better than a Negro driver." On the list of species grown in Richard Toll were priority crops: indigo, sugar, and cotton, and others like tomatoes, avocados, coffee, and cacao. They experimented with other crops, too, that in hindsight seem crazy—olive trees and cherry trees that need proper cold periods to be at their best. Both *Vigna subterranea* and *Arachis hypogaea* were grown there, too. As a consequence of his work, Caillié may have understood that they were different plants.

As soon as he gathered enough money to make the journey, Caillié made plans to join a small Mandinka caravan going first into the highlands of Fuuta Jallon and then following the Niger River to its bend at the Sahara Desert's edge. He went disguised as a Moor, dressed in robes and with his pockets full of pages from the Koran. Caillié constructed an elaborate backstory as a lost Arab from Egypt who had been abducted by the French as a child, and was now trying to get home to his country. Incredibly, his interlocutors seemed to believe his yarn.

The caravan was following trade routes that such Mande traders had probably been using for centuries, routes that linked parts of the Mali Empire from the desert cities of Gao and Timbuktu to the outer reaches of its influence along the coast, and the routes that some of those early Portuguese envoys had taken three hundred years before him.

And as Caillié followed the trade routes into the interior, he may have also been following the peanut's path of migration.

5

A Peanut Ruse

One of the first regions to answer the call of the peanut was an area that traced the littoral for more than six hundred miles, from the Gambia to Liberia. Here, what looks like land on a map is instead a combination of peninsulas, islands, and wetlands stretched across a meandering maze of interconnected rivers, lakes, and streams.

Viewed from the ocean, the shores of this region look flat and monotone. It is only when you get closer that you can see how variegated the environment is, full of dense concentrations of mangrove trees that are half submerged in the water. The mangroves genuflect and creep on their branches up and down the estuary.

From the point of view of nineteenth-century French administrators in Gorée and Saint Louis, this area was called les Rivières du Sud, or the Southern Rivers. The British administrators in Freetown had the opposite perspective and called it the Northern Rivers in their documents, staking their claim to the area. This land between their traditional zones of influence was a disputed region between the French and British for many years. It's clear, though, that the Portuguese got there first and gave their names to rivers, capes, and islands: Bissau, Cacheu, Nunez, Verga, Pongo.

The area was not what experts would come to think of as good peanut land; the soil was neither light nor sandy and the rainy season was, if anything, a bit too long. But this area had a few critical advantages: it had already established trading posts and, crucially, had a lot of labor—the arms and backs of thousands of enslaved people.

The Rio Pongo was known for its treacherous shallow mouth where ships risked running aground depending on the season and the tides, and farther up one of the river's branches, a whirling channel called Hell's Gate could catch and destroy unsuspecting ships. But when the British government and the American government outlawed the slave trade in 1807, what had been a liability during the days of the legal trade—the difficulty of navigating the tangled mess of waterways— became a key advantage for the illicit trade.

Although the British government deployed its Royal Navy to Free- town to patrol the coast against British slavers, it could only detain ships flying under flags of countries with whom the British government had binding treaties. After all, it would be some time before other countries would ban the trade for their citizens: the Netherlands only in 1814; 1818 in France; 1831 in Brazil. Each country's abolition of the slave trade had loopholes manufactured by competing interests, loopholes that kept the bans from being fully enforced. And even when there were treaties in force, their terms made it difficult for the navy to make any seizures.

On the Rio Pongo, the labyrinthine layout of the swamps meant that slavers with knowledgeable pilots could go places that the British anti- slave-trade squadron could not follow.

Many new slave traders only established themselves in the Rivers after the abolition of the slave trade. Stiles Edward Lightbourn was born in Bermuda and had a list of prominent siblings who had settled in Savannah, Georgia, and Charleston, South Carolina, and become politicians and merchants. Stiles, "an accomplished rogue who . . . preyed on all comers," came to the Rio Pongo in the early 1800s, where he married a woman whose father was a long-established Luso- African trader and whose mother was from an influential clan. Many other traders also established mixed-race dynasties on the river with people with British, American, and French surnames.

When, in 1822, a British patrol ship managed to catch a slave ship at a local trader's wharf just as the trader started to load up the men and women he had waiting, chained up in his barracoons, it made some traders reconsider the long-term profitability of the area's clandestine slave trafficking. Bureaucrats in Freetown wrote to the Colonial Office in London saying that some of the traders had finally seen the light: "The other chief traders on the river [Rio Pongo]," said the letter, "are strong in profession of having altogether abandoned the trade, with a determination not to return to it under any circumstances, but to pursue the fair course of legitimate industry and commerce as planters and general merchants."

Their chosen economic activity was farming, and on a grand scale. By the end of that year, Stiles Lightbourn had received 1,000 coffee plants from a British merchant in Freetown to start exporting coffee.

The British authorities must have congratulated themselves on a job well done, since they thought they had succeeded in changing the hearts, minds, and habits of the region's trans-Atlantic slave traders. But those authorities made a mistake: they thought that merchants could either deal in slaves or deal in legitimate commerce. They were wrong; the traders could and did do both. At the end of the rainy season, the coffee was harvested and sold to merchants in Freetown and then exported to Britain or France; the slaves were harvested and sold to buyers in Havana, Salvador, and Charleston.

And if the British ever suspected differently, they would be hard pressed to prove it. In fact, since their plantations needed so much labor, the Pongo traders could explain away their large numbers of slaves as only being put to use on the land. The slave trade may have been illegal, but slavery was not. And even when European countries pushed through an abolition of slavery, it applied only to their own citizens or in their own territories. Since these European traders usually had African wives, the women could always claim that the slaves belonged to them.

One of the biggest perpetuators of this ruse was the Lightbourn family. The Lightbourns may have had several thousand slaves at any one time, according to some, possibly exaggerated, estimates at the time. While Stiles Lightbourn may have been the slaver on the books, everyone knew that it was his missus who made the whole operation work. Her name was either Elizabeth or Isabella, but for decades she was known to most people on the river as Nyara Bely, the influential daughter of an African woman and a mixed-race trader on the river named Emmanuel Gomez. *Nyara* was an honorific in the area, a derivation of the Portuguese word *senhora*. Nyara Bely's husband would disappear from the river by the 1830s, either dead or having returned across the ocean, and Stiles Lightbourn Jr. took over in name, but in practice his mother was the one in control until the day she died. In the words of one foreigner, she was "the Zenobia of West Africa."

Some of the most interesting sources on Nyara Bely come from her later years, when Protestant and Catholic missionaries and European colonists were pushing into the river and trying to subdue it, via treaty, gun, or religion. Some wrote that she went about in men's clothes with two pistols holstered on her waist, and personally inspected the many cannons around her fort every day to ensure that they were in good repair. Other sources reported that she dressed in pagnes, those colorful traditional woven fabrics, which she matched with bare feet and thick gold jewelry. A British captain writing in his journal in 1856 seemed to admire her: "She appeared to be about 50 years of age, possessing striking traces of beauty. Her colour, although very dark, had a depth and richness that cannot be understood by those who have never seen an African beauty; her hands and feet would be a study for a most imaginative sculptor," wrote the officer. She had studied in England and spoke English, but, in what was surely a power play, always chose to speak through a translator.

The price of coffee fell precipitously in the 1840s, so the Lightbourns and most of their neighbors reoriented their sizable plantations to grow peanuts, which were starting to be in demand in Europe and the United States. Their early involvement, with their large numbers of laborers both free and forced, helped that crop gain prominence as a key object of trade.

When a French naval captain from Marseille visited the neighboring Mellacourie River in the early 1840s, he noted there was a robust demand for slaves. Louis-Edouard Bouët-Willaumez, who would become the governor of Senegal a few years later, was an abolitionist, but was not at all troubled by this commerce; he admired the plantation owners for their industriousness. "The natives still buy captives from the interior, but they no longer buy them for exportation," he wrote. "They employ the slaves on their numerous fields of peanuts, which earn them a great deal of profit."

6

The Legend of Ndakaaru

Several hundred miles up the coast from the Rio Pongo where the Lightbourns were doing a brisk business in peanuts and people, there was a place called Ndakaaru.

In those days, Ndakaaru was not yet the large city it would become, with its name altered and shortened to Dakar, but was still a series of fishing villages hugging the rocky promontories of the Cap Vert peninsula. This was the continent's finger, stretching itself as far as it could into the great ocean, and it was covered with a carpet of grass, flowers, and fat baobab trees whose spindly branches reached out to scrape the sky.

The people of Ndakaaru were best known to the French for their habit of pillaging the ships that sank off the coast, of which there were many. Since they were just a short boat ride from the narrow streets and bustling warehouses of the prosperous island of Gorée, where the French government had a fort, they did a brisk business in provisioning that island's people with anything they might need or want.

One day in 1840, in a historical story that feels like a legend, the chief of Ndakaaru approached the representative of a French trading house with some slaves to sell. The French merchant responded to the chief, "Keep your slaves, they are our fellow men, but I will give you anything you want from Europe for peanuts."

There and then, the chief had an epiphany. He went to tell his people about this new idea. "Because each slave can bring in enough peanuts to equal his selling price, instead of selling them, let's use our slaves to cultivate our fields," he said.

From that moment on, the people of Ndakaaru promised to not only dedicate themselves to peanut farming, but also to tell their cousins and neighbors about it up and down the coast and into the interior, in the land between the rivers Senegal and Gambia and beyond.

They preached the gospel of peanut farming far and wide. And so it spread.

It was a peanut rush.

7

The Caravan

The caravan master steered his convoy of people and animals away from the coast, through Dakar and Yoff and onto the trail that led to the interior. It was February 1851, and the weather had turned gusty. Encouraged by the wind at its back, the caravan crossed the dunes and moved through a forest of elephantine baobabs and skeletal acacia trees full of needle-sharp thorns.

Caravans led by Moors from Trarza had long traversed the area on their traditional migrations from the deep Sahara, connecting places like Marrakech, Algiers, and Qayrawan to Chinguetti, Walata, and Timbuktu and ending at areas just south of the desert's edge, across the Senegal or Niger Rivers, where they picked up their precious cargos of gold, ivory, and slaves.

A caravan was a singular thing, but it was also multiple, made up, as it was, of men and women of all the shades between black and white; and of animals—camels, donkeys, cows, sheep, goats, and the occasional horse, too. Their pace was always slow, but steady, a relentless trickle that created grooves on the earth for future caravans to follow. Some of these paths were well worn, crevassed from centuries of movement; others sprang up and shriveled away within just decades. The paths could change, but the form stayed the same.

The caravan would keep moving, by foot or hoof, sloughing off and picking up travelers and goods, contracting and expanding, bulging sometimes—a snake digesting its meal. Here it took on salt and there it sold millet; here it passed a burning village—no one to buy anything there anymore—and there, some of the former inhabitants had been sold now as slaves. Join the caravan!

The caravan master in this case was not a Moor headed to Chinguetti or Marrakech, but a mulatto from Gorée named Hippolyte. And he was accommodating when two French priests joined them at the last minute, rushing to the caravan at sunset just as everyone was making camp on the edge of a lake for the night. Hippolyte must have understood that it was rarely prudent to travel alone in so unsettled a country.

That night, they slept close to a dense patch of Palmyra palms, which, along with several bonfires, served to "shelter the whole caravan from the cold gusts of the northern wind, which began to blow with ferocity and with such a chill as to make us forget that we were living in the torrid zones," wrote one of the priests. "Everyone squeezed and muddled together around the blazing fire, while to the side the donkeys, oxen and camels were tied up, chewing their cud and yet serving as a buffer against the brisk night's breeze. The couscous and the fish that had been prepared for the voyage were happily eaten; then, after merry words exchanged on all sides, they all stretched out on the ground and wrapped themselves in their wide pagnes, and fell asleep in a jumble."

In the morning, Hippolyte gave the signal to wake at three when it was still dark, to beat the scorching sun. The days were often the same: walk or ride until the sun became too hot; the people and animals panting from exertion or fainting with fatigue; rest; and then start all over again. One evening, they arrived at a sizable village called Tayba, where they were "greeted by the sound of tam-tams and the noisiest clapping of hands." The caravan was here!

The people of Tayba were so enthusiastic because a caravan coming from the coast like this one may have been full of desirable items: glassware, ceramics, trade beads, tobacco, l'eau de vie, guns, foreign textiles from the lowliest percale to sumptuous fabrics in brilliant shades of indigo, tourmaline, and the brightest vermilion, as well as more useful items, including paper to write on, tea to drink, and dried fish and shellfish to flavor their sauces. Maybe, too, the caravan would bring news from the rest of the world and some entertainment. Any aristocrats or important leaders who traveled with the caravan would have been accompanied by their gewels or griots, those court bards who were sometimes dancers whose feet moved so fast it was if they were afraid to touch the ground; and other times they were musicians with an assortment of drums for every occasion, and a few xalams—string instruments similar to lutes; and sometimes historians who could recount, through epic poems, the annals of their lord's lineage and would be sure to share his latest battles and exploits. The campfires would have burned late into the night.

The next day, the caravan gathered its folds and set off again. Hippolyte's terminus for this particular caravan was not far away, just a few days of traveling into the heart of the kingdom of Kajoor, a stretch of land between Saint Louis and the Cap Vert peninsula. There were boats waiting at Gorée and nearby Rufisque for the cargo that Hippolyte was charged to bring back. In exchange for his foreign goods, he had come prepared to buy peanuts from the people of Kajoor.

In the village of Karsala, the chief said he had been a big "slave hunter" and waxed nostalgic about the days when he was young and could capture the *baadoolo*—free peasants—that he sold "wherever the slave ships were stationed." "Where have these happy times gone,'" the man bemoaned. "Now that the whites no longer buy captives, I will soon find myself reduced to cultivating the land, and if it were not for the trade I do with Mr. Hippolyte, I would be in a state of near poverty."

The commercial evangelization of the French merchant and the chief of Ndakaaru had worked; the chiefs of Karsala and Tayba and points north, south, east, and west had decided to use their slaves to grow peanuts. That French merchant had only managed to export seventy tons of peanuts in 1841, but by 1850, he was able to fill an entire ship. And most of Senegal's peanut exports were coming from Kajoor.

8

Those of the Sand

Kajoor would not seem like promising agricultural land to the un-trained eye. Much of the area is covered with lightweight ochre sands, what the Wolof call *joor*. Here, the dry season lasts most of the year, so winds can combine dried-up creeks and harvested fields and whip them up into sand spouts that move across the horizon as if propelled by an unseen hand.

Those soils give the kingdom its name. *Kajoor* literally translates as "those of the sand."

But the joor of Kajoor was ideal for something. The joor of Kajoor was the peanut's apotheosis.

The peanut we eat is also a seed. And if you don't roast it or boil it first, you can take it from its shell and put it into the ground, where, with a little bit of water and a warm sun, it will start to find something new within itself. Roots will grow as slender tentacles, slithering into the soil; a stem will push up to breathe the air and feel the sun. Leaves and branches will form, then discreet flowers, warm yellow with sunset-colored striations, curved like tiny fans. The flowers will bloom and die in one day, because their real purpose is to develop a protuberance, a secondary stem commonly called the peg.

But the lance-like peg will not grow up to the sun like the plants' leaves; it contains the new embryo, and its objective is to grow down-ward in an effort to penetrate and impregnate the soil. Once nestled in the ground, it will start to develop horizontally—creating a shell and eventually filling that shell with seeds.

This imperative to bury its fruit in the ground is called geocarpy, and it makes the peanut a rarity in nature. Geocarpy is practiced by only a handful of known plant species (sixteen by one count), ones that mostly grow in areas at two ends of the climatic spectrum—in the tropics and in semi-arid zones. Scientists speculate that geocarpy is a plant's adaptation to harsh environmental conditions and a way to hunker down and protect itself; it literally buries its head in the sand.

The peanut is at its happiest in a sandy soil. Its peg can burrow into the ground with ease and the shell can have space to develop. When it comes time to harvest, the sandy soil is an advantage there, too, allowing workers to pull up the plant from the ground with an intentional tug, and not lose too many shells in the process.

Once the peanut came to Kajoor, it spread with ease. "The peanut grows almost spontaneously in the areas of Kajoor with low fertility," early French merchants reported to geographic societies and chambers of commerce. It was the fact that it grew so well that made many early botanists wonder if the peanut had originated there in the drylands of West Africa.

By the time that French business interests started looking at Kajoor with a speculative eye, households there may have been growing peanuts between their millet plants or alongside their cowpeas and watermelons for centuries. They likely used it as an occasional food or to thicken or enrich a sauce. Perhaps it seemed simple enough for merchants to ask the people of Kajoor to add more plots of peanuts to their fields.

Kajoor was also a natural place for peanut cultivation to expand since it sat between the poles of French colonial influence in Saint Louis on one end and Gorée, Rufisque, and Dakar on the other. The people of Kajoor were used to responding to demand in those outposts; coastal traders sometimes sent their livestock to graze in Kajoor's flat pastures, and the kingdom provisioned those coastal outposts with millet, meat, manioc, butter, and salt.

But there were constraints as well. Kajoor had no natural rivers by which to easily evacuate its peanut harvests. Instead, they depended on the camel and mule caravans driven by Moors or people like Hippolyte to transport peanuts to the main ports.

The biggest constraint, though, was that in order for the people of Kajoor to increase their production of peanuts enough to satisfy the growing demand from beyond, Kajoor farmers needed to do more than plant their seeds and pray for rain. They needed young arms and strong backs that could tend to more fields and produce more peanuts; they needed workers—friend or stranger, willing or unwilling.

9

A Middleman

As the peanuts moved back and forth across the Atlantic, through deserts and savannas, drylands and forests, people did the same. They were voluntary adventurers sailing on the high seas, people fleeing war or violence, and, of course, people who were enslaved because of those wars and that violence. They all dispersed from their homelands to lands unfamiliar. Neither the trade in people nor that in peanuts was just a movement from point to point; it was a rotating flux that pulsed in different directions, gathering people up here and spitting them out there. Sometimes the "there" was Charleston or Havana or Salvador da Bahia. But sometimes the "there" was a region a few hundred miles away, across a river, at the other end of the desert or up or down the coast. It was a diaspora that was both near and far.

This was the story for Walter Taylor's parents, who had been freed, not from slavery in the Americas, as was the case for so many in Sierra Leone, but directly from the belly of a Portuguese slave ship. The ship was brought back to Africa by the British Navy, but the people on it were not brought back to their own countries. Instead, they became a part of the abolition project that had originally inspired the establishment of the province of freedom in Sierra Leone—Freetown.

Walter Taylor's parents were called Sally and Samuel, although, of course, those were not the first names their own parents had chosen for them. Their true last name, likewise, was not Taylor, which could have been adopted by them voluntarily or given to them by some colonial bureaucrat or missionary or even a benefactor in England whose donation included a chance to bestow their name upon a newly freed person.

Freetown is almost cut off from the continent, sitting as it does at the tip of a peninsula that juts out into the Atlantic Ocean, and with the mountains at its back. At the time, the biggest attraction of Freetown was its immense natural harbor. That harbor meant that during the height of the slave trade, ships had an easy time docking there. And after the British outlawed the slave trade for British citizens in 1807, that harbor seemed like the logical place for the British Royal Navy to base its anti-slavery squadron, chasing down and capturing rogue slavers.

Nearly 100,000 enslaved people, including the future Sally and Samuel Taylor, were liberated from these slave ships and brought to the Freetown colony to settle. These newly freed people were first called "captured Negroes" or "recaptives"—captured first to be sold as slaves and then captured again by the British, this time to recover their freedom. Or at least a kind of freedom. The most common name was aspirational: "Liberated Africans."

After having experienced the trauma of capture and sale in their own countries and embarking on ships to sail on the big, salty lake, the early Liberated Africans were set aground in a world that was not so far away, but that was, nonetheless, a new one. When the slave ships docked, the people who had been their cargo were bustled into a building near the wharf—the Liberated African Yard—where they were registered and dispatched on to their new lives.

Adolescent and adult Liberated Africans may have been conscripted into the military, or may have joined voluntarily, or may have been shipped to the Caribbean on work contracts (indentured into something less free), or, often, may have been sent to work as apprentices in trades such as carpentry or shingle making, then in demand in Sierra Leone. Some, through their own initiative, attempted to make it back to their far-flung homelands. Still others went to work for the more established members of the community of liberated people: the freed slaves and free Blacks from the West Indies and Britain who had formed the initial settlement of the colony in 1787; and the Nova Scotians, ex-slaves who had fought on the British side during America's Revolutionary War and who formed a second wave a few years later.

In the early days, the Liberated African Department provided new arrivals with an initial stipend and supplies. According to the regulations, every man would receive a meager allowance for six months. Women only received the allowance for three months, since the colonial government supposed that women would soon marry and no longer be a burden on the system. Each liberated person also received some supplies: "one mat, one blanket, one duck frock, two duck kilts, one or two tin plates or wooden bowls, one iron spoon, one tin cup; and one camp kettle and one iron pot to a group of four or five men." The men also were given hoes and bill hooks, cutlasses and axes. In this way, they chopped down forests, both to sell the timber and to clear the land for new villages in the tree-covered mountains.

We do not know at what age Sally and Samuel Taylor came to Freetown, or when. But their son Walter was born sometime in the 1840s and grew up in a farming community called Hastings that was nestled in what one mid-nineteenth-century visitor called an "amphitheatre of mountains." Water was abundant in the community, and settlers grew ginger in the rocky earth. Most of the people in Hastings were just like the Taylors, which is to say that most of the people came from the same general region of Africa that the Taylors had come from, worshipped a similar pantheon of gods, and spoke a similar mother tongue. They were known as Aku people in Sierra Leone and Gambia, an appellation based on their common salutation in a language people would now recognize as Yoruba.

Walter Taylor's parents found themselves in Sierra Leone in the early nineteenth century because they had been sold and exported, along with many others from the same region, during the turbulent collapse of the Oyo Empire. For more than a century, the Oyo Empire, which regrouped several Yoruba-speaking regions, had controlled a stretch of the Slave Coast's interior in what is now Nigeria and Benin. The fall of the empire provoked decades of chaos as neighboring polities soon found themselves at war with each other; the decades of the 1820s and 1830s were full of rebellions, shifting alliances, violated agreements, and general unrest and violence. As the players took captives after their battles or raids, they sold their victims to other neighbors and eventually sold them to slavers, who packed them into ships bound for the Americas—a Yoruba wave reaching from Oyo-ilé, the capital of the Oyo Empire, to Havana and Salvador da Bahia. In the nineteenth century, about 445,000 people were shipped from the region, many of them Yoruba. Only a fraction were intercepted and brought to be settled in Sierra Leone, but by the 1830s, Aku people predominated in villages like Hastings.

Many Aku went on to get a British education, learning to read, write, and sum in English, and were converted to Christianity by assiduous missionaries. But some maintained close cultural, linguistic, and religious ties to their places of birth and kept to the old ways of worship, even after converting to Christianity or to Islam. For some years, Hastings was known as a center of such Aku religious practices.

In the years just before Walter Taylor's birth, the resident missionary in Hastings, a German called John Ulrich Graf, waged war against Aku ceremonies and sacraments, their sacred objects and their "gree-grees," the charms that people wore on their bodies. He confiscated idols; was vigilant over the smallest food or drink left as an offering at doors, in the forests, and at crossroads; and wrote screeds about the Egungun masquerades that often traversed the village and caused much excitement.

The drums usually started first, a talking drum there to transmit a message to the others, followed by a rhythmic base meant for dancing. The masked form of the Egungun was surrounded by drummers and dancers with sticks, all ready to mete out justice.

An Egungun masquerader in motion is inchoate; the form seems to move on its own, floating over the ground and whirling. Its eyes are obscured, covered with a veil of cowrie shells, and its body draped with panels of rich fabrics in clashing colors: red velvets, periwinkle flowered damasks, yellow silks embroidered with beads, woven country cloths died in deep indigo. It makes its own music with its beads and cowries that tinkle and rattle as it goes.

Bishop Samuel Ajayi Crowther, the most famous Yoruba convert of the period and the first African bishop in the Anglican church, explained that the Egungun "was an inhabitant of an invisible world, that he was [the] spirit of a dead man, which had made its appearance again on Earth as a heavenly messenger, whose dress must not be touched or the delinquent will be punished with immediate death by a supernatural power." The ancestors that the Egungun dancers represented saw everything and were charged with the duty to make sure that everyone was held accountable for their deeds. They came sometimes to administer justice, and sometimes to clear away sorrow and leave blessings behind.

But the missionaries saw the collective Egungun masquerades as devil worship, calling the central figure a kind of demon. They saw it as an embodiment of everything that was wrong with the "heathen" faiths. So they attacked it, by every means they could. Graf once dared to beat the Egungun masqueraders with a whip. "He began to castigate [the dancers]; but he only flogged a mass of empty Egugu [sic] clothes. The bodies inside the clothes had mysteriously and inexplicably vanished," according to an account later written by a Hastings citizen. Graf must have felt a sense of satisfaction, feeling that he had literally beat the devil out of them. But the townsperson added a detail that surely Graf did not know. "The [missionary] marched back to the Parsonage; his whip had dropped, but a broom belonging to one of the . . . Egugu [sic] escorts, followed him to the Parsonage, gyrating, in fact executing a little dance of its own behind the worthy cleric's back."

A Church Missionary Society (CMS) agent in Hastings named William Marsh soon noted that their repression of the old ways was working. "Comparatively speaking, order and decency are growing gradually; heathens who are fond of making noise publickly [sic] are ashamed of themselves and their practices," he wrote. "Fortune tellers are ashamed of carrying on their practices openly and publickly."

What he doesn't say is that the old ways carried on in secret. The Aku culture was stronger than the missionaries thought. The people of Hastings increasingly used subterfuge to keep practicing their rites and worshipping their gods behind the backs of the Christians, just like the broom dancing behind Graf's back.

Walter Taylor said that he did not join a church until he was living in the Gambia. "Up until then, I had been indifferent," he wrote. It's possible that this was an exaggeration, meant to make his conversion seem more miraculous. But maybe he really had resisted conversion like so many of his neighbors. Maybe he had danced with the Egungun in the town square as a young man. Or left offerings at the crossroads or at the base of a sacred iroko tree: piles of corn, cowries, or coconuts, along with bottles of palm oil and rum. Maybe he knew what it was like to stand in the scrim between the seen and the unseen, to talk to deities and the spirits of ancestors gone long before who were waiting for their chance to come back again.

The missionaries were resilient, though. If they couldn't truly convert the first generation, they would play a long game and target the community's children by instituting an extensive system of mission schools across the country. Top students of Liberated African origin would go on to attend the Grammar School, the flagship institution of CMS where young men would learn Greek, math, geography, and, of course, the history and teachings of the Bible. An even smaller fraction of these students would end up attending Fourah Bay College, a university initially started as a seminary to train young Africans to become ministers themselves.

Hastings village schoolmaster turned historian Aaron Belisarius Cosmo (A.B.C.) Sibthorpe attended the Grammar School with Walter Taylor and mentions him a few times in his *History of Sierra Leone*, first published in 1868 and subsequently revised and expanded in 1881 and 1906. He remembers young Walter as a "sharp fellow," a top student who passed his finishing exams the same year as A.B.C. Sibthorpe himself.

The Grammar School furnished British colonies from Bathurst to Lagos with bureaucrats, doctors, barristers, and, of course, men of the cloth. They were a kind of talented tenth, a small minority of exceptional men who were primed for leadership, long before W.E.B. Du Bois ever popularized the term. Early students included a number of firsts: the aforementioned Samuel Ajayi Crowther, Fourah Bay's inaugural student; Crowther's son-in-law George Nicol, who would become the first Black colonial chaplain; James Africanus Horton, a pioneering doctor and scientist; and Sir Samuel Lewis, a barrister who was the first

African to ever be knighted. These men embodied the idea that Black men could aspire to the British ideals of respectability—that they could be well-educated, capable, and responsible stewards of their own communities. Their achievements were aspirational, and their attitudes were generally assimilationist, privileging European standards. Although they stopped far short of the more radical ideas of early pan-Africanists of the era like Edward Blyden, who believed Africans could and should create their own models for their own societies, many of these men would go on to espouse something like self-governance.

Perhaps Taylor absorbed some of these ideas at school, which imbued his worldview with a constant eye toward self-determination. "I left the institution," he said years later, "determined to dedicate myself to politics with other young people, to fight against the colonial government, which we considered to be overly exclusionary and oppressive in its governance."

Like so many of his social class, he first became a schoolmaster when he finished his studies. As the second master in the government boy's school, he would have been an adolescent of sixteen or seventeen teaching smaller children their sums and their letters. It was a common path as a way to earn money and save up for further studies; even Bishop Crowther had been a schoolmaster in his day.

We don't know if young Walter had larger plans for his life, but his career as a schoolmaster took a turn in 1865 when he was probably about eighteen years old. He was arrested for petty theft and hauled before a magistrate. The stolen object was a book—Jeremiah Joyce's *Scientific Dialogues*—and the complainant was his boss, the colonial chaplain. The charges were also linked to a student at Fourah Bay College who had gone on a book crime spree, filching nearly sixty books over the previous months that he then sold to local schoolmasters, who resold them to their students in turn. The Fourah Bay administrator chased down the books when the guilty student confessed, and approached Taylor and the other schoolmasters to get the purloined books back. Taylor said the *Scientific Dialogues* was long gone, but gave the administrator his own personal copy. The Fourah Bay book thefts were hushed up and, although most of the people who had gotten books from the student lost their jobs, no one was ever charged in the courts—not the book-stealing Fourah Bay student, not the other schoolmasters known to be involved—except young Walter Taylor.

That's because when Taylor delivered what he said was his own copy of the *Scientific Dialogues* to Fourah Bay, a copy of the book went missing from the colonial chaplain's collection. The coincidence seemed overwhelming. Whereas the Fourah Bay administrator seemed inclined to work with the schoolmasters to get back the books, the colonial chaplain did not hesitate to draw up criminal charges against his young employee.

At the trial, Taylor insisted on his innocence. He even produced two witnesses to say that the book the court said was stolen from the chaplain had been in his possession for some years and had distinguishing marks: a prominent ink stain on the cover and the name John C. Taylor inscribed on a fly leaf, maybe the name of one of his relations.

Nonetheless, the magistrate found him guilty. For the sake of a book worth five pounds, Walter Taylor was sent to prison for three months.

It's not clear why the colonial chaplain chose this harsh approach when the other aggrieved chose lenience. What is obvious, though, is that this incident knocked Taylor off the path he might have otherwise continued to climb in Sierra Leone. Maybe he would have expected to continue on to Fourah Bay to train as a reverend, like Bishop Crowther had after his own stint as a schoolteacher; or to continue his studies and become a barrister? Instead, Taylor had to choose another path.

In 1866 or 1867, he left his village in the mountains of Sierra Leone and settled on an uliginous, boggy island near the Gambia River's mouth where the British Navy had created a town. Bathurst was a new city, a planned city that was all perpendicular streets on the sand, but nature stood ready and eager to reclaim it by flooding that grid with regularity. That may have been why the island had no full-time inhabitants when the British settled there, only fields that were occupied during the rainy season. The floods nourished the island's rice paddies and oyster beds, but made its people ill with all the diseases known to the tropics.

Walter Taylor said he came to Bathurst to work as a clerk for the navy, although a search of some of the colonial documents from this time did not reveal his name. But details of such employees were not always disclosed, beyond their grades or their salaries. Even despite his previous troubles, it's possible Taylor could have found work as a low-level clerk. The colonial government was held aloft by moderately well-educated Africans like Taylor who could not advance beyond the lowest levels, but were indispensable; they staffed offices, worked as accountants and copy clerks, and traveled with colonial authorities as translators. The pay was notorious for its paucity, and many colonial clerks, Black and white alike, quit when they found other advantageous business opportunities.

Many of them found work as middlemen, not for the colonial government, but for European and American merchants. "The European merchant generally leaves for Europe by the June mail leaving this part of the trade to be conducted by his Native agent," wrote the Gambia's colonial administrator, an arrangement that kept Europeans from being too exposed to the feverish rainy season. In this way, these middlemen helped such merchants conduct business.

And the main business in Bathurst—and indeed the main business of the whole region from the Southern Rivers to Saint Louis—was the buying and selling of peanuts.

Part II

10

The People Who Came from the Sea

In the late 1860s, soon after Walter Taylor arrived in the Gambia, a sickness emerged from the desert, curved along the course of the upper Senegal River, followed caravan trails into Kajoor, Waalo, and Jolof, and sailed down the Gambia River. It flared across the region for nearly a year, and everywhere it went, it was conspicuous in its ravages. These were not quiet deaths.

"Bathurst for the last month has presented the horrible scenes of a plague stricken town and I doubt if in the annales [sic] of history a like story could be found of what has happened in this place," wrote the British administrator in the Gambia to his superiors in England. "Daylight each morn discloses a picture appalling to humanity and it is only the strongest nerves that dare to face what is to be seen. Dead bodies knawed [sic] by prowling rats lie about in all directions presenting a spectacle too horrible to contemplate and around each corpse are traces in the sand of the fearful midnight struggle of the poor creatures in the last cramping agonies of the fatal disease."

In Bakel, a fort town on the upper Senegal River, the French commander wrote the governor in Saint Louis that people died so quickly there that they couldn't keep an accurate count. "The cadavers remained for the most part either in the huts, or in the streets, or finally on the banks of the river or in it, where many of the unfortunate people who were affected believed that if they threw themselves into the water, they would find a way to ease their suffering. Unfortunately, there, as everywhere else, they had to resign themselves to death."

That governor would himself experience both this frenzy and resignation when he was infected and died from the disease a couple of
months later.

This was cholera, a disease that could progress at shattering speed.
Even healthy people could get infected, experience a progression of
symptoms, and breathe their last breath in just a day or two. Its victims died from severe dehydration and shock because when the disease struck, they would have to evacuate their bowels repeatedly and
vomit up everything in their stomachs until the body started to compensate by taking moisture from wherever it could find it: from the
mucus in their nostrils to the tear ducts in their eyes to the water in
their blood. Cholera victims died in agony, their skin turning slate
blue, their whole bodies convulsing.

The 1868–1869 epidemic killed broadly: about a tenth of Saint Louisians died officially, but scholars think the real numbers could have
been higher; Bakel lost a quarter of its people, and in Bathurst one out
of every three inhabitants succumbed to the disease.

Cholera was as devastating to the economy and trade as it was to
the people. In Bathurst, the disease struck just before planting season,
and the administrator worried about the effects. "The prospects of the
River Gambia which has been scourged from its source to its mouth
are without a parallel and I fear it will severely try the mercantile
interests of the community. The present year, independent of the epidemic shows a falling off of a third of the ground nut crop and a general opinion prevails that next year will not even produce a third. . . ."

What's more, the cholera epidemic followed several years that had
shaken the people of Senegambia in an elemental way: a yellow fever
outbreak in 1866–1867 killed nearly half of those who were infected in
Gorée and spread up and down the coast; a couple of years before that,
locust swarms destroyed crops across the region for two consecutive
years, pushing the whole region to the precipice of famine. In fact, oral
historians of the kingdom of Kajoor remember 1864 as "at um xiif ba,"
or the year of hunger.

The insects may have gone away from Kajoor unsatiated, though,
because other invaders had beaten them to the table. The kingdom's

fields were wasting away, and its people and animals were thin and hungry.

The principal cause of Kajoor's condition was a different kind of plague: a sickness called conquest.

For years, the French had contented themselves with occupying coastal, riverine, or island forts and operating as demanding neighbors. But a series of disputes in the early 1850s sparked a conflict between Saint Louis merchants and the leaders of Waalo, a kingdom located just outside of Saint Louis where a project to create cotton, indigo, and sugar plantations, as in the Antilles, had been tried and failed a couple of decades before the current tensions. The conflict offered the French military an excuse to invade, burn down the villages in their path, and chase Waalo's authorities from power in 1855. The French colonial government placed that kingdom under their direct control. Once the conquest started, it spread, like cholera would a decade later. It moved from Waalo to Fuuta Tooro, a state along the upper Senegal River, and the Saalum kingdom near the Gambia.

But most of all, the French coveted Kajoor. They ached for it beyond measure with its fields, so deceptively fertile; its copses of acacia trees, useful for construction or for cooking; its convenient pasturelands full of cattle; its coastal salt flats; the wide expanse of its flat body where a visitor could see far into the horizon; and its territory, which divided the principal seats of French power in Gorée and Saint Louis from one another. They tried to nibble at its edges, offering successive damels, Kajoor's kings, hardy horses, and military support against their rivals in exchange for some of the kingdom's prime trading villages, and a narrow strip of the littoral stretching from the Cap Vert peninsula to Saint Louis. Their plan was to build a telegraph line and a series of caravanserai so that French soldiers and merchants could halt their voyages, and rest themselves and their animals in peace. The stated goal was to make Kajoor safer for commerce, but successive damels refused this plan, perhaps seeing it for what it was—a staging ground for colonial expansion.

The French governor at the time, Louis Léon César Faidherbe, was a decorated military man who had cut his teeth on foreign conquest, building his career and reputation in Algeria in the 1840s. He was an engineer and an earnest scholar as the author of numerous works on the histories, cultural habits, and languages of the people he wanted to dominate. He brought stealth, spies, false treaties, and mind games to the French colonial strategy in Senegal, with Machiavellian tactics that included stirring up unrest among the Muslim clerics in the north of Kajoor and playing Kajoor's power-hungry factions of nobles against one other. That strategy was almost too easy because Kajoor was notorious for its restive political climate, and the reign of any damel was always challenged from within. Faidherbe also planted seeds of distrust in the border kingdoms of Saalum, Siin, and Bawol, writing to the minister in France that by doing so they could "isolate and surround Kajoor."

In early 1861, Faidherbe tired of waiting and invaded Kajoor to build the caravan stops under armed guard—citing a treaty by the previous damel. It was a ruse, for there was no such signed treaty. But Faidherbe understood that his action would show that the damel was weak and that rebellions in the interior and challenges from other states could chase him from power. And he was right. With that damel overthrown, Faidherbe knew there would be an opening, a seat of power ripe for the tampering.

The damel title was not one that passed from father to son; instead a new damel was always elected from a field of nobles who had the right lineage. His father had to be a Faal, a paternal descendant of the man who founded Kajoor as an independent kingdom, and his mother had to come from one of seven aristocratic families. The women of such noble families wielded strategic power to promote their sons, brothers, and nephews. In this way, the reigning Geej matrilineage had maintained a close grip on power since it had seized it in 1697. The word *geej* means "the sea" in Wolof, and one historian has posited that the conqueror and his family chose this name to remind everyone that "the weapons that had given him victory over his brothers had been sold to him by people from the ocean."

With the election of the new damel under way, the French used their influence to make sure that a more biddable damel would capture the throne. They helped elect Majojo Degen Kumba Faal in 1861, but he soon proved unpopular. The griots who sing the legends of Kajoor highlight Majojo's viciousness; he was reputed to keep a demon vulture and to have once killed one of his subjects so that the rapacious animal could feed on the man's entrails. The stories of griots, though, must always be read more for their themes than for their accuracy. What's clear is that he was not beloved and was unable to consolidate power in the fractious kingdom.

Majojo was soon overthrown, and another damel was elected and started his first reign. Lat Joor Ngooné Latyr Joob was a young man of nineteen or twenty with spindly arms when he came to power. As a Joob, he was the first leader ever in the history of Kajoor to not come from the Faal family on his father's side, but his claim through the matrilineal Geej lineage was strong, and so was his large army. In the legends of Lat Joor still sung by griots, they insist that, although not a Faal, his father's family descended from Njaajaan Njaay, the founder of the Jolof Empire to which Kajoor had once belonged.

Lat Joor was short in stature, but would soon be larger than life as a seasoned military leader whose nimble strikes were often unexpected, swift, and devastating. He saw what the French had taken away from Kajoor, so many key lands and towns. And he wanted them back.

Lat Joor had been damel for just over a year when, in 1863, Faidherbe decided that the young leader needed to go. In Faidherbe's own account of this time, he made the case for French intervention, calling Lat Joor a usurper who was "weaving plots," who was capable of violating the terms of a treaty on a whim, and who "gave himself unreservedly over to his instinct to plunder." The message was clear: Lat Joor was threatening the peace, and by that they meant he was threatening trade in that key Kajoor commodity, the peanut.

The French invaded Kajoor again. In the face of a French military column four thousand men strong, Lat Joor was forced to retreat. He sought refuge in an area of the Saalum region that bordered the Gambia, at the court of the evangelizing imam Maba Jaaxu Bâ, another leader who saw no reason to accept French or British power as destiny. Maba's holy revolution to convert the people of Saalum was bloody but successful, and he was ready to collaborate with other local leaders to fulfill his vision of a pan-Senegambian Muslim community.

From Saalum, Lat Joor continued to wage a stealth campaign. He was everywhere and nowhere, darting in and out of villages and across borders, recruiting soldiers, stealing meat and millet to supply his warriors, and burning the peanut fields of those who dared to oppose him.

It took the French several more months, thousands of foot soldiers and cavalry, a constant patrol of Kajoor's borders, and the burning of many villages that supported Lat Joor to convince the young damel that it was in his long-term interest to pull back.

The French reinstalled Majojo. But his second attempt at rule was no better than the first, so Faidherbe ripped away the scrim of independence and annexed Kajoor, dividing its land into five cantons, all directly supervised by the colonial government.

But once the French had disrupted Kajoor's delicate balance, the fire of war—civil wars, holy wars, wars of conquest—burned bright and raged. They consumed the region, leaving a monochrome palette of charred huts, carbonized trees, and blackened and bare fields where there had once been green plants, bricks made from ferric muds, tawny hay-covered roofs, and the deep indigo of cloths hanging in the sun. Afterward, some searched for shelter in the forests that bordered most villages, taking their chances among the lions and hyenas. Others fled to neighboring villages, which were set alight and razed in turn. And some went to the colonial cities where the soldiers and scavengers had taken their crops, their livestock, and their gold.

An official wrote in the late 1860s that Saint Louis regularly experienced an influx of the desperate after skirmishes in Kajoor: "After these expeditions, I saw more than thirty refugees from Kajoor die of misery and hunger in Saint Louis every day for more than a month." Indeed, all the French-controlled cities saw a similar movement of population, from Saint Louis to Podor to Gorée. But the people who made it may have been the minority, the official speculated, writing, "Who will ever be able to say the number of unfortunate souls who fell on the way, and whose unburied bones whiten the paths that lead to the sea?"

11

The African Business

It was not war, but the peanut that brought young Walter Taylor to the island of Gorée in 1867 or 1868. On the island, traders and their agents gave out seeds in advance, received pawned gold jewelry and rich fabrics in return, and had to keep track of their own merchandise of liquor, tobacco, crockery, and all manner of fine notions, all of which required a rigorous book of accounts. Taylor's accounting skills would have been in demand, and eventually a merchant asked the young Sierra Leonean to keep the books for a trading house on Gorée.

At the free port of Gorée, visiting merchants didn't have to pay duties on the trade goods they imported to conduct their business, and the export duties were relatively low. As the peanut trade expanded, this advantage breathed new life into an island whose raison d'être had seemed unclear since the end of the slave trade half a century before.

Gorée was a rock, a small volcanic island a bit more than a half-mile long and a bit less than a quarter-mile wide, on which lived about three thousand people when Taylor would have moved there. The island had few freshwater sources, little space to grow vegetables or grains in sufficient quantities to feed its people, no wood for cooking or for constructing houses, and not a lot of space for new houses or new arrivals.

Taylor may have been aware of these constraints and dangers since Bathurst had similar limits as an island itself. Taylor must have either been determined to make his fortune or had a strong sense of adventure.

Taylor never revealed the name of the merchant who recruited him to Gorée, but in 1872 Taylor mentioned in a letter that he worked for the company of an American shipping merchant named Samuel C. Cobb of Boston (Roxbury), Massachusetts.

Samuel Crocker Cobb would go on to become the mayor of Boston from 1874 to 1877, and, as befits a prominent member of Boston's political establishment, has left behind several years of handsome leather agendas embossed with his name, which are now stored in an acid-free box at the Bostonian Society's library, just across from the Old State House building.

Cobb's agendas are the sparest form of diary; most entries are just a few lines long with notes on the weather, the political climate, the price of gold, his society meetings and dinners, and, often, his shipping business concerns with his associate Francis C. Butman of Salem, Massachusetts.

Cobb, as far as the record shows, never set foot on the African continent, but for some years he and Butman owned or chartered ships that sailed to West African ports, mainly Bathurst and Gorée, to engage in what he called "the African business." They sold American tobacco and other goods in exchange for African cow and goat hides and peanuts that were measured by the kilo, bushel, and ton.

The hides, they sold to shoemakers. And the peanuts, Cobb's agendas confirm, were sold to middlemen like Paddock and Fowler, Manhattan-based brokers of foreign fruits and nuts. These "exotic" nut wholesalers, in turn, sold those peanuts to street vendors who hawked hot, roasted peanuts in cities like New York City, Bridgeport, Connecticut, and Pittsburgh, Pennsylvania, where new pastimes like baseball, and old ones like variety shows and circus big tops, were within reach for masses of people, rich and poor.

The peanut had long been associated in America with enslaved people who, although they did not grow the crop commercially, tended to it in their kitchen gardens. It was one of the foods they grew for themselves along with African staples like okra, black-eyed peas, and watermelons. This was all before circuses, Mr. Peanut, and Cracker Jack, and to be called a peanut eater was almost a slur.

A white booster of the peanut, the Virginian Thomas B. Rowland, started to keep notes on the commercial promise of the peanut after the Civil War, and noted that the peanut was hard to market because it suffered from a crisis of perception. In the early days, he said he had to beg New York merchants to carry peanuts, which they dismissed as "nigger trash."

In the years after the Civil War, it caught on. An article in *Harper's Weekly* in the 1870s noted that the "pea-nut" was universally liked, but considered "ungenteel." The columnist wrote about the curiosity of the pea-nut trend: "Outside of boydom the popularity of the pea-nut is chiefly confined to people who frequent such places of amusement as the Bowery Theatre, the atmosphere of which is always redolent of the peanut stand, and the beer gardens. Such people, indeed, munch them everywhere."

As the peanut started to become more popular in the United States in circuses, theater halls, and baseball games, American supply could not keep pace with the explosive demand. Merchants looked for peanuts in a place that made sense to them: Africa. Rowland noted that in 1867, the American crop amounted to only 200,000 bushels, while African ports exported some 6 million bushels, mostly to Europe.

Cobb was one of a handful of New England merchants and captains exploiting this trade niche throughout the middle part of the nineteenth century, although the trade had its ups and downs.

"News from Gorée of a decidedly unfavorable character," wrote Cobb in early 1870. His diaries reveal a string of recriminations about the African trade. Although the details of his grievances are largely unknown, they can be supposed. The business seemed plagued by high turnover from captains and Gorée-based agents, for one. Whatever the unfavorable news was, it seemed serious enough that he and his partner, Francis Butman, would send their clerk Joseph H. Hasty to Gorée on the next ship "to settle up our matters there." We don't know what Hasty found when he arrived, but it was so urgent that the clerk sent a telegram, which was no simple maneuver since the note had to travel by boat to France and then across a new trans-Atlantic telegraph cable whose per-word prices were dizzying.

The following year, Cobb wrote, "Business very *dull*. African peanut *a drag.*" The prices rarely seemed as high as Cobb would have liked, and a month later he went personally to talk to one of his Boston-based peanut buyers about the prices. And in January of 1872, the coup de grâce: during the height of the African trading season, they got another surprise telegram from Hasty, this time to inform them that one of their main shipmasters and agents had left Gorée precipitously to sail home via France. Details would follow in the Gorée mail a few weeks later, but would not be enumerated in Cobb's diaries, which only note that the trouble with the agent was "very discouraging." Some months later, Cobb learned that the agent was going back to Gorée with a new job—as an agent for their French competitor Maurel et Prom, one of the biggest trading houses in the region. "There really seems no end to our troubles in the African business," wrote Cobb.

While Cobb and Butman persisted in the African trade, the named agents and ship captains may have been aided by the unnamed Walter Taylor, clerk and accountant, whose thankless job made their business run. He said he accepted the proposition to come to Gorée because he wanted to improve his French and Wolof on an island where those were the two main languages. "A strange thing! I started learning [the languages] by myself, just to distract myself, at the age of nineteen," he noted. Both languages were necessary in a region where, along much of the coast and the interior, French was the main administrative language, and most small traders were forced to use Wolof since it was the most common language in the nearby peanut-growing lands of Kajoor and Bawol.

Since the island was so small, the buildings on Gorée were typically multi-purpose compounds: many were equally storehouses for peanuts, animal skins, or tobacco; boarding houses for visitors from faraway lands; bars with the most popular fire waters from gin and rum to port and absinthe; textile shops and haberdasheries selling cloth by the yard; pharmacies stocked with quinine for the fevers; bookshops offering maps and almanacs listing the high tides at the main ports of call; grocers with rice or millet, dried meat, and tinned vegetables for the people making those trips; and brothels, too, of course.

As was often the custom, Taylor may have lived where he worked, keeping a room above the storehouse. His job as an accountant meant he was in control of the company's registers that kept track of goods loaded or offloaded, loaned or sold throughout the season, but Taylor may have had other duties, too. He may have worked with the ship captains to find trustworthy buyers and sellers, to dry out fresh peanuts to make sure they didn't mold before the journey across the wide ocean, and to organize the treatment of new animal skins by preserving them, as was the standard practice of the day, with an arsenic solution to prevent them from rotting in the humid air. One American shipmaster wrote that the poison seeped into everything near it: "Our peanuts are stowed with the hides and must be more or less affected with the arsenic that forms the basis of the Hide poison and yet people eat the peanut both in their raw state and when used in confectionary. If people could always know the history of the 'nice things' which are given them to eat I think we should see some wry faces made."

Educated men of color like Taylor formed a "petite elite" of interpreters, clerks, accountants, successful traders, and administrative officials. They distinguished themselves from the much larger group of Black people living on Gorée who worked as skilled and unskilled laborers.

Manual laborers, whether enslaved or free, had always made up the majority of Gorée's population. The women were clothes washers, cooks, millet grinders, and domestic staff; the men were ship pilots and stevedores, carpenters and weavers, and general laborers for whom the only requirement was to have strong legs and backs. After abolition in 1848, Gorée's society converted their enslaved population into low-paid workers, apprentices, or, if they were minors, wards for whom a salary was still not mandatory.

The conditions these workers had to accept, Taylor later wrote, saddened him deeply. Their state, still so close to enslavement, he said, "made me think of what my own parents had been," and "what they had become thanks to the Gospel."

12

Unholy Wars

Lat Joor returned to Kajoor as a chastened former leader in early 1869, following the defeat and death of Maba and the dissolution of the movement the holy man had created. He had been allowed to settle in his home county provided, the French administrator said, "You promise you will not start any wars unless I give you the order." Of course, Lat Joor had other ideas.

North of Kajoor, in a village not far from the Senegal River and the new French fort at Podor, another holy man with dreams of expansion was gathering strength. Amadu Ba—sometimes called Amadu Seexu in the historical records or, often, just "the marabout"—issued from a clerical family with messianic tendencies from Fuuta Tooro. His father, Hamme Ba, had believed himself to be the "mahdi," a reformist figure in some traditions of Islam who appears at the end of time to cleanse the land, guide the faithful, and help them defeat the forces of evil. To prove his bona fides, Hamme said God demanded a public sacrifice to cleanse the country and he was prepared, like the prophet Ibrahim (Abraham) in the Book, to pay with the life of one of his infant sons. One day, in the center of the village, he slit his baby's throat.

Hamme Ba, the rest of his family, and some followers were banished from their village after this, but he soon founded another one.

When cholera broke out in the region in the late 1860s, Hamme's son Amadu fixed his mind on his father's message of cleansing the region. With its rapid, grotesque deaths, the cholera epidemic was seen by Amadu as the hand of God exacting his furious punishment. He preached about reform and revival, urging his followers to overthrow the French infidels and all African leaders who worked with them. As the disease spread, the scared and desperate people who had seen their loved ones and neighbors die in such agony were fertile ground for Amadu's message of divine retribution.

Amadu's adherents multiplied and his military spread as fast as the cholera that had preceded them. "Wherever he goes, he preaches about the holy war and fanaticizes the local people," the administrator in Podor informed the governor. He said this movement was "far from being a fleeting outpouring of excitement. It is expanding more and more every day."

Not long after Lat Joor had returned to Kajoor, the colony's official newspaper reported he "had let himself be seduced by Amadu Seexu's promises and made common cause with him." Maybe Lat Joor had taken note of Amadu's new challenge to French rule and, always a habile strategist, saw in that movement a force that could help him reclaim his own throne.

In July 1869, Lat Joor and Amadu Seexu brought their combined armies together in the Kajoor heartland village of Mékhé. There, the armies set a trap for the French forces who were in pursuit of Lat Joor. They lured French troops into a part of the village that was surrounded on three sides by prickly thickets of spiky succulents and chunky baobab trees, acacias with thorns as sharp as small weapons, and overgrown shrubs whose branches tangled together to provide good cover for any who might need it. The same edition of the colonial newspaper reported on the battle: "As the soldiers [for the French] went through narrow and winding paths, the enemy was hidden in the village's huts and greeted them with an extremely heavy attack at close range." More of the combined Kajoor and Madiyu forces were hidden in the bush and pursued the French soldiers who tried to retreat. It was a rout; about a quarter of the French cavalry column lost their lives, including the French officer who had led the charge, and more than half their horses were taken as booty.

The French who survived only did so by hiding on burr-covered paths and finding their way through the dry, spiky bush on foot. They hid on trails that had few wells and, therefore, less traffic from any adversaries who would be in search of them. July in Kajoor is always blistering hot and, if the rains had not yet come, the air would have been filled with suffocating gusts of stinging sand; only the desperate would take a route where there was no water. One of the officers wrote that water was so scarce he was obliged to drink his own urine.

The songs the griots still sing today trumpet the triumph of Kajoor's brave warriors over the French at Mékhé. What's more, Lat Joor prohibited farmers from cultivating in the areas near French fortifications, leaving parts of central Kajoor deserted.

Many people of Kajoor moved on, just as they had been obliged to do throughout history, in those baking lands where water was often scarce. As one observer wrote, the area had "no mountain to climb, no river to cross, no river to bypass. It is a horizontal landscape, ideal for moving along a direct path, for riding, for taking action."

French reprisals soon came; the Kajoor army's arsenal of lightning-fast guerrilla strikes and clever tricks continued, too. In the north, Amadu's followers had taken control of part of the Senegal River, and the French were fighting there, splitting their military focus between the river and the flatlands of Kajoor.

None of this conflict was good for business, and the Kajoor region was less safe for trade than ever. One French military bureaucrat wrote: "The resounding failure of our attempts to conquer Kajoor after those bloody expeditions that have ruined this magnificent province must correct us from the system of direct government, even a mild form, beyond the outskirts of our cities."

In France at the same time, the government was fighting a war with Prussia, a war that would soon lead to the capture of Emperor Napoleon III and would end the Second French Empire. So when the biggest merchants in Bordeaux and Marseille lobbied the colonial government to abandon both the military campaigns and the direct rule of Kajoor in order to keep the country safe for peanuts, their arguments found receptive ears. And after the governor died of cholera in August 1869, his replacement, François Xavier Michel Valière, seemed open to pursuing a conciliatory agenda. By mid-1870, he was having regular discussions with the colonial council and with the nobles of Kajoor about restoring the monarchy with Lat Joor as their leader. Valière wrote to the minister, "If I have authorized Lat Joor's bid instead of fighting it, and if I have also easily accepted his nomination and sponsored the projects of this person who was, the day before, our enemy, it is because I am convinced that he is the only possible damel for Kajoor."

Lat Joor soon became damel again and turned his back on the alliance with Amadu Seexu. In a way, Amadu's movement *had* helped Lat Joor reclaim his throne—by giving him another bargaining chip to play with the nobles and gatekeepers of Kajoor, and with the French. But the Kajoor that was newly released from colonial control was only a shell of its former self. The French insisted upon the restricted borders of Kajoor, keeping the spoils of previous treaties that had allowed them to absorb Gandiole in the north and an area outside of Rufisque in the south, the key ports of the peanut trade.

13

A Word on Slavery

Defining slavery here is imperative, and yet it is also fraught. From today's vantage point, many if not most people tend to see the New World experience of slavery as the reference, but it bears underscoring here that slavery was a system of exploitation, marginalization, and domination that existed on nearly every continent and in most societies. Slave labor may have built many of the world's marvels, from the pyramids of ancient Egypt to the Roman Empire's extensive system of tunnels and roads to the Great Wall of China.

But there were as many forms of slavery as there were forms of freedom. What it meant to be enslaved depended on the society. In some societies, the enslaved person strengthened the group's demographic weight or military force. Others had ritual uses for the enslaved. Still others insisted upon the economic uses of enslaved people and their labor, as in chattel slavery.

What it meant to be free also depended on that society. Some groups established a slave class or caste, for whom the barriers to freedom were high. Others were integrative, offering attainable methods of manumission, which meant that within a generation or two or three, the descendants of the original enslaved person could be born free and even aspire to have slaves themselves.

Long before the trans-Atlantic slave trade from Africa began, desert caravans conveyed captive people across the Sahara, along with gold, ivory, and spices, all of which would fetch fine prices in the cities hugging the Mediterranean or those across the Red Sea and the Indian

Ocean. And long before that, many African societies with robust militaries would occasionally raid other polities to capture artisans with specialized skills, wives for whom no dowry was necessary, or simply more general laborers.

In general, the enslaved were typically strangers, outsiders from neighboring countries or even just neighboring villages, who were deprived in some ways and to varying degrees of their autonomy. As such, their bodies and labor no longer fully belonged to them and, often, neither did the labor or the bodies of their children. Slavery differs from other forms of labor exploitation and dependency, such as corvée, indenture, debt peonage, or pawnship, because slavery is of indefinite duration.

In West Africa, there were many different systems of slavery, some of which approached the New World understanding of the enslaved as chattel, and others of which allowed the enslaved to assimilate into their societies over time and be made into something close to kin. Sometimes these systems even co-existed; the recently enslaved could be treated poorly or sold at will, while the enslaved of the second or third generations would be treated as integral parts of the clan or family—even if some distinctions always remained.

For centuries, many of the enslaved in West Africa were captives of war or the victims of raids. Some had been convicted of crimes, were witches or sorcerers or members of groups that somehow angered their leaders. All were stripped of their families, their histories, their sense of themselves in the world, and, to different extents, their personhood. Many were put on the market and sold, dispersed like spores in the wind.

"In the marketplaces, there are slaves as well as horses, millet and all such products as can be sold," wrote a nineteenth-century French doctor and amateur ethnologist who was posted to Senegal in the 1870s. "The Wolof who wants to sell peanuts at the end of next season is there looking for a farmer to work his land." Other merchants, he wrote, were looking for porters, laborers, and concubines. "You can see that this unfortunate human flesh is destined to be used for this or that at random according to the prevailing circumstances."

On the Rio Pongo, where Nyara Bely may have kept a barracoon to confine the men and women who would tend to the peanut fields while awaiting the next slave ship, it was said that she used occult practices to make her new captives biddable. The stories told by elders in these communities place an emphasis on the mystical tools used by both the enslavers and the enslaved. One story reported that the captives were seated on a special black stone, made to drink a special decoction, and bathed to wash away their pasts and tame their spirits. The goal wasn't to beat them into submission, but, according to the keepers of this history, to "to make the slave accept his fate, which he can never change and which nothing can alter." The newly enslaved person was to accept his or her *maaragiri*, a word that means something like "unchangeable destiny."

Once transformed from free into enslaved, the ones who stayed on the continent experienced a spectrum of conditions. They may have labored in fields, sure, but may also have tended to livestock, aided in temples, or worked as foot soldiers, porters, domestics, or concubines. Sometimes they even became wives. Others learned the trades of their masters and became weavers, blacksmiths, and shoemakers. An infinitesimal number of them became elite administrators, tax collectors, and royal advisers who had enough money and power to have slaves themselves.

Some were living pieces of money, who could be sold and resold at any moment at markets and private sales. Others would, over the course of some years, save enough to be able to buy their own freedom and that of their family. Some of the enslaved, as the first generation gave way to the next, would be given a place within the hierarchy of the family or clan or caste, becoming a part of them and finding a place within the body politic. They were to become members of the family, sure, but lesser members, restricted from marrying the sons and daughters of those who had enslaved them, and still consigned to cooking, cleaning, and tending to animals. Their place in society was assured, but they were never supposed to forget it.

Not even the rare elite slaves, who in most ways could not be called slaves, were exempt from the dual sword of place. Eighteenth-century

French slave trader Dominique Harcourt Lamiral, who spent many years in Senegal, wrote that one of the damel's high officials was always a slave. "He always has to have irons (chains) suspended at the head of his bed, so that when he is lying down he constantly has them before his eyes, continually reminding him of his servile status." Lamiral speculated that the practice served an important function in a society where the free minority dominated the many enslaved, and served "to check their pride and ambition."

14

This Black Man from Gorée

Gorée's brisk crosswinds drew visiting ships to the volcanic rock on a regular basis, but also drew people who came to escape the vapors, the fevers, and the relentless heat of the continent. "Although situated in the torrid zone, like our other establishments in Africa, here we breathe in cool and temperate air all year round because of its island location," according to French colonial statistical records about Gorée in the 1830s. "And it is rightly considered the healthiest place occupied by France in West Africa."

In 1871, one of Gorée's visiting ships brought the French Protestant missionary François Villéger and his wife, Marie, to the island.

Saint Louis, Senegal, was Villéger's first posting after finishing his training at the Maison des Missions in Paris and being ordained as a reverend in service of the Paris Evangelical Missionary Society. The young missionary couple had been in Saint Louis for just over a year when Marie fell ill. Fevers had forced the retreat of the two other missionaries who had originally traveled with them to Senegal, and caused the death of at least two previous Protestant missionaries in the swampy Casamance, so the couple felt it prudent to travel to Gorée, where everyone said the air was more pure. They were to stay there for several weeks until Marie recovered.

Villéger wrote to his superiors in Paris that the people of Gorée were chafing from the "yoke" of the Catholic priests. The Protestants of France were critical and distrustful of Catholic leaders and with good reason; for nearly two centuries Protestantism had been largely outlawed in France, and its practitioners were forced to hide or flee. It was only after the French Revolution that the French government formalized a new policy of religious freedom that allowed Protestants to come out of the shadows.

Villéger said that on Gorée, "the population was thirsty for light." This thirst must have revealed itself as apathy, for Villéger himself noted that the people of Gorée were not avid churchgoers of any kind.

Despite his initial disappointment, he soon made a happy discovery: "There are also about 50 Protestants from Gambia in Gorée. I believe many of these people to be pious, and I did not hesitate, after speaking with them, to give communion to one man and two women."

We can't be sure, but the man may have been Walter Taylor and one of the women may have been his new wife, Elizabeth, a woman of Liberated African heritage, but from Gambia instead of Sierra Leone.

Walter Taylor said that not long after he moved to Gorée, the Reverend George Nicol, the Gambia's colonial chaplain based in Bathurst and a fellow Sierra Leonean, wrote to him: "Dear Mr. Taylor, Do you want to be a centre of light for all the Protestants of Sierra Leone who live in Gorée, by bringing them together every Sunday at your home to read to them the word of God and the Anglican liturgy, and to address them words of exhortation? I will help you as much as is within my power by sending you religious texts. . . ."

Nicol had been a lecturer at Freetown's Grammar School when Taylor was a student there and had since become the first African to be named to the high-level colonial position as chaplain. Taylor responded to this call and started to hold services for the community of Sierra Leonean and Gambian people on the island, most of whom were working, like Taylor, as clerks and agents for European or American trading houses. He also invited them to prayer sessions at his house three times a week.

The records do not show how Taylor met Villéger, but the island was small—both in population and in surface area—and they were both of a similar age. They seemed to be disposed to think well of one another.

After Villéger went back to Saint Louis, he and Taylor kept up a slight correspondence. Taylor wrote to Villéger in mediocre French full of Anglicisms, saying that the Protestants of Gorée needed a proper shepherd to lead their flock: "We very much regret that a pastor with our religious views does not reside in our midst." Taylor also shared how he converted someone, a poor laborer who "longs to be baptized and looks forward to your return here with impatience." Some months later, after Elizabeth gave birth to their first child, a son they would call Walter Jr., Taylor asked Villéger to come back to Gorée: "If you can come on April 15th to baptize my child, I would be very pleased."

Villéger took up his pen and responded to Taylor, sharing that he had finally finished translating the Gospel of Matthew into Wolof. Taylor responded in turn, praising Villéger's efforts in this respect: "To demolish the fortress of gross ignorance and superstition in which the people of Senegal are held captive, the Holy Bible must be in the language of the country so that everyone can read it and understand what is being read."

In Sierra Leone, many Liberated Africans learned enough English to read the Bible on their own, thanks to an extensive system of schools run by both religious missions and the colonial government. The goal of the schools and the government, after all, was conversion by turning Africans into model Christians and emissaries of British culture and ideas.

What Sierra Leone had that Senegal didn't, Taylor speculated, was enough people to spread the "good news of salvation." "The harvest is plentiful, but the laborers are few," Taylor wrote, quoting the scriptures. He suggested there were many pious Sierra Leoneans and Gambians who had received enough training and education that they could be tasked with this heavy work of evangelization.

He was also signaling that *he* could become one of those assiduous spreaders of the glad tidings of Protestantism, and by so doing, rejoin the path he had been forced to leave after the book incident in 1865. In the same letter Taylor wrote: "Since I know the language of the country, if you think it is appropriate, I would like to go to France to study in order to devote myself to the advancement of the reign of God and give you help after a few years."

Villéger shared the strategy Taylor had articulated to recruit "native" missionaries with the director and committee in Paris, writing, "It would be most helpful if we could have native workers who could withstand Senegal's climate, which is so dangerous for Europeans; I believe this would be the best approach for success. I would urge the committee to bravely embark on this path."

Villéger also backed Taylor's candidature for the Maison des Missions in Paris where the missionaries were trained before being ordained, writing: "As for the Black man from Gorée who I know, I think you would do very well to admit him."

15

Lat Joor Wants His Slaves Back

The only known image of Lat Joor
appeared in *Le Monde Illustré* in 1875.
Digitized by Gallica/BNF

The newly reinstalled damel of Kajoor regularly wrote reams of letters
to a succession of French governors and administrators in the 1870s
and 1880s, or rather, he had people write them for him, because he was

probably illiterate and only marked his letters with a special stamp that said, "LAT JOOR, DAMEL OF KAJOOR." Qadis, the Muslim judges who resided with his court, wrote the letters in Arabic script, but with Wolof words, which were then translated into French by people with differing degrees of skill. The missives varied in levels of politesse because Lat Joor had a complicated relationship with the French. They were occasionally obsequious, often belligerent, and almost always clever.

Sometimes he wrote flattering greetings like, "From Lat Joor to his father and mother, the Governor," or "From Lat Joor to his close friend, the Governor," or, what seemed to be a personal favorite, "Praise be to God, to the Emir of Saint Louis."

Lat Joor wrote to the governor about the taxes that peanut merchants and camel caravans were supposed to pay when they traded in his kingdom; about his grinding obsession with invading the nearby Bawol Kingdom, which had previously been attached to Kajoor; about murders and cow thefts; about his grievances with other leaders; and he wrote letter after letter asking for the governor's help in tracking down his captives.

October 29, 1874: "The son of the King of Saalum, named Fakha, married one of my sisters, the princess of Soguer [Kajoor], who received as dowry a female captive named Guinar who managed to gain her trust. Last year she came to St Louis, but she met a man named Laëti Diouf who made her believe that she was free; from then on she no longer returned to Kajoor; I am certain, and I can swear, that this woman was born a captive. . . . Please give her to the person carrying this letter."

September 20, 1876: "Die Guèye and his brothers have escaped from our country and are now in your territory (at Amadou Diama's house in Gandiole). We are sending you this letter for you to permit us to bring them back to us. We are counting on the friendship that exists between us. Slaves here are like silver [money] in your country. I did not do anything to Die Guèye or his relatives, only they learned that every captive who comes to Saint Louis is freed. We are scared that any of our slaves should stay long in Saint Louis."

December 27, 1876: "One of my captives has fled to your territory and it is certain that she is in Guet Ndar. . . . I am counting on our friendship for you to take care of this business about my captive."

Often Lat Joor was too late; the people had already gotten their freedom papers. At other times, French officials might expel the would-be freedom seeker before they could go through that process. In those cases, once outside of the limits of French authority, Lat Joor's men could capture the person on their own. And sometimes, the French did the deed themselves, just as Lat Joor might have hoped.

In 1870 or 1871, a French official wrote to Lat Joor: "I received the two letters that you sent to the commander of M'bidjem to claim a captive. I have examined this case and I find your claim fair," the official wrote. "I order the commander of M'bidjem to give her to the envoy you choose."

These dry directives appear repeatedly in the archives. On the other end of the transaction was a real person who was subsequently dragged back into servitude.

The same year that Lat Joor got his captive back from M'bidjem, a similar case unfolded on the island of Gorée—one that the missionary Villéger wrote about, saying he had witnessed it firsthand. It must have been when they were staying on the island during Marie's convalescence.

Gorée was rarely the destination for runaway slaves, since, as an island, it was tricky to travel to there. But in the latter half of 1871, an enslaved woman from Kajoor decided to seek refuge on Gorée. "Six months after her escape, she was discovered and captured," wrote Villéger. "The state prosecutor wanted to save her, but Gorée's highest-level commander gave him a written order to deliver this woman to her owner, which was done. The woman was a mother, she carried her child on her back. It was heartbreaking, the poor wretch, screaming and crying for help from her mother when police officers beat her and put her in a canoe that carried her to Dakar on the mainland."

What happened after is a matter of some contention. Villéger wrote, "When she arrived in Dakar, about five or six hundred meters out of town, her master killed her with a shotgun and took the child away!

The murderer has not been punished." That version of the story was disputed several years later by Gorée's commandant, who said the woman was still alive and still with her master. But, in a way, the truth didn't matter. The story itself seemed possible and horrified all who heard it.

Walter Taylor, Gorée resident and accountant, must have heard her cries from his desk in a dusty stockroom or heard about it from his wife or his friends over dinner. Could he have started wondering then if he might have a role in helping such people in the future?

Part III

16

A Sickness with No Name

Peanut harvest, Bambey. *Cirad collection*

In Senegambia, June was the precipice of the *nawet,* or the rainy season, which spread out heavy and thick after some seven or eight months of dry desperation. The world would be crispy and monochrome, all brown leaves, brown grass, brown sand, and, when the Harmattan was blowing, brown skies. The first rains were a release of a forgotten breath. Ah, yes, this is what air smells like after it is washed by the rain. This is the earth returning to itself.

The first rain was sometimes a ringer, a false hope sent to trick the anxious. After the second or third, farmers could feel confident enough to take to their fields and plant their crops. But if the skies teased them with cloudless blue vistas, and the rain kept its distance, people might plead for its return, mimicking the sound of drops of water on the dry sand.

Dugub jaa ngiy dee	*The millet is dying*
Rippoo-ripp	*Rippoo-ripp*
Gerte jaa ngiy dee	*The peanuts are dying*
Rippoo-ripp	*Rippoo-ripp*
Mboq maa ngiy dee	*The corn is dying*
Rippoo-ripp	*Rippoo-ripp*
Ñebe jaa ngiy dee	*The cowpeas are dying*
Rippoo-ripp	*Rippoo-ripp*
Lii metti na lool	*It is very difficult*
Rippoo-ripp	*Rippoo-ripp*
Sunu àddinaa ngiy tukki	*Our whole life is ruined*
Rippoo-ripp	*Rippoo-ripp*

In some villages, even farmers with large families and an extended network of nephews to labor could work only a portion of the land available. So they bought slaves. And if they couldn't afford slaves, or not enough slaves, they might come to an agreement with people from lands distant and near who came to help both those farmers and themselves. These migrant sharecroppers worked the land and sowed the fields that local farmers could not farm and, in return, gave the landholders a portion of the harvest as rent. Along the Gambia River such men—for they were always men—were called "strange farmers," but in Senegal, they were called "nawetaan"—"those who came for the rainy season."

On the Gambia River, Soninke traders from the desert's edge, what is now eastern Senegal and western Mali, were pioneers of this practice. During the long centuries of the trans-Atlantic slave trade, they would rent out land along the lower river and grow grains such as millet and rice to provision the cities and forts along the coast, as well as the slave ships that docked there.

When the slave trade was outlawed, some Soninke traders still used their long-established commercial routes to transition to legitimate commerce, just like the crafty farmer-slavers on the Rio Pongo. But instead of employing a system in which slaves were worked for a season and then exported, as the Rio Pongo farmer-slavers did, the Soninke took to commodity farming with unparalleled industry. Some sent their trusted slaves to the lower Gambia River or even as far as Sierra Leone to become strange farmers, along with their sons and nephews, who went as free men. At the end of the season, the free men might be able to buy a slave or two themselves whom they could send back to their home villages to tend the land there. And the trusted slaves might save enough money to buy their own freedom.

In the 1860s, a French officer traveling from Senegal to Segu in the heart of Western Sudan wrote about encountering one such Soninke trader on the road. The man had left his home country five years before and spent several years growing peanuts. "He left poor; he came back with a decent fortune," the Frenchman wrote. "He was bringing back five captives, a wife, and a child."

The French traveler was struck not only by the trader's story, but also by the state of his captives. "A vigorous captive carried the child, and three other young girls, crippled by the long journey they had just taken, were attacked by Guinea worms; with their swollen legs they followed, with the help of a stick. . . . No matter how hardened I was, I could not look at these unfortunate souls, who, when it was time to leave, could no longer get up with their numb limbs; then their master arrived and struck them, and sometimes a tear ran silently down their cheeks. No doubt they were thinking of their birth places and of their mother's hut, as slowly, painfully, they resumed their journey."

Although many farmers, strange or otherwise, saw the winds that blew in the nawet as uplifting to the spirit and bringing the hope of a better future, their immediate condition at the beginning of the rains was often a precarious one. The rainy season was a time of crisis. Even if the gods were smiling on them and the rats had not gotten too fat on last year's stocks of millet or sorghum, this time of year required balance; farmers' available grains would have dwindled, and they would have to wait another few months until the harvest to eat until their bellies were full.

As luck would have it, small traders, many of whom were African, would choose this time to sail up the river or trek into the interior to sell the food that farmers increasingly needed and could not provide for themselves. The administrator in the Gambia described the process: "He [the native trader] conveys rice and corn, the property of his European employer, the items most in demand at that time in the upper river. He recovers in exchange pagnes [trade fabrics] or country cloth, manufactured from cotton grown in the country in the native towns by their means and dyed by the women from indigo grown in small quantities near each town; in November he receives groundnuts, hides and wax, in exchange for these same pagnes."

In between the wars, epidemics, and famines, merchants even started advancing stricken farmers with millet and peanut seeds at the beginning of the season. It was a seemingly benevolent idea that in reality trapped farmers into a cycle of trade that soon created a cycle of debt. Along the Casamance River, farmers who received a bag of seed before the nawet had to repay the merchant with two bags of seed after the harvest. Plus, after the harvest, when the trader reappeared to buy his peanuts, he brought with him goods—guns, spirits, and imported fabric—to entice the farmers to spend more and save less and, crucially, to acquire more debts and push into more land to make more money. Despite the sometimes unfavorable terms, cash crop peanut farming continued to grow since it was still the means by which farmers could gain money for goods and dowries, cattle and slaves.

But in the late 1860s, the French commandant in Sédhiou, a large town with a fort on the river, started sounding the alarm about another problem in an extraordinary report. "A disease, for which I have no name, attacked a number of [peanut] plants in this province last year," he announced to his superior, writing at the tail end of the rainy season. "This year the affliction has spread and entire fields have been so affected that their owners have abandoned them."

The nature of the sickness was mystifying; the plant seemed normal at first—the seed would sprout, its stems and leaves would grow as expected. But the plant would not branch out as it should, and, most important, it would not flower. If there were no flowers, there would be no pegs to slowly drive the plant to bury itself into the dirt so it could develop pods and seeds.

"It is a disease that has caught us by surprise and if left unchecked, threatens to spread throughout the country," the commandant warned.

At first, he thought the sickness only attacked old fields, where farmers had been growing peanuts for several seasons. But the next year, farmers were finding the sickness even in new fields, and still he had no idea what was causing it.

He undercut the impact of his warning, though, as he continued: "Although this disease is causing great havoc, especially in the highlands, I still believe that because of the large amount of fields being cultivated and because of the extreme fertility of the healthy plants, this year's harvest will not be less than last year's." And he was right about that. The amount of peanuts exported from Sédhiou that year didn't even register a dip from the previous year's numbers. The trade kept expanding in the hands of enthusiastic landholders and strange farmers whose industry, in spite of the troubles, helped the economic wheel continue to turn.

There doesn't seem to be any record of the commandant following up about the sickness with no name in the following seasons. Maybe the plants started producing again, or maybe new strange farmers moved in with new seeds and new fields? Whatever the case, it was a missed opportunity, because the problems that emerged in Sédhiou had their parallels up and down the riverine coast, from the Gambia to Sierra Leone. Everywhere in that rich region of swamps and mangrove forests, farmers were starting to encounter problems: some peanut plants weren't growing, others would produce empty shells, and still others would rot even with the barest caress of a humid wind.

The peanuts in the Southern Rivers were dying. And this wilting crop endangered a whole system of labor and trade that would soon have to seek fresh lands elsewhere.

17

A Native Evangelist

Walter Taylor. *Courtesy of Defap*

The director of the Paris Evangelical Missionary Society, Eugène Casalis, eventually responded to François Villéger's letter about Taylor joining the mission. Casalis said that, in theory, the idea of hiring a "native" pastor in Saint Louis was a good one, if they could trust that the man's faith was sincere. "This is indeed the future of the Senegal mission—if we can find men truly devoted to Christ and capable of being completely committed to his principles despite the misfortune of their pagan origins." Casalis wrote that the board of trustees would consider inviting Taylor to the Maison des Missions in Paris— eventually. In the meantime, Villéger was to bring Taylor to work with him in Saint Louis: "You will use him at school, you will see him close up and when we write to you in a formal way, you will be able to better decide if it is appropriate to open the doors of our institute to him," wrote Casalis.

This response from Casalis and other letters from Villéger disclose a key weakness in their missionary project: they did not seem to respect the people they set out to convert. They may have been men of the cloth, but they went to Africa with a set of assumptions about their own superiority vis-à-vis the continent and the people who lived there. They did not question the colonial orthodoxy that the French culture was better, that the French systems of law and education were better, and, of course, that their religions were better, too. They were people of their time, and their racism was often explicit. When Villéger first arrived in Senegal, he wrote that he was determined to love the natives even though he "at first experienced a kind of repugnance for Negro people." It was, nonetheless, his firm belief that the Gospel was for everyone, for all races and creeds. The force of his faith changed his mind. "Now, I love them more than ever," he wrote. "When I meet them, I would like to hold them to my heart and carry them to the heart of Jesus."

His stated desire must have been more metaphorical than literal, because early letters show that Villéger did not spend much time among Black people. His evangelical outreach was mostly limited to holding services for a handful of French Protestant soldiers who were posted in Saint Louis. He and his wife also ran a school that targeted young Black children whose parents wanted them to learn their sums and read enough French to ensure their future jobs in the colony's trade. But Villéger's lack of ease among Black people meant that the actual mission of the mission was not promising.

From the beginning, the Protestant mission occupied a strange position in the French colony, a small minority religious organization within a governmental structure that had long been oriented to privilege Catholics and was increasingly trying to become completely secular. Protestants were part of the system, but were also in opposition to it.

In general, after nearly a decade in Senegal, the Protestants were losing ground. Between the competition from the more populous and more well-funded Catholic Church, and the resistance of much of Saint Louis's long-standing Muslim population to evangelization, the future seemed grim.

But Taylor must have felt some optimism, for he accepted the terms and the place laid out for him, and moved to Saint Louis in October of 1872 to work as an evangelist for the mission.

The population of Saint Louis was mixed between Europeans; the established mixed-race families of traders, lawyers, and clerks who dominated the political and social life of the city; some Sierra Leoneans, just as on Gorée; and local Africans, from the Wolof to whom the land had originally belonged to others from Moorish regions to the north and the Pulaar-speaking regions to the east. The main island of Saint Louis was much bigger than Gorée, but the same housing patterns remained with a blend of European-style and African-style buildings and merchants who lived above their stockhouses and shops. Most Europeans tended to live on the main island, although some also built beach houses on the Langue de Barbarie, not far from the "native village," Guet Ndar, to take advantage of the fresh ocean breeze. Many Africans lived on the main island, too. Everyone lived in close proximity, if not in intimacy. Maybe some crossed paths on the palm tree–lined promenade near the governor's palace, which was, according to one European visitor, "a veritable oriental palace with verandas and terraces and surrounded by a zoological garden."

After Taylor arrived in Saint Louis, Villéger wrote that the Black man could not "replace a European colleague." The lead missionary would later learn that Taylor was also disposed toward illnesses, with countless migraines, asthma attacks, and bouts of malaria, but was

unmatched in his zeal when he was well, and energetic in his outreach. "He fetches the Blacks and brings them back to his rooms to
talk to them about God and salvation through faith," Villéger wrote to
Casalis.

There is little correspondence from Walter Taylor to the Paris office
during these early years, an indication that he was not a decision-
making member of the mission. Nonetheless, Taylor opened the mission up to a different approach to evangelization, not by longing for
their souls, but by befriending people, by eating alongside them, by
going to their homes and letting them come to his, by listening to their
concerns and mediating their conflicts. The letters show that many of
the small strides the mission would make in the following years would
come from Taylor.

A couple of years into his stay in Saint Louis, Taylor started a "young
people's Christian association," where he spoke about the Gospel and
served the people a good meal, "harder aliment," Taylor wrote, "that
they can well digest."

Taylor's own social status as part of a petite elite also broadened
the reach of the mission and helped them target an influential class of
Black leaders. His good friend was a brother to the customary leader of
Waalo, Sidya Joob—who subsequently asked them to establish a school
in his territory. The Protestants did, eventually, but long after Sidya
had been pushed from power.

Taylor was also friends with a lieutenant of the tirailleurs, an African unit of the French colonial infantry, named Mamadou Racine Sy,
a high-born and well-connected man from Fuuta Tooro. "He's no ordinary Negro," wrote Villéger. He and the committee in France knew
that such a high-profile conversion could have a catalyzing effect on
the soldiers he led, who were themselves well placed to influence people in their own villages. "He [Mamadou Racine Sy] comes to service,"
wrote Villéger, "and he talks often, almost every day, with Taylor. All
this seems to show a very real beginning of God's work in his heart."

Taylor had written in 1875 that he had befriended a marabout, a
flexible designation that could mean a Muslim teacher, an imam, or
even a healer or prognosticator. Whatever kind of marabout this man,

Daouda, was, Taylor knew that he often had unscrupulous methods. "I have had some months ago many and many a time," wrote Taylor, "to call attention to the way and manner he, as a priest, has been practising on the credulity of his less educated coreligionists to deceive, cheat and rob them of money and other valuable articles by most unjust, shameful and unlawful teaching and representation." After several months' acquaintance with Taylor, Daouda felt a sense of guilt and repented of his ways. Some months later he decided to join the church and was baptized on Easter Sunday in 1876.

Walter Taylor preached on this red-letter day, for he was a skilled orator with a palpable presence in the pulpit. The chapel wasn't full, but spectators crowded in the street. "It must also be said that the baptism of a Mohammedan priest was an extraordinary event in Senegal," boasted Villéger. Many spectators were not members of the church but were rubberneckers hoping for a bit of excitement.

Taylor read from the Gospel of John: "Ye worship ye know not what: we know what we worship," a pointed message for an evangelist presenting his beliefs to skeptics. Villéger recounted the ceremony in a letter to the director: "He managed to capture the attention of his listeners with a substantial, solid, well-thought-out message that would not have been out of place even outside of Senegal." When the service was nearing its end, Taylor led the assembly in a hymn in Wolof.

The seeds of the work the mission would later go on to do were planted by Taylor, too. In 1877, Villéger wrote that one of their newly converted church members, a certain tirailleur named Moussa Dialo, was trying to get enough money to buy his wife out of slavery. It is possible and even probable that Moussa Dialo had himself once been enslaved; many early tirailleurs signed up to serve because the signing price they received allowed them to claim their freedom. In the early days, the signing bonus was sometimes given directly to their masters. During his time as a soldier, Dialo had been able to save some money to buy his wife. "The ransom price had been set at 350 francs," wrote Villéger. "Although Moussa had only 200 francs to offer, he was able to take his wife with him, promising to complete the sum as soon as he could. Since then, he has not been able to find the 150 francs that were still due. He has absolutely nothing. Knowing his position, our brother Taylor had the idea of taking up a collection among Protestants and even some Catholics in Saint Louis. They contributed 120 francs, so only 30 francs remain to be found, which I will provide."

Following this happy event, Villéger also helped a man that Moussa knew get his freedom papers from the courts in early 1877 and escape being pressed back into servitude. Taylor wrote that Moussa's friends and neighbors, many of whom shared similar experiences of servitude, were impressed. "They are very well disposed towards us and listen with great attention when we proclaim the Gospel of Jesus Christ to them," he noted.

Moussa Dialo lived in Sor, a large island just across the river from the main island of Saint Louis, a trip facilitated by a pontoon bridge. Wolof may have been the lingua franca of Saint Louis, but Taylor said that many of Moussa Dialo's neighbors and friends in Sor spoke Bambara, a Mande language that marked them as coming from somewhere deep in the interior in what the French called the Western Sudan, but what its people called then, and still call now, Mali. Although Taylor, Villéger, and most of the colonial records would call them all Bambara, this broad category masked important differences among the people who spoke the language; many of them were actually from zones farther south, like the Wasulu, which had long been dominated by the central Bambara states.

Taylor and Villéger observed that although some of the runaways had Muslim names, they seemed to have little concern for the practice of that religion, preferring their own gods, rituals, and prayers. The missionaries saw these Bambara people as pagans, which were a missionary's dream; they seemed like fair game to these Protestants on the prowl for souls. "The natives in Sor are almost all farmers; their humble homes belong to them; they are therefore, in a way, independent," wrote Taylor. "Their position differs from that of many natives in Saint Louis who have Catholic or fanatical Mohammedan employers and who, for fear of losing their positions, or of displeasing their bosses, will only become Protestant Christians with extreme difficulty."

Taylor knew, too, that parts of the Gospel had a special message for these recently enslaved, just as it had for some of the people in his community in Sierra Leone, with its stories of liberation from slavery in the Book of Exodus or its New Testament, which said, "Come unto me, all ye that labour and are heavy laden, and I will give you rest." Here, he told the director, was a possible way forward for the mission: "I believe, dear director, that God has opened a door for us in Sor and we should enter with little delay."

18

Ceebu Jën

Senegal's national dish is called ceebu jën. The basics of ceebu jën are fish and rice made in one pot. That's what it literally means in Wolof: *ceeb* is rice and *jën* is fish. A good ceebu jën takes hours to prepare and should include carrots, turnips, eggplant (the regular purple one and jaxatu, the bitter green one), a chunk of tough cassava, a bit of cabbage, and maybe some yams. It should have at least two kinds of fish, the interiors stuffed with roff—a fragrant mix of garlic, parsley, and pepper. The classic ceeb is red, colored with tomatoes, but some cooks hold the tomatoes and keep the rice uncolored. It can be cooked with a kind of putrid, fermented mollusk called yéet; a bit of a salted, dried fish called guedj; or sprinkled with a funky powder called netetu that transforms its flavor into something transcendent. Sometimes it also is served with a sauce made from tamarind pods or another made of the bright-tasting green leaves of the hibiscus plant. All this and a lime or two, ready to be squeezed on the fish, and a hot Scotch bonnet chili pepper for a little more excitement.

If you ask Senegalese people where the original ceebu jën is from, they will tell you that it is *lekku ndar*—Saint Louis cuisine. And they will say that the person who invented it was a woman called Penda Mbaye.

People say Penda Mbaye was a real person, although the stories about her feel more like folk legends. The collective popular history reputes that she was born in the nineteenth century or the early twentieth century, and was either cook to the French colonial governor, a peasant or slave fresh in from the nearby Waalo or Kajoor kingdoms, or a griot known for her skills at entertaining who would cook and then perform bawdy and energetic dances at weddings, baptisms, and other grand events with her skirt and limbs flying. Maybe she was all of those things?

If she existed, maybe she lived in Saint Louis around the same time that Walter Taylor did or not long after—after the peanut had gained so much ground in the economy and society. That's because the peanut and ceebu jën are connected—a moral cause and effect.

Some of the letters Villéger and Taylor wrote to the home office in the 1870s were lists of their accounts and other money matters: their salaries—Taylor was then paid exactly half the amount Villéger received in 1875; rent on the parsonage; the going prices for cooks and washerwomen; the cost of keeping a horse; and the price of food. The Europeans in Saint Louis, Villéger included, ate à l'européen: meat, wild game, guinea hens, fresh vegetables, bread, and potatoes. But for the children who came to study in the Protestant Mission's schools, at least one letter mentions that they were served rice decorated with a bit of fish.

A species of rice is native to West Africa and was a common crop farther down the coast in the Southern Rivers and even in Sierra Leone, where the thirsty grains thrived in the river plains and boggy lowlands. A young Walter Taylor would have been accustomed to eating it. The French army also served rice to its tirailleurs. Anyone who had enlisted or had been forced into its service would have gotten used to that grain, no matter where he had grown up.

But most of Taylor's friends and neighbors, including Mamadou Racine Sy and new church members like Moussa Dialo, as sons of Fuuta Tooro and the Western Sudan countries respectively, would have spent their childhoods eating millet—a hardy grass that grows well in the sandy soil across the desert's edge.

"The specialties of the Senegalese people are couscous and sanglé [sanxal]. The first is called cere, the second laax," according to a mixed-race priest who had been born in Saint Louis in the early nineteenth century. Both products were made from millet and sometimes sorghum or corn. He noted that sometimes cooks would prepare rice, but it was not as common as couscous since the people of Senegal didn't find it very nourishing.

Two young pileuses pounding millet to make couscous. *Courtesy of Archives du Sénégal*

The transformation of millet stalks into couscous was a labor-intensive affair requiring scores of pileuses—women who processed the harvested hard grains into something more usable. They would pound millet in deep wooden mortars to shake the grain free of the hull and turn it into flour that would then be hand rolled into the tiniest balls the size of grains of sand. "Using the mortar and pestle is grueling work," wrote a French doctor in the 1860s who traveled around Senegal and wrote at length about the dietary habits of the people he met. "The Negro girls try to make this chore enjoyable: They sing along. . . . They throw the pestle in the air, clapping their hands several times before it falls; they join together to beat in rhythm." The songs were often nonsensical and sometimes made up on the fly, using hard consonants and alliteration to accompany their makeshift drums:

Kur kandang	*The pestle reverberates*
Kandang ndang	*The pestle reverberates*
Lekk ci dugub ji	*To eat millet*
Naan ci ndox mi	*To drink water*
Soo galaxndikoo	*After you wash your mouth*
Tuur téll	*You'll pour out the water you used with a splash . . .*
Xanaa dugub dafa ñor	*Could the millet be ripe*

This had always been the work of the women with the least amount of power in a household, often the enslaved since they were usually charged with the most disagreeable tasks. And in places where slavery was no longer supposed to exist, many newly liberated women could find work as pileuses. It was hard work, but an enterprising pileuse could sell couscous or processed grain for extra money and, by so doing, move up the economic ladder from worker to trader.

Although there were many opportunities for work in the city, life there was more controlled than life in the village; a pileuse's work was confined to certain hours and was to be done with a certain discretion. Women who sang and danced to pass the time during this repetitive, physical work violated new colonial rules and could sometimes wind up in court. In November 1871, the paper reported that three pileuses on Gorée were sentenced: "each fined 11 francs, for noise and causing a racket at night, disturbing the peace and quiet of residents."

Most of the millet that people ate in Saint Louis and Gorée came from their cantankerous neighbors up the river and, of course, from Kajoor, where the golden grains grew well in their famous "joor" soils. But, of course, those soils were perfect for peanuts, too.

Savvy farmers knew they should rotate crops, alternating between millet and sorghum or corn to help manage crop diseases. They knew, according to the French doctor, "you can't produce a depleting cereal for more than three years in a row on the same field." Peanuts could be and were beneficial in rotation with such cereals. The doctor said that Senegalese farmers had noticed that the peanut, "far from depleting the land, enriches it," an astute observation since peanuts and other legumes fix nitrogen and make it available to other plants, functioning as a kind of fertilizer when used in a seasonal rotation.

In some places, though, farmers were increasingly choosing to grow peanuts year after year instead of millet or other grains. Their decision would have a swift effect on the colonial outposts with their large populations, and on legions of pileuses, dependent on millet from Kajoor and Bawol. Already in the 1840s, some colonial authorities saw this could become a problem in the areas where peanut agriculture was starting to become popular: "The natives of these territories, seeing that peanuts were highly sought after, began to cultivate a great deal of them, and as a result began to neglect their millet crops."

As traditional millet farming started to be replaced by intensive peanut farming for export, there was simply less millet to go around. People in cities started to switch over to a new staple food: rice, imported first from the Gambia or the Southern Rivers and then, eventually, from as far away as India and Indochina. From the 1840s to the 1850s, the amount of rice imported in Gorée and Saint Louis tripled. This was helped along as the military, which employed many Africans as soldiers, started to serve them rice as part of their provisions.

In 1859, then-governor Faidherbe said that this growing dependence on a foreign staple food could have a couple of silver linings for French merchants. "If the Blacks simply eat the millet they grow, it doesn't produce any business for us. It would be to our advantage to make them grow peanuts, beraf, cotton . . . etc., instead of millet and sell them rice imported from India by French ships for their sustenance."

And so Penda Mbaye's ceebu jën, with all its careful elements, was the fruit of this policy and a chain of causes whose effects could not, at the time, be predicted.

19

A Steamboat on Land

As the peanut quality in the Southern Rivers started to become a concern, smart merchants looked north toward Kajoor, where peanuts could be grown under ideal conditions.

Kajoor had two main doors, exit points through which caravans transported their peanuts for export: Leybar in the north, just a short distance by boat to Saint Louis, and Rufisque in the south, whose deep port sat just across the bay from Gorée. But Rufisque was separated from the productive peanut lands to the east in Kajoor and Bawol by a crescent blockade—a chain of cliffs covered in spiky grasses and speckled burrs and fortified with a dense tree cover that stretched from the north to the south. A caravan trying to reach Rufisque from some villages in Bawol or Kajoor could go around that obstacle and take a longer route, veering north to brave the dunes and the marshlands where their animals would labor, or going south to scramble over the rocky cliffs along the coast; or it could follow the ridge to a gully, a convenient passage made of hard-baked earth instead of melting sands or bogs, on the other side of which was a more direct trail to the coastal port. The problem was, though, that the villagers around the gully were hostile to all strangers—Black or white—and when they could, they would swoop in with terrible rapidity to claim the caravan's goods as their own.

The Seereer groups who lived in and around those hills belonged to no big kingdoms and paid tribute to no leaders. At least a couple generations before, they had gone there to flee the region's wars, raids, and kidnappings and take refuge in the rugged cliffs and dense woods. Their Wolof-speaking neighbors in Kajoor knew little about them, but called them *Noon*, a word that means "enemy."

When the French started to use this route, they encountered these "Noon" and gave a name to this gully. They called it the *ravin des voleurs*, the thieves' ravine. As the port of Rufisque docked an increasing number of ships waiting for the bushels of peanuts being carried on the backs of camels and mules, caravans could not resist the allure of a shortcut. Many if not most caravans that took the ravine must have made it to the other side unscathed, and that's why they always pushed their luck. Some lived to regret it when they were ambushed, wounded, and liberated of their goods. Others had no regrets because they died in these attacks.

In April of 1872, for example, the commanding officer of the nearby post in Thiès wrote to his superior in Gorée that in just over a week, three different caravans had been attacked on the road to Rufisque: "On the 12th of this month . . . a man on horseback was murdered. . . . On the 13th, a new attack was carried out on the road from Pout to Thiès near the large fallen baobab tree in the ravine. Two Blacks were seriously injured and then looted of their cargo, which consisted [of] guinées [trade cloth], tobacco, gunpowder and 75 francs of silver. Finally yesterday, on the 16th, at the same place and time (about 6:30 in the evening) a caravan of 50 camels driven by some Moors, was attacked by Blacks, posted in the bushes. A single rifle shot was fired and wounded one of the Moors; his unarmed comrades were terrified and fled, leaving in the hands of the robbers: three camels, guinées, and 1000 francs of silver that had been placed on the camels that disappeared."

And still the caravans came, because still the merchants bought and still the peanut trade grew.

In the 1870s, monthly situation reports the Gorée commander sent to the governor regularly cited some kind of theft or death in the ravine: caravans that had been attacked; shootouts that ensued; camels, mules, and money that had been taken; and the gang that had vanished without a trace like the mist that developed in the valley at dawn and burned off as soon as the sun peeked over the hills. The dispatches about the region often ended with some variation on this phrase, "As usual, we couldn't find the culprits."

This sense of lawlessness served as the background for a shift in the ambitions of the colonial government. In 1876, Colonel Louis-Alexandre Brière de l'Isle became governor of Senegal following his distinguished military service in the new French colony of Cochinchina, where he was based not far from Saigon. As with Faidherbe, his predecessor who had come to Senegal two decades before, Brière's experience in conquering a far-flung foreign land and making it into a piece of the French empire had given him a large appetite for colonial expansion. Almost as soon as he took office, Brière dusted off a plan to facilitate and protect the transport of peanuts, a plan that had been moldering in some military engineer's back office for years; they would build a railroad through Kajoor.

The real goal, just like Faidherbe's telegraph all those years before, was obvious. Conquest was the ultimate goal. And this time, instead of hugging the littoral like the telegraph had, the rail would be a trail, a narrow strip of French land, that would run through the heart of Kajoor.

The official who conducted the initial technical study of the project suggested a route that would "serve the most populous, the best cultivated, and the most productive part," and he was frank about their ulterior motives. Such a path would, he wrote, "ensure our domination over these Black peoples."

Even before getting authorization from the government in Paris, Brière started to lay the groundwork with the main person they would need to convince: Lat Joor. Brière sent an envoy racing across the plains and patchy forests with a letter for the damel in January of 1877: "In consideration of the friendship that exists between us, I am looking for a way for your subjects to be able to earn as much money as possible from their products, which will make your country richer, and I found that a railroad from Saint Louis to Dakar through Kajoor would be a way to do so. On this route, there will be stations at some intervals where your subjects could sell their pistachios [peanuts] almost as high as in Saint Louis or Rufisque and they would no longer have to pay for the transport that is so expensive for them today." He kindly informed Lat Joor of his plan to soon cross Kajoor with his men in a preliminary survey for this project. And he offered Lat Joor a gift: "Thinking that a beautiful horse would bring you pleasure, I intend to bring one for you as a gift."

Lat Joor took the horse, for he was an equine collector and always kept a well-stocked stable. But he did not agree with the plan. He wrote back to Governor Brière de l'Isle a few months later: "You are attempting to create a railroad, like a steamboat on land: it is as impossible as putting one hut into another hut, or a bottle into a bottle. . . . Know that if, today, you create a railroad and set up trading posts along the route, you would be taking my country away from me and robbing me of everything that I own. A friend should not do such a thing on the land of his friend."

Lat Joor may have thought that this straightforward refusal would be the end of the conversation; it was not a letter with much ambiguity. But he had called upon the French for help so many times before, changing his mind and his alliances so frequently, the governor must have felt there was cause for persistence and measured optimism. The governor was determined to cash in on the many investments, both financial and social, the French had made in Lat Joor as the damel of Kajoor, and if he could not help them, they would find a way to help themselves.

20

The Ebbs and Flows of My Courage

When Walter Taylor first joined the mission in Saint Louis as an assistant evangelist in 1872, he thought it was a temporary situation, a way station for some months before he went to France to study and be ordained as a full reverend. But the temporary situation dragged on for a few more months and then a year and eventually more than five years—during which he nourished his hopes with the crumbs of vague promises.

Since he had thought his initial stay in Saint Louis would be brief, Taylor had originally sent his wife and child to Gambia to live with friends or relatives. But as his voyage to France was delayed again and again, Elizabeth and Walter Jr. moved to Saint Louis in the middle of 1873 to join him. Missionary wives were always a big help for evangelization efforts and performed countless hours of unremunerated labor, visiting sickbeds, swaddling babies, and dispensing advice to female congregants and children, so it can be supposed that she was a welcome addition. Elizabeth Taylor did not speak French well, but that was no problem since most of their new members didn't speak it either. She did speak Bambara with some fluency, having grown up in the Gambia where a sister language was widely spoken, and so would be doubly useful when it came to evangelization.

"She seems like a very good woman to us," wrote Villéger, a praise undercut by everything that followed. He did not seem to like Elizabeth Taylor. Although they lived in separate houses, the Villégers wanted Elizabeth to help with housekeeping duties and were not pleased when she was reluctant. "[She] unfortunately possesses to a high degree those great defects of her race: sluggishness and carelessness," Villéger wrote. "Instead of having in her the active help needed for the interior of the house, my wife quickly discovered that she could in no way count on her in this respect and that she would have to give Mrs. Taylor lessons little by little, which would not be so easy as for an ordinary Negress, because Mrs. Taylor was raised in the European style; but since she lacks energy rather than will, I hope that things will improve little by little."

In Mrs. Villéger's estimation, it would seem, Mrs. Taylor did not improve. A few years later, Taylor confided to the director that Mrs. Villéger had been cruel to Elizabeth. She "made fun of my wife—her dress, her walk, her hair, and who knows what," wrote Taylor. Others later told him that aboard a ship to Senegal from France, Mrs. Villéger had told some of her neighbors, "Mrs. Taylor is just a lazy woman—she is uppity and needs three or four servants."

The mission in Saint Louis in those days constantly suffered from interpersonal conflicts. When the mission society sent another European in 1873 to look after the school, Mrs. Villéger fought with the instructor's wife over every small thing related to their household and the mission. Soon, the instructor and Villéger himself developed a rivalry so vicious, it eventually involved many other colonists and divided the partisans of each missionary into intractable camps. Taylor was a bystander in that conflict since he had been away in Sierra Leone for much of 1874 recovering from a series of illnesses—his acute asthma and anemia, to which was added diarrhea and occasionally "neuralgic pains in the regions of the heart." He wrote to the director to describe the situation he found upon his return in early 1875: "The mission, I am very sorry to say, is still in a very deplorable condition." The strife between his two European colleagues "sits as an incubus on all our energies,—paralysing all our efforts; hindering further progress in our labour of love; and even undoing in a great measure the little good we have, under the blessing of God, effected during the past few years with so much pain and tears." Their bitter infighting was bad publicity for Protestantism.

Salimata Ndiaye, schoolteacher with the mission,
circa 1890. *Courtesy of Defap*

The schoolteacher was fired in 1875, and Villéger survived as the
head of the mission. With the schoolteacher gone, peace reigned for a
couple of years. A new helper soon emerged: a young woman from the
Casamance region named Salimata Ndiaye.

Salimata was about twelve years old in the mid-1860s when the
Protestant missionaries who had been posted in the Casamance town
Sédhiou sent her to France to study. When she returned to Senegal
nearly a decade later in 1876, she was sent to Saint Louis to work for
the mission's school. Salimata wanted to go see her mother in Sédhiou
upon her return, a natural request since she had been away for so long,
but Villéger, ever vigilant, denied the request, saying he was worried about the sicknesses so prevalent in the area, and about another

more existential fear: "It's almost certain that if Salimata were to go to Sédhiou they wouldn't let her come back," he wrote. He said that Salimata's mother would marry her off, and advanced a controversial proposal: "Perhaps we should give this woman a certain sum so that she would be willing to leave her daughter with the mission." In effect, he wanted to buy Salimata from her mother. Director Eugène Casalis pushed back right away, writing, "We do not believe it is possible to enter into any kind of agreement based on barbaric, anti-Christian mores." But this exchange shows something of Villéger's shabby opinion of Salimata's mother, of Salimata herself, and perhaps of African women in general.

Villéger's questionable actions vis-à-vis Salimata did not stop there. About six months later, he wrote that Salimata had gotten an offer of marriage. "A friend of Mr. Taylor's from Gambia, an employee of an English trading firm, wrote to Brother Taylor saying that he wants to get married and would like to find a suitable young lady. He asked him if Salimata would consent to marry him," Villéger wrote. "Unless the mission were to employ this young man, who, Mr. Taylor says, is a very good fellow, it is clear that Salimata would be lost to the mission." There was not any more surviving correspondence on the subject, so it's not clear if either of them informed Salimata of her proposal. But Salimata did not marry the man from Gambia, or, indeed, any other man during the next twenty years that she would spend doing the mission's work.

Soon the cracks began showing in Villéger's interactions with Taylor, too. Taylor, for his part, was tiring of the indignities he had forced himself to swallow over the years.

For one, the house Villéger had found for the Taylors on the southern part of the island was a typical Saint Louis building with storerooms on the bottom floor and living spaces above, but their rental did not include the ground floor storeroom. The owner sometimes filled the storeroom with peanuts, which gave poor Taylor terrible asthma attacks.

Taylor was paid much less than his European colleagues, even though by the end of the 1870s he had three children—Walter Jr., Sally

Margaret, who had been born while they were in Sierra Leone in 1874, and Samuel, born in late 1876. It was the schoolteacher who confided to Taylor that Mrs. Villéger opposed any raises for Taylor, even with his expanding family, and had once told her husband, "Let the Taylors starve, don't increase their wages."

And soon, it seemed to Taylor, Villéger was trying to tighten his grip on him, perhaps fearing for his leadership position at the mission. "I have the right to demand a weekly report of everything you do," Villéger told Taylor. "I don't know all the natives you know who visit you every day." When one of their students started spreading gossip about Taylor, he saw Villéger's meddling behind it. Taylor said this young man "told the natives that I was merely a servant at the mission; that they shouldn't listen to me."

According to Taylor's telling of it, Villéger repeatedly tried to assert himself and reclaim his authority, but he could rarely accomplish what Taylor could. When Villéger tried to take over an evangelization group that Taylor had been meeting with on Sunday evenings, no one came. "He didn't succeed because he needed to visit them during the week, to encourage them," Taylor explained, "so that on Sunday we could gather them; that's what Mr. V didn't do."

Still, Taylor continued. In May 1877, he started to learn Bambara himself. He was tired of depending for interpretation on his wife or Salimata, who also grew up speaking the language. Taylor said he wanted to learn it "to be able to help them [his parishioners]."

Sometimes Taylor fell into bouts of melancholy because he was so discouraged about his situation. He wrote to Director Casalis in late 1877 about his life—an emotional letter and a plea for help: "Certainly, as a soldier of Christ and as an African, it is my duty wherever I am to work to help the benefactors of my race in their noble and divine task to spread in Africa the religion of Jesus Christ, who alone, through his sanctifying influences, can tear the Negro from the state of moral degradation in which he finds himself, break his chains and dispel his darkness. It is a duty that every converted and enlightened African cannot refuse. But let me tell you, dear director, my position in Saint Louis is exceptionally difficult and prickly, and I am so unsteady.

Today I'm up; tomorrow I'm down. These ebbs and flows of my courage and self-confidence are very upsetting to me. I always ask God to let me know His will for me, or to give me more grace and faith, if that is His divine will, for the fight I have to withstand."

At the end of that year, the highs and lows had taken their toll; Taylor felt he'd had enough. "I have suffered too much, dear director, and I will end up, I'm sure, dying. Maybe it is God's will that I leave the work having accomplished what He has brought me here to do. I am sending you attached an account of the amount I need to be able to travel to Sierra Leone with my family." He needed 1,025 francs for the boat to Sierra Leone with his wife, three children, their ward, who was a formerly enslaved girl who had been living with them for some years, and the assorted baggage of a life spent abroad.

The board did not accept Taylor's resignation. Instead, they accepted Villéger's. The French missionary had sent one in a fit of pique around the same time. His provocation was not about his conflicts with Taylor, but related to the finance committee's repeated admonitions about his outsized budget. The Villégers, it seemed, liked to live well, and Saint Louis was an expensive place to set oneself up in the style to which they aspired.

Between Taylor and Villéger, the mission society weighed who was more important to the work being done in Senegal. Who knows what their full deliberations may have been; the meeting minutes only say that after some serious consideration, they decided that Taylor was indispensable: "He has shown himself to be too hard-working, too intelligent and too wise in his conduct for us to accept the loss of his services."

At the beginning of 1878, the director wrote his happy response to Taylor's desolate letters: "Instead of accepting your resignation and permitting you to return to Sierra Leone, the committee has instructed me to write to you that they invite you to come to Paris without delay." They would finally ordain Taylor; he would come back to Saint Louis as a full-fledged reverend and the leading pastor of the mission.

Part IV

21

Saxayaay

The time it takes for freshly sown peanut seeds to grow into maturity and be ready for harvest in Senegambia is between 90 and 120 days, depending on the variety, the soil conditions, and, of course, the rains. The best time to harvest the peanuts is not too long after the rains have ended, when the ground is no longer wet but still has some give. After pulling the plants out of the ground, farmers leave them in the fields for a few weeks and wait for them to dry. Then they gather to separate the tangle of peanut pods, peanuts leaves, and stems—the peanuts to eat or sell, and the leaves to feed the cows, sheep, donkeys, horses, and goats. It is time-intensive work that was and still is mostly consigned to women and children.

Determining when to harvest sounds simple, but isn't. One agronomist, writing at the beginning of the twentieth century, gave the peanut harvest a more precise time period: between October 15 and November 15. But if farmers are too hasty and pull out the peanuts too early, a late-season rain could cause them to rot right in the field; or, especially in areas with heavier soils, if the farmers wait too long, the dirt could harden around the pods, making it difficult to pull them out without significant losses. When that happens, it is also the job of women and children to dig in the dirt and glean what they can from the fields.

Even after all of this effort, some peanuts always remain in the ground. There they wait, biding their time until the conditions are right for them to be born anew. The following year, when the rains start again, pounding the thirsty sand and the hard-baked soils, they get their chance. Sometimes, in areas where no harvest happened at all because of conflicts or plagues, whole fields of these leftover peanuts push out their stems, their leaves search for the sun, and their flowers bloom all over again.

The Wolof have a special word for such plants; they call them *saxayaay*, seeds with no mothers.

22

Springtime in Paris

Walter Taylor prepared for his trip to Paris right away, settling his household accounts and ordering warmer clothes, since he must have needed an overcoat and woolen suits to be able to confront a Parisian winter. A diligent researcher would learn of this from Villéger's letters, since no correspondence exists from Taylor from this period; we can only speculate about how he felt leaving Africa for the first time. Maybe he was excited to discover a new culture and to finally achieve what he'd been working toward for so many years. Maybe he was apprehensive for the same reasons. Villéger had agreed to stay on in Senegal until Taylor's return so some of the day-to-day activities of the mission could continue in Taylor's absence.

The Paris Evangelical Missionary Society's journal reported on his trip with breathless excitement: "Mr. Taylor, the native evangelist of Saint Louis, well known to our readers, was summoned to Paris.... The Committee decided to bring him here in order to establish the basis of a personal and intimate acquaintance with him and to confer upon him the pastoral charge by the laying on of hands. Our brother has had a successful journey; he is at the Maison des Missions, where he is preparing for a serious examination. . . ." The Anglicans in Sierra Leone and Nigeria had built a substantial "native pastorate," an army of ordained Africans to evangelize among their cousins and their neighbors, but for French Protestants Taylor was a rare commodity. He would be one of the few Africans to join their brotherhood of ministers.

The Maison des Missions was a run-down, cramped, and musty

building on a tiny street in the Latin Quarter. It was not yet spring when Taylor arrived in March of 1878, but even in the cold gray days of the waning winter, he must have wandered the narrow streets, browsed new texts in bookshops, and read about biblical exegesis or moral philosophy at a neighborhood brasserie while he took in the life unfolding on the cobblestone lanes. A few streets over from his lodgings, the Parisian reproduction of the Pantheon sprung up, a white stone temple to the French intellectual; Taylor may have visited this secular mausoleum to walk among the graves of Voltaire or Rousseau.

The Paris Evangelical Missionary Society had moved to the Latin Quarter from the outer suburbs a few years before to be closer to the country's leading educational institutions. Students at the Maison were expected to study a theology that was theoretical as well as practical—and to be well rounded, versed in Greek and Latin, history, and geography.

A few days after his arrival, Taylor attended a mission board meeting. It was the first time most of the board had met him, although they had received correspondence from him for about five years. They were impressed by his "profound piety, lofty views and modesty." And they wondered, marveled really, at "how he managed to speak French so well," even though they knew he had lived in a French colony for the better part of a decade.

Occasionally, he may have been invited to dinner or to visit at some committee member's house where they would discuss religion, sure, but also politics and culture. French Protestants were a global lot, many with roots from other European countries more friendly to Protestantism. Taylor mentions at some point having borrowed a book from one member about the Fisk Jubilee Singers, an a cappella group from a new Black college in Tennessee, many of whom had been enslaved. Throughout the 1870s, they toured Europe, singing spirituals in front of packed audiences in Germany, the Netherlands, Brittany in France, and England, where they even performed for Queen Victoria. Taylor may have been inspired by their example and excited by their project to raise funds for their college.

Taylor gave his first big speech at the May general assembly meeting of the "religious societies," where he addressed a crowd of influential Protestants from across the country. He started by saying how happy he was to see "your keen interest and the work you are doing to ensure the spiritual and material uplifting of the Negro race." At the time, there had been several debates about how best to go about evangelizing Africans who couldn't read the white man's language or his Bible.

Taylor's speech was a sophisticated rhetorical gambit that asked the crowd for their help and support while also taking them to task for their high-handed assumptions at the same time:

> There is nothing that pains me more than to hear some people say that it is better to attempt to civilize the Negro than to convert him to the Gospel of Christ, and that we will be more successful by this means. If you put before the savage the benefits of civilization, he will have the right to answer you that, in his condition, he is as happy, perhaps happier than you are;—that he does not see the need to eat with a knife and fork, to put on stockings and shoes;—that it is a matter of taste;—that he does not feel the need to obey all the demands of civilization by renouncing his natural inclinations, in order to seek a happiness like the one you need for yourselves.

Taylor was a diplomatic voice, but was also a true believer, and as a missionary he saw his fight as not so much against African cultures than as a competition with the "Mohameddans" for African souls. "The Mohammedan religion is one that has a great affinity with human nature," he said in the speech, asserting that it was not difficult to get people in Africa to convert to Islam. He said that although Islam had obligations to fast, give alms, and pray five times per day, it also had polygamy, charms and amulets similar in design, if not in function, to the ones they would have used in their traditional religions, and a strong trade network. Nonetheless, Taylor believed that if only Christianity had been introduced first, many Africans would have accepted it. The call, he said, was clear: "The obvious Christian obligation is to not permit the Mohammedans to precede us in those Negro countries that are still pagan."

After this speech, one minister stood up and said that he was sorry

Mr. Taylor was planning to go back to Africa. "What the French would gain by hearing this! The people who attended this evening will not forget it."

It was a triumph for Mr. Taylor, who had proved his quality as an orator and evangelical strategist.

This general assembly had been scheduled to coincide with the 1878 Exposition Universelle, or the World's Fair, which was to open to the general public in late May. No documents confirm that Taylor went to the Exposition Universelle, but how could he have missed it? It was not just the talk of the town, but drew visitors from around the world. In Senegal, the buzz about the fair had reached a crescendo just before he left, as the organizing committee for Senegal's exhibit presented to the general public a taste of the colony's contributions, including fine leatherwork, a pirogue or two, fetishes and masks, a collection of several thousand live birds, and twenty-one dolls dressed in costumes representing local styles. The Catholic establishments sent an exemplar of their Bible in Wolof and a Seereer language catechism, but Villéger would not let the Protestant mission be outdone and sent along a collection of Wolof language hymns.

Certainly, once in Paris, Taylor would have been eager, just like hundreds of thousands of other visitors, to get a peek at the curious objects and people from around the globe and marvel at a world in miniature crammed onto the green esplanade of the Champ de Mars and in the Trocadero gardens. Maybe he visited the Indian pavilions, designed in a mishmash of styles that even spectators of the day called a "fantasy," filled with silk-covered divans, a palanquin made from ivory, and shields adorned with pearls and emeralds; or the Japanese garden, striking in the simplicity of its bamboo fences and tatami mats designed in the traditional style. Perhaps he wandered by the display dedicated to the guano of Peru with jars of the fertilizer surrounding a rock, complete with model birds to remind visitors who was really responsible for the stuff. Maybe, like so many others, he crawled into the newly completed head of the Statue of Liberty, which was a gift from France to the United States. The view from the top of the head offered the opportunity to observe the gathered company from a moderate elevation. And perhaps he went to see Mr. Thomas Edison's new invention in action, a tool to record the human voice, to capture and engrave sound onto a disk, which the local press called "the most amazing experiment that has ever been conducted in France." He may have even gotten to take a ride in Giffard's *"le grand captif"* in the Tuileries garden, a steam-powered dirigible capable of taking forty to fifty passengers at a time to rise some seven hundred yards into the air, floating above the city and observing its patterns and colors—the geography of its life.

One July evening, just a short walk from where visitors would be able to hover in the *grand captif,* a substantial crowd gathered at the Protestant Temple de l'Oratoire for a spectacle of a different kind. The temple had formerly served as a royal chapel and, having been built in the baroque period for a king, was much more ornate than a Protestant church ought to have been, despite a great deal of unwilling simplification during the looting and destruction of the revolution when mobs had decapitated marble statues and pulled down ornate paintings of saints and kings. The building still retained its shell with soaring, vaulted ceilings and colonnades inlaid with cherubs. It was in this place—a king's chapel that had been torn apart and then restored to its original vocation—that Walter Taylor would receive the laying on of hands and be consecrated into the holy order of workers dedicated to the advancement of Protestantism.

It started at eight o'clock at night, and even though many people would normally have left Paris during the hotter months, the ordination drew a large crowd of Protestants in the long, narrow sanctuary, eager to see the rare ordination of an African man. The crowd was so large, too, because instead of receiving his ordination from just three or four ministers, Mr. Taylor would receive the laying on of hands of no fewer than thirty pastors. Everyone, it seemed, wanted to be associated with Taylor and the promise he held for the future of their churches.

After some prayers and recitations of Bible verses, as well as a hymn or two, Pastor Georges Appia, a Lutheran from a prominent Italian-Swiss family, preached his consecration sermon. He picked up the thread that Taylor had laid down months before. "The Church is not sending you to civilize Africa," he said. "No, the Church is sending you, in the name of the Lord, to be a fisherman of men. Go, it is telling you, go and tell the people and nations of your African homeland that a God of mercy and love has seen their ruin as He has seen ours, and that we, the elder brothers through the love of a common Father, have sent you in His name to bring them the message of freedom, forgiveness and heavenly life."

Once ordained, Taylor made his arrangements to return to Senegal, despite a bout of poor health, undoubtedly the fevers, migraines, and asthma toward which he was prone. But one obstacle remained before he could go. Just after Mr. Taylor's departure from Saint Louis earlier in the year, Villéger wrote to the director, "The Catholic clergy of Saint Louis is plotting to expel Mr. Taylor from Senegal as soon as they see him in charge of the mission, and that it is necessary for Mr. Taylor to have the support of a French pastor."

Taylor, as a Black man from Sierra Leone who was also a Protestant, would suffer from triple discrimination: from the whites who didn't feel that Black people should have authority; from the influence of the Catholic majority in the government and in trade who may have a lingering antipathy to the Protestant minority who had been massacred across France for generations; and from French expansionists who would always consider him a British spy since he came from British-controlled Sierra Leone. He was a Black man from Africa in a power structure dominated by white Europeans.

The committee members sought the opinions of their influential friends about how to proceed, including certain friends in the Senate and Admiral Jean-Bernard Jauréguiberry, a former governor of Senegal who was then high up in the naval ministry. One such official suggested naturalization as a solution. A flurry of letters was sent and the procedure started. Toward the end of the month, the committee reported that it was successful. "Thanks to the benevolence of the Minister of Justice, he is leaving with a residence certificate that gives him all civil rights and in three years he will be fully naturalized."

So much had changed in less than six months. Mr. Walter Taylor, the catechist from Sierra Leone, was now the Reverend Walter Taylor, a pastor of the Reformed French Protestant Church and a soon-to-be-citizen of France.

23

Reports from the Rivers

According to interested accounts, Nyara Bely—the peanut farmer, slave holder, and, generally, head woman in charge in her corner of the Southern Rivers—had long resisted proselytization by the region's Protestant missionaries, either of her people or of herself. But in August of 1878, when she was over eighty years old, Nyara Bely was somehow persuaded to change her mind. Once converted, she threw herself into it, ordering that a house for the missionaries be built in the village so they might settle there and start a chapel and a school.

The missionary who converted her, a Black man from Trinidad who had, by then, spent a decade on the river, said, "It is no sudden change which has come over the old lady. There has been a gradual disintegration going on for some time." Who can say what that disintegration may have entailed, but the Rio Pongo and the rest of the Rivers had changed significantly since she first began her reign some fifty years before.

For starters, the region had gone from being a no-European's land—both the Northern and the Southern Rivers—to seeing the beginnings of a colonial division, sectioned off into silos as defined Portuguese, French, and British territories.

And, up and down the Rivers, from the Casamance to the area just north of Freetown, another change was happening. The crop that had given the region its second flush after the clandestine slave trade was starting to disappear. Like Nyara Bely's conversion, it only seemed to have happened suddenly, but was, in fact, the fruit of years of trouble.

The causes were manifold, but the most important one, the one from which all the others stemmed, was probably the market for peanuts itself.

In 1869, on another corner of the continent, the great strides Europeans had taken to bend to their will what they saw as the unruly natural world and an unruly African country had paid off in a key achievement: the completion of the Suez Canal. The French developer Ferdinand de Lesseps had used subterfuge, bullying, and corvée—unpaid, forced labor—to get it done, and had driven the Egyptian government into crushing debt in the process, but it's not an overstatement to say that the canal would change the world.

The Suez Canal connected the Mediterranean to the Red Sea so that ships coming from the Arabian Gulf or the Indian Ocean no longer had to circumnavigate the African continent to get their goods or passengers to Europe. The canal shaved off some 8,000 kilometers and at least a month from the journey. In the 1870s, more merchants based in points east—East Africa, the Middle East, and especially India—took advantage of the new route and flooded Europe with their products. By the end of the 1870s, the market in Marseille, a city that had once been desperate for oily seeds to mill, was awash in peanuts and sesame seeds from the east. Those products, coupled with the growing use of petroleum for lighting, pushed down the price of peanuts overall.

This overstock of oilseeds was soon compounded by a new obstacle: weakening demand because of an economic downturn in Europe that would soon be felt around the world. The "Long Depression" started in the early 1870s and would last more than two decades, years in which peanut prices continued to fall.

In 1880, the Marseille buyers would pay at most about 43 francs for about 100 kilograms. In 1885, that price would drop to 31 francs, and by 1895, it would tumble further to 24.50 francs.

Once peanuts from West Africa arrived in Bordeaux or Marseille and were transported to a factory, they were prepared: cleaned of foreign elements like pebbles, hay, and horse hair; shelled and skinned; and the kernels ground up. The first cold-press extraction was done using scourtins, large bags made from reeds or other vegetable fibers, the same tools that for centuries had been used to extract oil from olives. This first pass on the peanut yielded the best-quality oil, superfine or even sometimes extra-superfine, which was a yellowish, edible oil that was light with a mild nutty taste. The second cold-press extraction yielded "fine" oil, a lower-quality product, but was the one used in soap-making. The mix was then reground using hot water and pressed for the third and final extraction, which would produce lampant oil, a poor substance only suitable for oil lanterns.

The peanuts from Kajoor could "withstand all competition," according to administrators. They were a sought-after commodity that created "an excellent cooking oil with an agreeable hazelnut flavor," a superfine oil that provided the most profit per kilo.

Farther down the coast, though, the peanut quality was inferior. The Gambia was on the second rung, with lower-quality peanuts, although some portion was still capable of producing superfine and fine oil. But in other parts of the Southern Rivers, the peanuts had always been poor quality, rarely producing the top-of-the-line golden oils that fetched the highest prices in Europe. These peanuts from the *bas de la côte* always sold for the lowest prices on the exchanges, and the prices were only getting worse.

This was what the commandant in Sédhiou had noticed all those years before, "a sickness with no name." Merchants were increasingly calling it *dégénérescence*, or degeneration, as they noticed the crops had more empty shells and smaller peanut kernels. Whatever it was, it was making Southern Rivers peanuts much less profitable than before. Lower-quality nuts produced less oil, after all.

Initially, watchers wondered if the problems were just related to the late rains. Or maybe it was the region's constant conflicts that hampered farmers who wanted to grow their crops in peace? Or it could have been that the farmers weren't rotating their crops as they should. Or maybe opportunistic farmers were harvesting the free-growing saxayaay plants instead of cultivated peanuts? Or perhaps there was trickery by greedy traders looking for an advantage who weighed down their baskets with pebbles? The causes were unclear, but the effect was obvious: poor-quality nuts were bad for business.

Most often these bad peanuts were discovered in Bordeaux and Marseille, when oil factories tested the freshly arrived seeds for their oil quantity and ascribed damages or bonuses depending on what they found. In the early days it didn't seem to matter to shipmasters eager to fill their hulls on a return trip to Europe. But now that lower prices were affecting the whole industry, merchants were reconsidering the numbers.

For a long time, traders bought peanuts for 2.50 francs for a bushel, which added up to 20 francs per 100 kilograms. As the prices went down in France, merchants squeezed their suppliers in the oldest exporting region of West Africa, where the peanuts were literally third-rate. In the early 1880s, boatloads of peanuts from the Casamance, Bolama in Portuguese Guinea, Rio Nunez, and Rio Pongo were selling in Marseille at a rate that was barely profitable, sometimes even 10–12 francs below the prices for peanuts from Kajoor. In the Casamance, an influential merchant crunched the numbers one year in the early 1880s and discovered that to turn a profit they could not pay the farmers more than 7.50 francs per 100 kilograms!

Smart merchants recognized that unilaterally cutting their farmers' prices in half would not endear them to their suppliers; they engaged in various forms of subterfuge to make the change less visible and more palatable. The most popular trick up and down the coast was that instead of changing the price per bushel, they changed the size of the bushel. In the Gambia one year, all the merchants conspired to rethink what a bushel could be. It had been 13.5 square centimeters, but they decided to stretch it to 16 square centimeters, a change that netted them about five kilograms more peanuts per container.

In other cases, traders increased the prices of the goods farmers bought with their peanuts. On the Rio Nunez in 1882, the commandant wrote to the governor that "they [the trading posts] have used an all too common subterfuge in order to gain access to the market. . . . they increase the price of trade goods. At present, they have almost doubled those prices."

Of course, the farmers of Senegambia and the Southern Rivers weren't stupid; they could tell they were getting a bad deal. Many

Weighing peanuts at a trading post in Senegal. *Courtesy of Archives du Sénégal*

farmers resisted, protesting by withholding their peanuts and refusing to sell them on such disadvantageous terms. In the Gambia and Casamance, the farmers called it a *tong*—a seller's strike. "The 1881 harvest in Sédhiou was one of the most lackluster," wrote one large merchant, "all the more so as the Mandinka people refused to sell—the 'tong'—as long as the bushel's size was not reduced."

Usually, the traders on certain rivers fixed their prices, but farmers from the Casamance could go a short distance to the Gambia where the terms were sometimes more advantageous. In other years, the opposite happened as farmers from the Gambia transported their peanuts to the nearby French trading area, Foundiougne, or even as far as Rufisque. But this was untenable; the farmers were so indebted to the traders, some even reliant on them for staple foods. If they refused to sell up to pay their debts one year, they might find themselves starving the next.

Nyara Bely breathed her last breath on the fourteenth of April, 1880. "This was no ordinary news in the neighbourhood of the Rio Pongo," wrote the resident missionary. "The news was not communicated till the next morning, when one of the largest cannons that are being used for the protection of the town was fired, and all her people present at once shouted in tears."

On the Rio Pongo that she left behind, another crop was gaining ground. The vining rubber plants were native to Africa and grew wild all over the region. Tapping the plants for rubber quickly progressed as a commercial activity since the same volume of product could be sold for at least ten times as much as the peanut could. By the 1880s, farmers were abandoning the peanut trade en masse to wander the forests in search of rubber plants. "The peanut harvest has begun, but it will yield very little," wrote a French official on the Rio Nunez in 1883. All the migrant workers, he said, had gone away to look for rubber.

Soon, the peanuts that once were grown on huge plantations in the Southern Rivers and exported for such profit in European ports would disappear from markets, ships, and factories almost completely.

24

A New Appeal

When Walter Taylor left France in August of 1878, he carried with him some carefully chosen gifts for Elizabeth and the recognition of a new set of French supporters. From Paris, he traveled to Bordeaux to get a packet boat bound for Senegal. In that city, he spoke at two churches and so moved the congregants about the mission's work with runaway slaves that he collected some 200 francs in donations, almost enough to buy a person freedom. His new friends and supporters, according to the mission's journal, accompanied him to his ship and "took their leave of him by embracing him with deep emotion."

The ship sailed down the coastline to Lisbon, a choppy crossing, and Taylor, whose health was delicate even on dry land, was sick the whole way. It docked there for several days to take on mail, passengers, and cargo. "Today I'm feeling weary," wrote Taylor to the director in Paris. "I'll be going ashore today after lunch, though, to see a bit of the city and put this letter in the mail." In it, he wanted to fill the director in on his warm departure from his new friends in Bordeaux and their promise to support the mission's work. "A ladies' committee will be formed to look after the work in Senegal in a particular way. . . . Many souls have promised to support me in my work in the future. All these demonstrations of sympathy and interest in the Senegal mission only increase my duty, already so great, before God, before the committee and before the churches of France."

From Lisbon, the packet boat slid into the Canary Current, an oceanic conveyor belt, and glided down the west coast of Africa with the wind at its back. Taylor arrived in Dakar less than a week later only to discover that yellow fever had broken out there and on Gorée. He and his fellow shipmates immediately boarded a waiting aviso bound for Saint Louis, but were kept from disembarking on that island in the middle of a rushing river, for all ships from Dakar and Gorée had to be quarantined at sea or risk spreading the disease.

When Taylor finally arrived on solid ground two weeks later, he expected to find Villéger still at the mission house, caring for the flock, but discovered that the French minister had left the month before. He had been in a hurry to avoid the yellow fever outbreak.

"The hasty departure of M. Villéger for France made a bad impression among Europeans," Taylor wrote to the director. "The priests did not fail to draw attention to the words of the gospel that say that the mercenary flees because he . . . does not care for his flock, while the good shepherd lays down his life for his sheep."

The committee in Paris took offense at Villéger's actions—considering him to have "failed in his mandate as a missionary and disgraced his title of Protestant pastor." But the committee also took exception to Taylor's fundraising efforts in Bordeaux, mostly because the fruit of this effort went directly to Senegal and did not go into the general fund. Casalis wrote right away to Taylor in the strongest terms: "Do not encourage direct donations for this or that special project."

But Taylor did not back down. He said that this work with runaway slaves wasn't just any special project. "In France, I pleaded for the cause of runaway slaves because I really do feel sorrow for them from the bottom of my heart," wrote Taylor. He was determined to continue this work and for that he needed money, which the friends in Bordeaux and some in the Alsatian city of Rothau were happy to give. "I'm sure that if I gave up direct donations from Rothau and the Bordeaux Ladies' Committee, the general fund wouldn't benefit at all. Instead, these people would become less enthusiastic, or they would go do something abroad for a special project which always interested them more. If you wish, I will inform you of all the donations I receive from these two groups, and let you know how I will put them to use. . . . However, if you insist that I shouldn't receive anything directly from these two sources, I will give it up."

In the end, the mission society conceded to Taylor's demands, allowing him to make direct appeals to these French communities, and he would soon form the Asile des Esclaves Fugitifs—the Shelter for Runaway Slaves—as a formal project of Senegal's Protestant mission, operating out of Taylor's own home and with close collaborators in Bordeaux.

Taylor rolled up his sleeves and got to work on his new mission, holding regular services and greeting old acquaintances and new ones. He had been anxious about how Mr. Villéger's friends and partisans would treat him upon his return. He was also concerned about how Europeans would treat him now that he was a leader in the community. After all, the racial views of Villéger must have been shared by many, even those who were not the man's friends. But Taylor wrote that his fears seemed to be unfounded: "To my great surprise, I was well received by the Europeans and by the natives, and everywhere with respect and sympathy. God has been working for me," he wrote. "I admit that I was too fearful in France, but it is always better to be scorned for fearful apprehensions than to be ruined by overconfidence."

Not long after his return, he decided to reach out in different ways to the African community of Saint Louis. He started a weekly prayer meeting, a Sunday school for both children and adults, and a Bible class where those who were interested could learn more about the faith every day except Sunday and Thursday. That September he also celebrated the Eid-al-Fitr holiday with his Muslim neighbors and friends, which marks the end of the holy month of Ramadan. A friend loaned him some appropriate clothes, maybe a billowy boubou in the brightest white, as wide as it was long to better catch the wind, and he headed to the Saint Louis mosque for the Eid-al-Fitr prayers. "The news spread through the mosque that the Protestant minister was among those present. All eyes turned to me,—and there were many different comments. 'Maybe he wants to become a Muslim,' some said.

'No danger,' replied the others who know me well. He's an eccentric man that Taylor—he wants to know everything, and he only comes to know what we do in order to criticize us in his sermons." The last remark was true, for Taylor had come to refine his methods of evangelization, he later wrote. He wanted to know more about the practices of his Muslim neighbors and about the sermons of their religious leaders, all so he could be "in a position to facilitate useful discussions with Muslims."

In October, he wrote to the director that he planned to baptize six new members "to give the mission, compromised by Mr. Villeger's hasty departure, a little bit of a boost." True to the strategy he articulated the year before, they were all Bambara—four men and two women.

"On the day of the baptism my house was filled with Bambara people three hours before the beginning of the service. I had to provide them with dinner. At six o'clock in the evening these brave souls sat down to eat and after doing justice to the food I offered them, they all went to the chapel."

At the chapel, other Bambara people, a handful of Sierra Leonean merchants, and a Swiss clockmaker came to witness the happy event. Taylor, resplendent in his pastor's robes, preached the gospel in Wolof and Bambara. "After the sermon, and the reading of the ten commandments in Bambara, I questioned the candidates, and on their solemn promise to live for Christ until their deaths, I baptized them in the name of the Father, the Son and the Holy Spirit."

After only a few weeks, it looked like Taylor's strategy was working. "The newly baptized put me in touch with other Bambara who ask me to teach them," he informed the committee in Paris. The strategy spread on whispers and rumors, eventually reaching the ears of the desperate and afraid, the poor and dispossessed. It was unlikely that they were looking for the gospel, but since many were newcomers to the city, they needed support and patronage to find housing and jobs. Some had surely decided they would accept their freedom in whatever form it came.

25

The Fifteen Captives of Ndiack Ndiaye

In 1878, the court in Saint Louis deliberated on a novel case—the affair of the fifteen slaves of Ndiack Ndiaye who were discovered at a farm just outside the city. Investigators said that the enslaved people "have clamored for their freedom." They said they were overworked beyond reason and were fed meager amounts food that was often of poor quality.

The summary court documents listed some details about each enslaved person's path to servitude:

1. Malick Cissé is a man about fifty years old; he was employed as a foreman on the farm; he lived in Bajoum with two wives, captives like himself; one of them, the first in consequence according to the Muslim custom, gave him a child, born in captivity; he complained that he was often mistreated; at the time when he was called to testify, he bore on the back of his neck the marks of blows that he said he had received a few days earlier.

The discovery was the result of a chain of events that started with a fight between Ndiack Ndiaye, a self-made son of former slaves and upstanding resident of Guet Ndar, and that village's chief, one Marabat Guèye. The two gentlemen were often at contretemps and so had, some time before, agreed to settle their grievances on a humid day in July via fisticuffs on the beach.

2. The woman Barka Sankaré had been a captive at Ndiack's for seven or eight years; she had married Malick Cissé; she has the status of second wife to him; now about thirty-five years old, she was once bought in Medina for a quarter [kilogram] of coarse salt, worth three francs; she complained in her deposition of overwork and lack of food.

Ndiack Ndiaye was the clear winner, according to the records; but Marabat Guèye was soon proven to be a sore loser and pressed charges against Ndiack for battery. Guèye was unhappy with the outcome of that suit since Ndiack's sentence was only ten days in jail and a fine of just 16 francs, or the price of about six bushels of peanuts. So he soon decided to reveal another fact to the court and the public prosecutor. Marabat Guèye said that his rival had regularly been involved with slave trading and introducing enslaved people into the colony— never mind that a member of Marabat Guèye's family had sold Ndiack Ndiaye some of the aforementioned people with the help of Guèye himself.

3. Bala Sirasinassy is a young man of eighteen; taken into captivity after the destruction of his native village, he was bought by the Moors who sold him to Ndiack for twenty guinées [trade fabrics].

Ndiack Ndiaye saw no reason to deny the facts of the complaint, but he said he thought this was permitted outside of Saint Louis, since many of his neighbors also bought, sold, and currently kept more enslaved people than he ever had. Even the fact of buying people within Saint Louis itself, he thought was permitted, since the enslaved cargo would not stay in that city. But the law clearly stated that on French land there could be no slaves and no French citizen, which Ndiaye was, could own slaves.

4. The woman Sira Courma is about forty years old; she has given birth to two children (since she has been in servitude), one of whom died long ago; she is currently pregnant as a result of the efforts of Malick Cissé, for whom she is the first wife. Sold by Toucouleurs (Fuuta) to Sarakolés [Soninke] (Guoy Kamera) who sold her to Ndiack in Kajoor about four years ago.

All people born in Gorée and Saint Louis were French citizens who could exercise their civil rights while living in the colony and had representation in the French National Assembly. But French citizens were also barred from possessing slaves on French land or outside of it. It was this law that Ndiack Ndiaye, as a colony-born citizen of France, violated. But Ndiaye also had friends who were citizens of local kingdoms not bound by French authority or who were only French subjects, not citizens—born in Waalo or in the towns the French had progressively nibbled away from Kajoor. These friends could keep people enslaved or sell them as they wished. Some French citizens engaged in a slave shell game, buying and hiding their slave holdings at farms in surrounding areas; only a handful were ever pursued in court for such stratagems.

5. Carpha Sara is a fifteen-year-old boy; he was born to free parents; the Sarakolé, who reduced him to captivity after his tribe's men were slaughtered, gave him as payment to the king of Medina Sambala who sold him to Yaguemar Guèye, brother of Marabat Guèye. Ndiack had bought the boy from him . . . at the gates of Saint Louis about five years ago and brought him to Ndiago and to his property in Bajoum, where the boy remained.

When it concerned the enslaved people who belonged to their friends and allies, colonial authorities realized it was better to turn a blind eye to violations of the "free soil" principle. When Lat Joor, a key ally during this period, traveled to Saint Louis or to a French fort with an entourage of captives, those men and women were almost never allowed to claim their freedom.

6. Young Fa Diama, who is about twelve years old, is Bambara; he was born to captive parents; brought to Medina by his masters the Moors, he was bought by the same Yaguemar Guèye who sold him to Ndiack at the same time as young Carpha.

As for the runaway slaves, the colonial government had long articulated a policy that made it difficult for the "free soil" principle to be effective and established a procedure for the on-demand expulsion of runaways. A service note from 1862 expressed this clearly: "Article 5.—When runaway slaves from friendly countries are found in Saint Louis, Gorée, or at the trading posts of Sédhiou and Carabane and their masters prove that they did everything possible to find their trail immediately after their disappearance and they come to claim them within a reasonable period of time, these slaves will be expelled as vagabonds who are a threat to public order and peace and will be conducted over the borders of the French territory where their masters will be able to take them back."

7. Young Samba is seventeen years old; he was born to free parents in the Wasulu; he was taken prisoner as a child by Bambara (Kaarta country) who had attacked and defeated the men of his tribe; sold to Sarakolés who sold him to a trader in Saint Louis named Ousmane who sold him to Ndiack about fifteen months ago.

Members of the colonial government contorted themselves to not know more about the details of the slave trading that was happening in and around the cities and forts they administered. A close reading of a letter the governor sent to the commandant of Dagana in 1879 is illustrative. The commandant had written in a previous letter about confiscating some captives and the governor objected, writing back to him: "In your letter you add 'that these captives were intended to be sold in Dagana.' By expressing yourself in this manner, you seem to be reporting this as something completely natural, whereas your duties and instructions require you to outlaw all such traffic in our port. I would like to believe, Mr. Commander, that in the future your official correspondence will not contain remarks about a similar state of affairs, which, if true, would be an indictment of the district's management, the district that you command." The governor's reproach does not focus on controlling the traffic in slaves; it did not, for instance, say that the commandant should crack down on known slave markets. Instead, it focused on the appearance of language about such traffic in official letters.

8. *Miama is a man of very lofty stature; he is between thirty-five and forty years old; he does not speak any of the dialects in use on the west coast; brought to Saint Louis around December 1877 or January 1878, he was sold to Ndiack by the Moors of the caravan that he had accompanied; Ndiack, who had initially declared having bought him from Ndiago, recognized during the course of the proceedings that he had bought him in Bou-el-Mogdad's house in Saint Louis.*

What the administrators always found preferable was that these runaway affairs be managed with discretion, and out of their earshot. They wanted the runaways to free themselves, probably—but, again, they preferred not to know—by coming to a financial arrangement with their contentious masters, as was customary. When Taylor and Villéger helped the tirailleur Moussa Dialo raise enough money to pay for his wife in 1877, this was what they were doing; presumably the master had found the woman before three months had passed and, rather than see her dragged away, Moussa Dialo purchased his wife. Many of the enslaved people listed in the *Moniteur du Sénégal* as receiving their freedom papers had found the means to pay for their liberty.

9. *Labèye is a young man of seventeen years of age; he was born of the union between a Moor and a Black slave woman; his master, who was presumably also his father, gave him to Ndiack as payment for a debt he owed; he had been in Ndiago for about five years.*

The French colonial military had long used these tactics themselves to recruit African soldiers, tirailleurs like Moussa Dialo. Many of the early tirailleurs had been enslaved, but, upon joining the military, were given a signing bonus—money that was often given to their masters as the price of their freedom. The men would then be bound to the tirailleur unit for a set number of years of indenture; they were no longer enslaved, but were not yet exactly free.

10. Teneng Conaté is a young girl of about twenty-two years old; she was born to free parents in Wasulu; stolen by some Bambara, she was sold by them to the Moors who took her to Saint Louis and sold her to Ndiack about four years ago; she said the sale took place in the house of Bou-el-Mogdad.

The Ndiack Ndiaye situation highlighted the shifting and uneven application of justice when it came to slavery and the slave trade. After all, he was a French citizen and this farm was on French land; by no stretch of the statute could he be allowed to own other people. But the procedure was not simple. More highly placed authorities, including the governor and eventually the minister, repeatedly asked the judicial service to stand down.

11. Awa Sidibé is a captive of about thirty years old; stolen, like the previous woman, by some Bambara, she was bought by some Moors who brought her to Saint Louis and sold her to Ndiack.

One reason for the administration's concern was the location of some of the sales: in the house of Bou-el-Mogdad Seck, a well-traveled diplomat, holy man, and brother-in-law of the top Muslim religious leader in Saint Louis. He nurtured deep connections in the Moorish countries to the north as far as the Adrar Plateau, persuading caravan leaders and traders to bring their objects of commerce to Saint Louis, where they could then buy French goods in return and enrich the colony. And, perhaps most important, Bou-el-Mogdad had an official colonial function as one of the governor's most trusted interpreters. The French had invested in him for years, decades by this point, even sending him to Mecca twice to make hajj. The allegations would tarnish his reputation. The governor wrote to the minister that the prosecution of

Ndiack Ndiaye seemed designed to embarrass Bou-el-Mogdad, even if there was no proof linking the cleric directly to any of the sales. "The authors of the reports are well aware," wrote the governor, "that his [Bou-el-Mogdad's] house is simply a large caravan and was open to all Muslims from North Africa, the desert and the Sudan."

12. *The captive Diama Sankaré was born free in the Wasulu; she was reduced to captivity in a war between tribes; when her freedom was taken from her, she had three children and she has remained in complete ignorance ever since about their fate. The Toucouleurs who had taken her sold her to a blacksmith who sold her to the Moors; those sold her to other Moors who took her to Saint Louis and sold her to Ndiack.*

As always, the political administrators were also worried about the geopolitical impact of such proceedings. That year, yellow fever had already broken out in Gorée and the interim governor was worried about securing the cooperation of their sometimes friends and often enemies in the interior of Kajoor and Waalo, on whom they depended for food and for commerce. In the case of another severe epidemic, he posited that their position would become difficult. "Would Kajoor, undergoing quarantine measures, disappointed in its export sales, not see these measures, which would affect their property rights over their slaves, as a new kind of attack, and would they not seek revenge for it?"

13. *Fatma Touré was born free in the Bambara countries; she was captured by Sarakolés and sold to an individual in Richard Toll, whose name she does not know, and who was obliged to sell her to Ndiack; she is the oldest of the captives in the possession of the accused; before her freedom was lost, she had three children who, like her, were taken into captivity.*

This was sound logic, because the fate of the captives was still an active subject of dispute across the region. In Kajoor, Lat Joor, as his endless letters of recrimination show, was always preoccupied with his runaway slaves. He would use any pretext to renegotiate his treaties with the French, and one of his favorite threats was that he and his people would just move somewhere else. French officials often worried that slaveholders would vote with their feet and that the French would soon reign over an empty territory.

14. Mbarrick is a young boy of sixteen years of age; born in the territory of the Dowich Moors, he was sold to Trarza Moors from whom Ndiack bought him for twenty guinées.

The territory defined as French land where slavery would have to be abolished was increasing, expanding from just Saint Louis and Gorée to Dakar in the mid-1870s. And in 1879, Rufisque was to be rid of slavery and its captives set free. The slaveholding population was worried. "The trading period has begun; it is said that there will be many more peanuts this year," the commander in Gorée reported to the governor. "There is, however, one small dark cloud. It is the upcoming liberation of the slaves."

15. Lastly, a female child of approximately three years of age was born from the marriage of Malick Cissé to captive Sira Courma, his first wife; she is considered a captive by the accused under the general principle that the child must have the same status as the mother.

In the end, Ndiack Ndiaye was sentenced to just six months in prison, the minimum sentence for his offense. If he had been made an example, it's difficult to say of what. His captives were set free; most of their names feature on the *Moniteur*'s list of those delivered to themselves in August of 1878. But what happened to them after their liberation, we do not know.

26

The Future of France

The European explorers of the nineteenth century were a rampant herd. They sailed to the main coastal cities of Africa and raced on flat riverboats, or on the backs of horses, donkeys, or camels, or sometimes even on foot into the interior, each with a fervent dream more arcane or extravagant than the next: they wanted to map the course of the Niger River or find the source of the Nile or make contact with far-flung groups and bring them the twin gospels of commerce and Christianity. Exploration was also the first step in being able to conquer a given land, and France in the 1870s, fresh off its defeat in the Franco-Prussian War, was ready to search for glory and territory in areas farther from home.

In early 1878, a French explorer with an impressive bushy beard disembarked in Dakar. For just 50 francs, Paul Soleillet was able to rent the services of a camel and a camel driver to take him and his bags all the way to Saint Louis. It would be the first time that Soleillet visited this part of Africa—having previously traveled only in the grand desert to the north and its Mediterranean coast—and he marveled at what he saw as he was accompanied along the way by gangly gazelles and birds dressed in radiant hues. "Kajoor, in particular," he wrote, "which for the past ten years has been completely peaceful, is in a state of great prosperity. It is an independent state, very well populated, very well farmed, and with beautiful trees and flowing waters." This was surely a bit of hyperbole, since Kajoor had no rivers that could flow, but the kingdom was prosperous when it was not at war.

Once he arrived in Saint Louis, he met with the governor: "Mr. Brière de l'Isle approves of my projects and promises to provide me with the means to undertake them. He will immediately provide me with a supply boat, a mule, and a native tirailleur who will be my servant and companion. The municipality of Saint Louis has also given me a grant." He also met with other Saint Louis notables and leading religious authorities to ask for their advice and their contacts, including with the qadi and tamsir Hamet Ndiaye Anne, the Muslim judge of Saint Louis and its top religious leader, whose family hailed from the upper Senegal River; and Anne's brother-in-law Bou-el-Mogdad Seck. Soleillet was especially excited about meeting Bou-el-Mogdad because he was known to have crossed the Sahara many times and maintained cordial relations with Moors across the region.

And so Soleillet set off, with the intention to go from Senegal to Algiers by land with stops in Segu and Timbuktu, tracing the possible route of a colonial white elephant: a trans-Saharan railroad.

A few years before this trip, Soleillet had written an impassioned appeal for the project and made his case to members of the French government, to geographical societies, and in public forums across France. The future of France, he wrote, was in Africa. A train connecting Algiers to Senegal was the means by which that future would be assured, allowing goods—ivory and gold, sure, but also peanuts and palm nuts from the African interior—to make their way across the Sahara, to traverse the Mediterranean, and to arrive in Paris in less than half the time it would take to go by sea, at least according to his calculations.

To those who would dismiss the idea as too ambitious, too technically difficult, or too much of a quixotic dream, he replied with the example of America's transcontinental railroad. "When the idea first arose, some fifteen years ago, of establishing a railway across the American continent, linking New York to Sacramento, the Atlantic to the Pacific, and giving the United States commercial and political dominance in the Far East, China and Japan, it was called a pipe dream, even in America, where dreamers have so often been right. Today a continuous railroad connects the two seas, over a length of about 5,300 kilometers. . . . Since its completion, the Pacific railway has produced the results that were expected and the Americans have been well justified in saying that the work of Christopher Columbus has been accomplished, and that this is the road that leads to the Indies." Such a triumph was within reach for France, too, he said, if only it would be audacious enough to take action.

Soleillet sailed up the Senegal River to Podor and then followed a land route to Segu, situated on the right bank of what the French called the Niger River, but what locals had long ago named the Joliba or the "great water." The Joliba "flowed in the direction of the rising sun" and snaked through so much of the region that Soleillet was certain that if the French could dominate it, they could expand their influence.

Awaiting more funds to continue his journey to Timbuktu, he sojourned several months in and around Segu and gathered information on the leaders there for the colonial authorities. The money never arrived, so, for lack of funds, he turned back and returned to Saint Louis in early 1879. Walter Taylor said he met Paul Soleillet then and described him as "intrepid," but didn't say where they met. Maybe he encountered Soleillet at the house or office of Saint Louis's mayor, Gaspard Devès, with whom Taylor was acquainted. Or maybe Taylor was in the chamber when Soleillet addressed the administrative council of the colony and they voted to accord him 20,000 francs for a full expedition the following year, which would be no less unsuccessful.

In France, railroad boosters would soon settle for a more modest proposal: one railway that would connect the Senegal River to the Niger River and a smaller one from Dakar to Saint Louis. But for that one, despite its limited scope, the biggest difficulty would be in persuading Lat Joor.

In September of 1879, diplomat Bou-el-Mogdad traveled from Saint Louis along well-worn trails edged with patches of euphorbia plants, through blotchy strips of forest, and across sandy dunes and windswept pasturelands into the heart of Kajoor. It may have taken him longer than usual, since September is the middle of the rainy season and menacing dark clouds could race across the savanna and surprise a traveler with a downpour, temporarily turning even well-trodden paths into streams of muck. But Bou-el-Mogdad's business, apparently, would not wait. He was headed to Lat Joor's home in Kër Amadou Yalla, a village on the kingdom's edge with an almost desert to one side and a forest on the other. Lat Joor had fortified his compound there in the Malinké style with half-meter-thick mud walls, watchtowers to survey in each direction, a moat, and, if any army could make it past those obstacles, a number of *trous de loup* to booby-trap them as they ran. There, the diplomat persuaded Lat Joor to sign a treaty that authorized the project to build a train through his kingdom; Lat Joor even agreed to an addendum saying he would provide labor for its construction.

"You must understand that it was difficult for us to accept what you ask," Lat Joor wrote to the governor a week later, "but we have done so because we can't refuse the person you sent anything. . . . Now that everything is settled between us, I ask, that you, as my friend, would make me a gift before too much time has gone by of three handsome horses, not counting the two horses you must provide to me at the end of each season, according to our prior agreement."

Lat Joor's change of heart was a political maneuver engendered by primal distress. For the brooding clouds of the rainy season mirrored the clouds of war that were gathering in Kajoor again and hovering just above Kër Amadou Yalla. Lat Joor had decided he needed reinforcements.

Over the years, one man had been responsible for Lat Joor's rise. This man had helped an adolescent Lat Joor make the crossing into manhood by presiding over his circumcision ceremony. Then this man had swayed Kajoor's nobles to elect young Lat Joor as damel and establish him on the throne. When Lat Joor was pushed from Kajoor a short time later, it was this man who had suggested that he align himself with the religious rebellion of Maba in Saalum. This man was not thought to be a person of the Book himself, but saw that Maba could be a useful ally against their common enemy, the French. He must have also sensed that the move would help win over the influential Muslim clerics of a certain Kajoor splinter province, a group that had resisted supporting Lat Joor in the past. And a few years later, when the region was electing a new damel, this man had proved his prescience. One of the clerics said, "We had heard that Lat Joor had become a Muslim and that is why we elected him," and that province went for Lat Joor. Over the years, this man gave the erstwhile damel keen advice, helped him administer his lands, led his armies, and collected some of his taxes. He was Lat Joor's right hand and his left. But in 1879, Lat Joor and this man, Demba Waar Sall, had a falling out, and the whole of Kajoor would suffer because of their discord.

Demba Waar Sall was what the Wolof called a *jaami-buur*—a crown slave. But he wasn't enslaved like Walter Taylor's parents or like Moussa Sidibé or the other unfortunates who sought refuge at the Saint Louis mission. He wasn't a stranger sold to foreign lands because of war. In fact, Demba Waar Sall had caught and was the proud master of many such enslaved persons himself. In Demba Waar's role as head of the *jaami-buur*, he was the commander of the slave army, an enforcer, a pillager, a brother in arms, and a political animal. But most of all, he was a kingmaker.

The reasons for the dispute between Lat Joor and Demba Waar are not entirely known, but have been the subject of wide speculation by historians and griots alike over the years. Even at the time, in the months before Lat Joor was persuaded to sign the treaty, the French didn't know what to make of his sudden repudiation of Demba Waar. When operatives from the colonial government's intelligence service visited Kajoor during that summer of 1879, they found that the situation between Lat Joor and his former supporters was tense. One report noted, "[It] is making Kajoor anxious and nervous, and although the region crossed by the mission was far from the big centers, the evening conversation in the village squares was on this very subject."

One of the first signs of trouble had come just a few months before Lat Joor signed the September treaty. In June of 1879, Lat Joor had written to the governor in the strongest of terms about all the members of his court—the free nobles and the crown slaves with whom he had just had a troubling meeting some days before: "When these people come to you," he wrote, "know that they are only slanderers, slanderers three times over! Who slander all the chiefs and even slander each other. I beg you to take them all, to incarcerate them and not to let them go free before we have consulted with them. They have always been my subjects, as well as their fathers, and their fate is to remain such and to submit to my orders."

On its face, the heart of their contretemps seemed to be Lat Joor's impressive fortified residence in Kër Amadou Yalla where he held court. It was far away from the traditional centers of power and the historical capital Mbul in central Kajoor. The nobles and crown slaves wanted him to come back; Lat Joor refused. "The people of Kajoor who want me in their midst have but one goal," he wrote to the governor, "that of keeping me under their control and keeping all the power for themselves." The whole issue had boiled over at a tense palaver in Mbul in June, the catalyst for his June letter on the slanderers. Lat Joor and his entourage stormed out of that meeting in anger. The damel then announced that Demba Waar and Sall's nephew, Ibra Fatim Saar, an influential leader in his own right who often acted as Demba Waar's surrogate, would be relieved of their duties.

Of course, even the French saw that the fight about the capital wasn't just about a place. It was also about how Lat Joor was replacing his old advisors with new ones—an old-fashioned power struggle. And the railroad project became an accelerant.

When Demba Waar and Ibra Fatim Saar first heard about the project, they seemed to support it, but Lat Joor hesitated. After some official engineers passed through to survey the land in early 1878, Lat Joor called Ibra Fatim and Demba Waar to his court and accused them of trying to advance their own interests.

Ibra Fatim recounted his version of that 1878 encounter to a French intelligence official sometime later:

Lat Joor: You saw all those men from Saint Louis planting stakes and marking trees there. Didn't that concern you?

Ibra Fatim: We were very pleased with it, and you yourself, Lat Joor, seemed to accept with pleasure this idea of a means of transportation that ought to enrich the country.

Lat Joor: But white people are very cunning. Do you know some of the things people are saying here? They say that your horse Ibra and yours Demba are the price of the land that the whites will take, and that the money I received has no other purpose than to make me close my eyes to the whole thing. If that were so, then you would be betraying me.

Ibra Fatim and Demba Waar were so offended by this accusation that they left in anger. Ibra Fatim said he knew that the words weren't coming from the damel's heart, but must have come from his new entourage of influential imams.

So, after the disastrous June 1879 meeting with all of the leaders of Kajoor that so angered Lat Joor, Ibra Fatim sought out the damel to defend himself, an impassioned litany that the intelligence officer quoted at length. Ibra Fatim said to Lat Joor: "Those who are inciting you like this would be embarrassed to show the same kind of loyalty that you know I have shown. Where are the ones who, in their youth, marched with you in difficult times, the ones who carried you in their boubous through the gunfire using their bodies as shields for you? Which of them brought you the scalp of an enemy king when we were in Wuli?"

In Ibra Fatim's interview with French authorities about the original failed Mbul meeting in June, he laid out this and more about the whole conflict, but assiduously left out one detail. The analyst noted that another informant had shared a widespread rumor, one that cast doubt on the righteousness of Ibra Fatim's complaints and helped explain Lat Joor's ire. That the discontented nobles and crown slaves had threatened to offer the damel position to someone else, they knew from Lat Joor's first explosive letter. But the new information intimated that the nobles and crown slaves had already picked out and approached that person: none other than Lat Joor's own nephew, Samba Lawbé Faal, who was still just a teenager. Ibra Fatim was also said to have told Samba Lawbé to inform his uncle Lat Joor about the plot, indicating that their informant might be playing a double game.

"What did Ibra want by proceeding like this . . . ?" the analyst speculated on what these underhanded dealings could mean. "To reconcile with the damel by giving him a sign of loyalty . . . ? To influence the mind of his king by hinting at a possible downfall? To prevent a certain civil war between two factions . . . ? Ibra could have wanted all of this. I believe that his hidden goal is to increase his own standing, to remain the indispensable broker between the two sides, to dominate each of them and to be powerful enough to be more formidable."

When Lat Joor returned to Kër Amadou Yalla, his fortress between the desert and the forest, after that June 1879 meeting in Mbul, he was so upset he ordered the drums of war to be beaten. But he must have soon realized that it was Demba Waar who was still really in control of most of the kingdom's soldiers, those men who could sweep through villages like hungry locusts and pick everything apart.

The September 1879 railroad treaty was a sign of Lat Joor's desperation and a way for him to borrow an army—the French army—and, in so doing, maintain himself on the throne. He must have thought that if Demba Waar and Ibra Fatim wanted to cooperate with the French, he could beat them to it and cut them out of the deal. Maybe it was the influence of his advisers? Maybe he was tired of being manipulated in Mbul? Maybe, over the years, he started to believe he had gotten his position on his own? What seems clear is that Lat Joor had started to forget an important lesson: that those who can make kings can unmake them, too.

27

A Word on Freedom

The 1848 French proclamation abolishing slavery in Gorée and Saint Louis was transmitted to the people on the twenty-third of August at eight o'clock in the morning; it was posted on a sign and also "published" via talking drum, whose high tones and low rumbles could be heard all over each island. Many of the new freedmen started that day by going to bathe in the ocean. Historian Mbaye Guèye wrote: "They hoped to leave their past souls in the water, because according to local beliefs, sea bathing not only purifies, but also confers immunity under certain circumstances. Thus the convicted person who goes directly to bathe in the sea upon his release from prison, will no longer return to prison. After their bath, the slaves, too, were assured that they would never again return to servitude."

At the end of that day, though, many newly free men and women found themselves on the streets of those islands; they had nowhere to live after leaving their masters. What is freedom, after all, in a place where you have no status, no clan, and no access to land? Without capital or connections, what could they do to support themselves? Some may have returned to their home countries, following those long caravans that ranged deep into the interior. But did their villages still exist? Were their families still there? They would not be able to find out before starting on the long journey.

Many stayed in Saint Louis and Gorée and made do on their own, choosing their own occupations as dockworkers and woodcutters, pileuses and cooks. The colonial authorities noted that the period after the 1848 abolition was also a boom time for prostitution. In 1849, the dispensary in Saint Louis was targeting prostitutes to control the spread of syphilis in the city since "prostitution, especially after emancipation, had reached a level that exceeded anything that could be described," wrote one health official. He said that even children as young as ten years old "practiced this infamous profession in the open."

Other newly freed people moved across the river or across the bay to settle and farm. Still others eventually went back to their former masters for help, accepting jobs and status as free men and women that differed little from the jobs and status they'd had when they were enslaved. In 1849, the governor at the time wrote to officials in Paris, "The new freedmen do exactly what they did when they belonged to their masters: the same work, the same way of living; they had, before, almost the same dose of freedom that they have today."

Later, as one century turned to the next, the French would establish "freedom villages" to receive the liberated near their forts, to protect them from raids, sure, but also to use their labor. The liberated rarely stayed in such villages for long.

This was always the dilemma for the newly freed: they still had to live in the societies that had captured, sold, and exploited them.

Only in a radical place could the newly liberated imagine something like total freedom.

On the Rio Pongo, the elders of today still retain the stories their grandparents passed on to them about the foreign and native slave traders who used to live on the river. As in many places in the Americas, there were runaways here, too. They managed to establish maroon communities, places full of people who had liberated themselves. The village of Konyéya was one such community, a place where, it was said, "any runaway who managed to enter, for whatever reason, automatically became a free man."

Underneath an old kapok tree in the village, an elder would perform a ritual to liberate the bodies and minds of the newcomers. The people would wash their faces three times with a special "medicated" water and, "when heaven and earth were sleeping at the same time," they would drink it and wash their whole bodies with it. "At the end of this ritual the man, now a free man, often changed his last name."

In the elders' stories, it is said that the powerful priestesses of Konyéya watched over the village to protect it from would-be conquerors or slave raiders. They used their powers to "suspend" the village in the air when its enemies came in search of it, leaving nothing but a quiet forest and the mist in its place. The raiders would look around in confusion, convinced they had taken a wrong turn somewhere. The village was safe. In this runaway utopia, the stories said, the people were able to live free from fear.

In another village in the north of Senegal, the oldest man, the great-grandson of the founder, said that freed slaves would come to consult his ancestor, a powerful sorcerer who could make people invisible. The man could give them charms to protect themselves, making it so that their enemies would walk right past them and never know they were there. This was how, the old man said, they were able to live in peace even when the country around them was full of unrest.

Across the region, even without mystical powers, many liberated former slaves established their own villages, clearing land with their own hands and constructing houses, enclosures for their livestock, and making space for people to gather. They would practice trades as blacksmiths, weavers, dyers, and leather workers, or they could farm—peanuts, of course. Some would cut down neighboring forests to make charcoal for sale on market days. They tried to make a new world for themselves, and sometimes they succeeded.

28

The Civilizing Mission

Refuge for freed slaves, 1879: from left to right: M. Taylor, Illou Seck, Dhimi Dhialo, Samba Coumba, Mademba (évangéliste), Moussa Konaté, Samou Dhiajaté, M. Sidibé. *Courtesy of Defap*

There is a photo of Walter Taylor and a group of liberated men and women from the early days of the shelter in 1879, although only Taylor and the men are listed by name in the caption. Taylor is at one end with a good-natured smile, looking comfortable in his coat, vest, and tie, hat in hand and pocket watch tucked away on a long chain; the women all wear light-colored dresses, and architectural scarves rise up from their braided tresses; and most of the men sport rumpled, ill-fitting dark coats—some too big and others too small—and faces that, like-wise, seem ill at ease. In the photo, a tall young man named Samba Coumba stands in the center and appears a bit more composed—his shirt a bit whiter than the others and his jacket a bit more proportional to his body.

Samba Coumba was among the newly liberated people that Taylor had baptized not long after returning from Paris. He was a young man of about twenty-five years, and, although he would stay with the mission for decades through marriage and children, epidemics and political upheaval, his early years remain a lacuna in the records. There is little personal information about him in the mission's archives, and the letters and reports that talk about his activities never even mention his family name.

Dogged research reveals only the barest traces of him either in other archives or in oral histories, for the world he lived in had no incentive to save his story. He was neither a white man nor a local political or religious leader; there were no griots to sing his praises, and no one kept written records about him from which people far beyond could draw a picture of his life. A determined investigator can only guess. All we know, all we can know, is that he was a man from the interior of the continent who had been enslaved, sold down the river, and then somehow managed to take back his freedom.

A month after Samba Coumba's baptism, Taylor wrote to the director in Paris about the young man. "He's filled with zeal for the Lord's cause. He's already introduced me to a Bambara man." Soon there would be others, for Samba Coumba was an assiduous spreader of the good news and would infect many of his friends. Some of the men in the photo are there because of him, including Illou Seck, the man standing next to Taylor, who was one of Samba Coumba's best friends, and Samou Dhiajaté, another one of his conquests. At the very end is young Moussa Sidibé, whom the reader met in the first chapter, and who found the mission through the Bambara whisper network of Saint Louis, fueled by people like Samba Coumba. There were others, too, who aren't pictured, men Samba Coumba worked with or people he met on the street or encountered in the homes of friends.

Since many, if not most, of the new members were people who were fleeing servitude, and sometimes traumatic and violent events only to find themselves setting up a new life in a foreign city, they needed a lot of help. Taylor often talked about the hidden effects of slavery—the toll that it exacted on the spirit long after the body had been freed. "Slavery debases the soul and intelligence to an extraordinary degree," he wrote to subscribers. "Some are hopelessly servile and seem to have lost every vestige of their own personality."

Taylor could not have known how much social work would be required of him when he started this outreach effort: the liberated needed housing, furniture, clothes, food, jobs, schooling, and a new sense of themselves in this new world. "We must instruct them carefully, give them constant advice, even arrange all their domestic affairs for them," he wrote. When some members had trouble with their employer in a nearby village, Taylor went to check it out. When a few others had difficulty finding jobs, he bought a boat so they could work on the river. Doing what, he doesn't say—but they would leave for weeks at a time, possibly transporting goods or passengers to the upper river.

In a short amount of time, Taylor found himself overwhelmed and way over budget, in spite of the donations he was getting from Europe. "I've spent more than I've been getting for freed slaves. It's very difficult to be able to support them in a colony like Saint Louis," he told the director.

Taylor promised in that letter to rein in his spending on the runaways: "In a little while, I will stop taking runaway slaves into my house."

But his pledge to turn away the enslaved wouldn't last.

Writing to contributors at the end of that year, Taylor said that, thanks to their contributions, they had helped thirty-one enslaved people "regain their freedom"—fourteen men, fifteen women, and two children.

On the days that Taylor held Bible classes, the new members would meet in his home, tucked away in an area far from the noise of the house: the maid pounding spices in the kitchen, the children playing with their neighbors or the household's pet monkey, and the many visitors who would drop by to exchange elaborate greetings and look around with curious eyes. The Bible classes seemed to be as much about teaching them to be free people in the world as they were about teaching them the Christian religion. Taylor recounted an interaction with one recently freed man who said "that owing his freedom to me, he accepted everything I taught him and that he was even ready to throw himself into the fire if I wanted him to." Taylor was often worried about such expressions in the newly freed, believing, as he did, that they reflected a kind of dependency of the mind—a lingering slave mentality. It also created a kind of conversion dilemma for him, making him question whether the student had converted out of gratitude alone. On that day, though, Taylor called the man's bluff: "I then arranged for a fire to be lit and ordered him to put his finger in it and leave it there until I had counted from one to a hundred. My good man stepped back. I then took this opportunity to make him and his comrades understand that we should be completely sincere in our words and promises."

Taylor also had to help the newly liberated combat the public opinion of them. Many colonial officials harbored stereotypes of the liberated—as lazy shirkers of their duties, and potential thieves or prostitutes, who would live on the streets, pose a sanitation problem, and generally lower the quality of life in the coastal cities. Even Taylor's acquaintance, the rich, mixed-race merchant and sometimes Saint Louis mayor Gaspard Devès, was known to speak in not-so-flattering terms about the people who came to the city in search of their freedom. "It is not the hardworking slaves, the ones who have acquired a good fortune, who come to us in search of freedom," Devès wrote in an 1882 letter. "The bulk is made up of the undisciplined, the lazy and the vagabonds."

Taylor must have been aware that to keep any good will and official favor on their side, and to keep up his reputation, too, the liberated converts of his Protestant mission needed to prove people wrong. In other words, he felt they needed to be twice as good to combat the discrimination that lived in the colony's air, undeterred by sunlight and sea breezes. This was an early iteration of respectability politics. Taylor wrote as much to a committee member in charge of the mission's finances: "The first converts were just like children and many people were ready to scrutinize them for their shortcomings."

One unstated but undeniable goal for Taylor was to turn his new church members into model subjects, for in a colony controlled by Europeans, Black men like Taylor and the new liberated members always needed to walk a fine line. Model subjects needed to speak French, go to school, cast aside their local customs, and control their anger, however justified. And it seemed to be working. "One of them recently refrained from taking the Holy Communion because three days before, he had responded angrily to insults from his European employer," Taylor explained. "What a touch of sensitivity for a freed slave who was converted to the Gospel at the age of 40!"

Model subjects also needed to marry according to the laws of their new society and new religion, in ceremonies overseen by ministers and the municipality. Taylor celebrated the members who managed to convert their partners in the process. The mission also waged a campaign against divorce, which was not as controversial for Muslims as it was for Christians, and against polygamy, although the receptivity for anti-polygamy messages broke down along gender lines: "We encountered more opposition from men than from women, " he wrote.

In 1879, the same year that the group photo was taken, Taylor bragged about officiating two marriages: "When I went to the Court to take the steps that the law requires for these two marriages, the judicial authorities welcomed me and were happy to see the influence that we exert on the natives who have dealings with us."

As more members opted for Christian and civil marriages, they helped build a community of respectable converts. Marriage not only helped people create social structures that encouraged them to conform, but was also a way to show that they respected French law over traditional laws, and that they accepted the colonial regime and its "civilizing" force.

Taylor often took exception to the idea of the mission "to civilize" Africa, and wrote as much to his friends and benefactors in France. In

1879, when he read about the war the British had waged against the Zulu Kingdom in Southern Africa, it so upset him that he wrote an extraordinary letter to the assistant director, unleashing the full force of his outrage about this subject. "As long as it is enough for a Negro tribe to demand their rights and their honor for their power to be shattered," he wrote, "and for them to be forced to accept a civilization that is hostile to all feelings of patriotism and moral independence, so that their conquerors may prosper and grow rich without difficulty, I do not see that within a thousand years Africa can take its place among the great family of nations."

Maybe he felt so free to criticize this openly because he was talking about British domination and not French. Even as he excoriated the British state, Taylor absolved religious leaders like missionaries of their roles in this conquest and pillage. "It is true that the missionaries of Jesus Christ are doing a great deal to set them free," he wrote. "But all their efforts are neutralized by their governments, whose administration is hardly based on the principles of freedom and equality when it comes to their colonial possessions."

From the analytical distance of more than a century, it can be difficult to understand how Walter Taylor could rationalize the contradictions inherent in his work. How could he decry European domination of Africans in one breath and in the next, embrace and support so many European values and customs? There are not any surviving writings wherein he might explain his position and process of thought. Some hints may come from the intellectual company he kept—other African men of the cloth with whom he corresponded or admired such as Rev. George Nicol, the colonial chaplain in the Gambia, and Bishop Samuel Ajayi Crowther, whose celebrity as the only African bishop in the Anglican church was unparalleled in religious circles. Both of them seemed genuine in their belief that Africans would benefit from receiving European educations, learning European customs, and, it goes without saying for clergymen, embracing European religion. Nicol had, early in his career, written that he believed that "Africa could be raised from its present degraded state of barbarism, superstition, and vice, to any equal with the civilized world," identifying that perfect ideal of civilization as European. But he also said that in this pursuit, Africans themselves should be the agents of their own uplift. Bishop Crowther articulated a similar vision, both conservative and radical—to save "benighted Africa," with some European ways and education, but to not lose track of native languages and traditions. They wanted to slightly Europeanize Africans, but also to Africanize the church to some extent. In their conceptual gordian knots, we can see Taylor's challenges as well.

No matter how little he himself may have agreed with some portions of the mission of "civilizing" Africans, Taylor was, nonetheless, an instrument of that project. Many of his interactions with colonial authorities revolved around the broad goal of influencing the natives to be more like Europeans. Either he was unaware of the contradiction, or, more likely, he knew how to play along to get along, since he must have seen how useful it was to seem to agree with the rhetoric when it came to getting political and monetary support for his causes. Not long after coming back from France, Taylor saw Mayor Gaspard Devès, who told the missionary to do his best "to civilize the natives." If Taylor was successful, Devès told him, the government might subsidize his work.

Gaspard Devès wasn't just a politician and a wealthy merchant; his trade empire stretched in every direction from Mauritania to the Southern Rivers to Mali, including but not limited to a fleet of riverboats on the Senegal River, a monopoly on trade cloth imports from India, the contract to provide grains and meat to the military; and, of course, he was a major buyer and seller of peanuts. He also held the considerable debts of many local leaders—including Lat Joor.

It is difficult to know how well Walter Taylor and Gaspard Devès were acquainted. Devès's deputy mayor, Jean-Jacques Crespin, was certainly friendly with Taylor, maybe because Crespin had spent years as a merchant in Sierra Leone, and his wife was reputed to be from either that country or the Gambia. Maybe she and Elizabeth became friends, bonding in that way that expatriates from the same place do when they find themselves in a strange land. She may have attended Taylor's English-language church service held for members of the Sierra

Leonean trade community, and perhaps that facilitated their husbands' friendship. Crespin and Taylor also belonged to the only freemason association in Senegal at the time, the Union Sénégalaise. Devès may have been a member, too, for he took an active interest in promoting its affairs. Indeed, the civilizing rhetoric in Devès's letters tracks with a key priority of Senegal's freemasons at the time: the creation of schools for liberated people to help them become "good French workers."

Devès was a powerful and generous ally for the mission, for Taylor and his parishioners, just when they needed it most. When one church member, a formerly enslaved woman, planned to get married, Mr. Devès gave her money for a wedding dress. On another occasion, Mr. Devès made a personal contribution to help a church member build a new house.

We can only speculate about Mr. Devès's motivation in so espousing Taylor's cause, especially since his own family's record on the subject of the enslaved was spotty at best and, at worst, hostile. Devès typically wanted what his clients, influential leaders like Lat Joor, wanted, and generally defended their rights to have slaves and reclaim their runaways.

One reason for his interest in Taylor's work may have been that Devès, like many a rich man before him, wanted to expand his political influence and power. On at least one occasion in 1880, Taylor helped seven liberated men register themselves on the colony's electoral lists. These men would be able to vote in the next elections and choose members of the colony's governing body, the General Council. Devès was opposed by the colonial establishment, but had a strong base among the Senegalese fishermen of Guet Ndar, a village on the sandy barrier island that separated the main island from the ocean, where his wife had family. He may have wanted more power from places where others were least likely to look for it and knew the value of a vote that others would ignore.

Although the record of which men he helped register to vote escapes posterity, can there be any doubt that one of them would have been Samba Coumba, the zealous liberated man who excelled in all domains? Soon after joining the church, Samba Coumba went to school and learned to read, write, and speak French. And Samba Coumba's family name, which does not seem to appear in contemporaneous mission records, is finally revealed in one public document in the *Moniteur du Sénégal* of 1880, where two lines of text read: "February 1st—There is a promise of marriage between Mr. Samba-Coumba Coulbary, woodcutter, 26-years-old, and Miss Lissa Sidibé, cook, 24-years-old, both living in Saint Louis."

29

A Stain That Must Be Washed

It was the first of March in 1880 when venerable elder statesman Victor Schœlcher took to the Senate floor of the Luxembourg Palace in Paris. At seventy-five years old, he had been fighting for the values of the Republic for most of his life, through coups, revolutions, repression, and exile. A few years before, he had been finally recognized by that Republic, the country's third, and honored with the title "Senator for life."

Even though a more respected member of that assembly could not be imagined, on that Monday, the audience interrupted Mr. Schœlcher's speech with rumblings and shouts.

"The Senate will please be silent and listen to the speaker," the Senate president shouted to call the legislators to order.

Mr. Schœlcher shouted in turn, "I'm dealing with a matter of national honor. . . . If the Senate will not hear me, I am prepared to step down from the gallery."

In response, the senators shouted, "Speak! Speak!"

He allowed himself to be appeased and raised his voice in that chamber again. His speech went on to describe a series of events that had been recently brought to his attention, events that occurred in Senegal.

He later read a letter from a correspondent who described the events. "In 1876, the author said, a woman who had taken refuge in Saint Louis and was sought by her master was seized by the police. While being dragged along, she was crying so it would break your heart. When she arrived on the Faidherbe bridge, she threw herself into the water, preferring death to servitude; she was saved by a Black man who handed her over to her master, who tied her to a camel and took her away."

Mr. Schœlcher's speech caused such excitement from those gathered for reasons not limited to his message; it was also because of the messenger. Victor Schœlcher was an elder statesman and a living legend in the world of abolition. When his father, a celebrated porcelain manufacturer on par with Sèvres, sent him to Mexico, Cuba, and the United States of America as a young man in 1829, he witnessed the terrors of plantation slavery firsthand and began to write about them in *La Revue de Paris*. After he came back to France, he began what would become a life of writing about and campaigning for an end to slavery. His father died in the 1830s, leaving the business to his son, but young Victor Schœlcher didn't have a head for business and eventually liquidated the company. He used much of his inheritance to support the abolitionist cause, writing articles and treatises about the ills of slavery and campaigning across the Antilles, Europe, and Africa.

In 1848, at the dawn of the new republic, he presided over the commission to abolish slavery on all French soil.

When noted American abolitionist and former slave Frederick Douglass, who was by then an elder statesman in his own right, visited Schœlcher's house in Paris nearly forty years after that momentous occasion, he was surprised by how much the man still surrounded himself with objects related to slavery. "There were old slave whips, which had been used on the backs of slaves in the French Colonies," wrote Douglass. "On the walls were handcuffs, broken chains, fetters, and iron collars with sharp prongs which had galled the necks and limbs of despairing bondmen, but which now gall them no more. These barbarous implements of a past condition were sent to M. Schœlcher by negroes from the Colonies in grateful recognition of his instrumentality in setting them free. One could easily see that the venerable liberator looked upon these iron testimonials with a sense of relief and satisfaction. There were not wanting other and more valuable tokens of negro gratitude to this noble philanthropist, grateful evidences that he had not lived in vain."

Abolition was more than a political achievement for Schœlcher, it was the moral center of his life.

And the news from Senegal that he was reading out loud on the Senate floor was an assault on his legacy, yes, but, as he saw it, it was also an assault on the very spirit of the republic. Mr. Schœlcher said that this traffic was "a stain that must be washed."

One of the letters he read had originally been printed in a newspaper with a religious bent published weekly in Nice—not the usual place to cause such a nationwide scandal. But the letter had gotten picked up by other newspapers and reprinted across France, where it elicited editorials from politicians and intellectuals and where it eventually landed on Schœlcher's desk some time later.

All this had started at a newspaper called *L'Eglise Libre* about six months before Mr. Schœlcher's display on the Senate floor. The editor had received a letter from a reader, a tease of information that invited more: "Dear Sir, *L'Eglise Libre* informs us . . . that the King of Choa [Shewa] has abolished the slave trade in southern Abyssinia and deserves the congratulations of all true friends of humanity. But why does France, despite the law of 1848, maintain the slave trade in the colonies, especially in Senegal? Why are there still slave markets protected by our canons in Gandiole, near Saint Louis, in Podor, Matam, Bakel, Medina, etc.? There are some interesting things happening in Senegal, there are facts worth mentioning. I will make them available to you if you wish."

Soon, another letter from the correspondent followed, this time with details: about the children who were bought at slave markets in the interior and taken into Saint Louis to be used as domestics; of a prominent citizen with a whole village of enslaved people farming for him; about the women expelled from French land and snatched back by their masters into servitude and sometimes death.

All of the letters were signed by one F. Villéger.

Part V

30

A Delicate Business

News of Mr. Schœlcher's stand in the Senate did not appear in the *Moniteur du Sénégal*; after all, that paper was an organ of the colonial government and the venerable elder statesman was attacking it at its heart. Walter Taylor was sure to have heard gossip about it in the days that followed, though, through whispers spirited from the halls of the governor's mansion or notes passed on from the telegraph office.

Taylor would get the full details via a letter from Paris a couple of weeks later; the society's director, Eugène Casalis, wrote to him the day after the Senate hearings and sent along a copy of the *Journal Officiel* that detailed the proceedings. The Paris Evangelical Missionary Society was doubly implicated in the affair. Besides Villéger's involvement, the Senate called the Minister of the Navy and the Colonies to testify, and that man was Admiral Jean-Bernard Jauréguiberry, who was a member of the society's governing committee and the director's childhood friend. Indeed, Jauréguiberry had helped to establish the Saint Louis mission when he was governor of Senegal in 1862. During that same year, he also signed a confidential memo on the policy of expelling reclaimed runaway slaves as vagabonds, a copy of which had found its way to a major newspaper nearly twenty years later and then into Schœlcher's hands.

Jauréguiberry defended the policy as necessary in order to keep the peace, and he refuted Villéger's assertions about open slave trading in the colony, never uttering his name but calling him "a man who, in spite of his holy garb, deserted his post." The Senate declared itself satisfied with Admiral Jauréguiberry's testimony, but many in the press denounced it, calling him an apologist for slavery.

"It's very unfortunate that our poor ex-missionary has meddled in this affair," Casalis wrote to Taylor. He noted that the status of the runaway slaves was unlikely to change anytime soon. "We do not even need to remind you to continue following the most careful and wise courses of action in all your dealings with these runaways."

Taylor wrote back with some admiration for Schœlcher's performance in the Senate: "Mr Schœlcher has a good heart. He championed the cause of the downtrodden with energy and conviction. I hope that the time will not be far off when, through the influence of the Gospel in Senegal, the fate of these unfortunate people will be changed."

The record does not show us Mr. Casalis's personal opinion about the whole situation or about Admiral Jauréguiberry's involvement, but he was pleased with one aspect of the minister's testimony: "You will see that the Minister, in a few words, has taken care of him [Villéger]."

No one on the Paris committee had been happy with Villéger's conduct at the end of his time in Senegal, and calling it abandonment, as the minister had, was justified in their eyes. Villéger's letters were baffling since, except for one fundraising letter, he had never evinced any special perturbation about the status quo of the servile either in Saint Louis or outside of it. And he had to know that speaking out in such a manner would not be well received by the colonial government.

When Villéger's detailed letters were published in L'Eglise Libre, Taylor was concerned right away about their effect on the mission. "What Mr. Villéger is currently publishing in the newspapers is making us very worried here. I fear he is only trying to get me in trouble with the government and the public in general and in this way hinder the progress of our work; for he has spent many years here, and knows very well how dangerous it is for the mission to have the government and the public against it."

All of this came at a busy time for Taylor; Elizabeth was pregnant with their fourth child, a boy who would be born in November of 1879 and would be named Alfred after Director Casalis's teenage son. In addition, Taylor was often in ill health with persistent headaches, asthma, and a gastrointestinal ailment he compared to dysentery. But as the controversy picked up steam, and after Villéger tried to get one of his old allies in the mission to make a stand, Taylor wondered what they could do to combat Villéger's maneuvers. He wrote in even stronger terms: "Mr. Villéger is very much betraying himself and showing his true character as a man who is shortsighted, unscrupulous, selfish, shallow, who seeks only attention in all that he does and is not concerned with practicing Christian wisdom and humility." And he reiterated that Villéger's actions seemed like they were designed to create a difficult situation for Taylor.

Taylor was right to be concerned. Even as Jauréguiberry defended the colonial government's policies in the Senate hearing, he pressured Governor Brière de l'Isle to do better, or at least to appear to do better. This was delicate business for the governor. He neither wanted to anger leaders like Lat Joor, who did not like to lose their captives and whose cooperation he needed in order to achieve his projects; nor did he want to give the merchants of Saint Louis, Gorée, Dakar, and Rufisque more fuel, for they were not silent about disliking his heavy-handed style of governing. Brière saw plots everywhere, and the issue of slave trafficking had been his bête noire almost since the beginning of his term in 1876. The Senate debate added to his world of troubles, and he was looking for places to lay the blame. So the governor in Senegal looked at Taylor with an increasingly suspicious regard.

A couple of months after the hearings, the governor wrote to Jauréguiberry about a new case, a section of a Moorish caravan that had been intercepted in Sor with ten children destined for sale in Kajoor. The children were confiscated, but one was later kidnapped by a Moor who hid in the house of the tamsir and qadi El Hadj Bou-el-Mogdad, and later successfully sold the child to a citizen of Kajoor. This again incited controversy in Saint Louis about Bou-el-Mogdad. Brière wrote, "I have given you these details, Mr. Minister, because I believe that this case has its origin in the actions of Mr. Villéger's representative in Saint Louis, a Black man from Sierra Leone with a dubious reputation. It could have been one of his accomplices who misled the Moors who were transporting the children and led them towards Saint Louis. It could be that they wanted to make more noise about the issue of slave trafficking here and be heard in France now that the justice system of the colony's principal city is pursuing it."

Of course, Taylor would have objected to being called a representative of Villéger; nothing could have been further from the truth. It seems unlikely he was involved. Taylor does not write about this caravan to his subscribers in Bordeaux or to the director in Paris, and he was, in general, averse to drawing attention to himself.

In fact, it would be hard to imagine Taylor getting involved in any complicated strategies around this time, because besides his constant fevers, anemia, asthma, and general ill health, he regularly made reference to feelings of sadness and despair during these months. From historical hindsight, it is clear Taylor was in the throes of a deep depression around this time. In March, he wrote to the director: "Since the beginning of this month and immediately following the weddings of Samba Coumba, and Illou Seck, a great sadness has taken hold of me. It is striking that it was at that time when everything was encouraging me to be happy that I suddenly found myself plunged into sadness and despondency." In a letter several months later, he speaks of it as a kind of spiritual crisis, from which he was still not delivered. "Dark and guilty thoughts rise up in my heart and take over with such strength and persistence that sometimes I am frightened out of my mind. I am amazed that with all this inner suffering I have been able, so far, to carry out my duties."

Taylor cited two main worries: about how to educate his growing brood of children in a satisfactory manner since Saint Louis was no Freetown when it came to educational institutions for Africans; and about how to keep his libérés on the straight and narrow. But he also must have been worried about his precarious position in the colony. In the days and maybe even months after the Senate hearings, a general spirit of distrust attached itself to the Protestant mission. Some officials in the government grew frosty toward Taylor, revoking certain courtesies such as helping runaways declare themselves to be freed by just providing their names to the judicial service and eliminating the need for them to come in person and risk exposure. What's more, the rest of the events of that year would not do anything to help him regain his spirits: his political ally Devès would be forced out of office as mayor, and yellow fever would break out again in the colony.

The deepest wound would occur at the end of the rainy season in 1880. Young Alfred, still an infant, got sick with a fever that would not abate, a fever that made his tiny body listless and weak. In October, after a month of suffering, baby Alfred died. "What a painful ordeal for me and my dear wife!" Taylor wrote to the director.

Throughout this period, Taylor continued to be overworked, over-extended, and unable to take many breaks, despite his heavy heart, a fact he shared with the director in nearly all of his letters. After Taylor's ordination in France in the summer of 1878, he had been told that the committee would choose a French missionary to follow him to Senegal without much delay; Taylor hoped that person would be one of his dearest friends from the Maison. "I eagerly await the arrival of my friend Mr. Marzolff," he wrote to the director when he finally arrived in Saint Louis, following his preventive yellow fever quarantine aboard his boat. "He mustn't be frightened by the yellow fever."

Henri Marzolff may not have been afraid of the yellow fever that stalked the coastal cities of West Africa, but his influential future in-laws were. After their strong objections, the committee decided it would be better to send Marzolff and his new wife to Lesotho instead.

It was for the best, since the 1878 yellow fever outbreak in Senegal was one of the worst outbreaks recorded; between mid-September, when Saint Louis registered its first case of the sickness, and mid-December, when it listed its last, nearly half of the city's Europeans died. As for the African victims, no numbers seem to exist tracking their deaths, but they may not have been as high proportionally. People who had grown up in areas where yellow fever was endemic, and may have been exposed to it before, could have been resistant to the disease.

The committee agreed that Taylor should not have to labor all alone in Senegal, but any would-be missionaries were frightened by the fevers in store for them during the bad season in Senegal. When the society had launched an appeal to the Protestants of France earlier in 1878, they had no responses.

One year turned into the next, but still, nothing changed. In September 1879, Taylor wrote to Paris, saying, "I am looking forward to having an associate join me." And in January 1880, another year and another plea: "We ask the committee to do everything possible to send us some colleagues this year."

Soon, a candidate emerged, although the young man still had at least a year of studies left before he could be ordained. He wasn't a born Frenchman any more than Taylor was, but with naturalization papers, the committee thought he'd do fine, especially since he was, for them, the right color. Georges Golaz, a young Swiss minister, and his new wife would go as soon as the yellow fever season had receded from the city in early 1881. Taylor would finally have someone with whom to share the load.

31

You Will Find Only
Jackals and Hyenas

Just as Governor Brière de l'Isle was leaving Saint Louis—having ceded his position to Commandant Louis Ferdinand de Lanneau in mid-April 1881—the agreement on the Dakar–Saint Louis railroad was falling apart. The now former governor was in Dakar waiting for his ship back to France when he got the first telegram announcing the trouble: a surveyor from the railroad company had come to Lat Joor's court bearing gifts, which the damel had accepted, but such things did not stop him from expelling his European visitor and his delegation, even though night had already fallen and they had nowhere else to go. A few days later, just as his ocean liner was lifting anchor, Brière received another. It said: "Urgent - Lat Joor absolutely refuses to let railway construction proceed. Writes me a formal letter on this subject."

Lat Joor had never been enthusiastic about the railroad project; he had only agreed to it as a matter of political expediency. And he soon changed his mind.

Following the tension about Lat Joor's residence, Lat Joor did move and an uneasy detente was maintained between him and Demba Waar. Lat Joor undercut the schemes of his enemies by starting to integrate his nephew Samba Lawbé Faal into his own sphere of influence and treating the young man as his heir apparent or a "petit damel," a reference more to his age than his stature since he was reputed to stand nearly two meters [six feet, seven inches] tall.

The treaty on the railroad project was the means by which this tentative peace was brokered, but the project was not popular with many of Kajoor's notables, who expressed themselves on the matter with some passion. One such notable was the aforementioned Samba Lawbé Faal, who had a sizable number of partisans. Perhaps it was the fear of letting his nephew appear stronger than him that persuaded Lat Joor to reverse his stance on the railroad.

Lat Joor was himself already concerned about the creeping control the French were having on his domestic matters, such as the issue of fugitive slaves. "We ask you to help us with our slaves," Lat Joor wrote to the governor just a few days before chasing the surveyors away. He used a comparison that he often employed in such letters to explain his demand: "Because in our country slaves are regarded as you regard silver for your money." Brière speculated that Lat Joor was testing the fortitude of the new governor.

The formal letter about the railroad Lat Joor sent to de Lanneau was not diplomatic; it was categoric: "The purpose of this letter is to let you know that I absolutely forbid the passage across my country and through my villages of your ship that moves upon the land. I would never accept such a thing that causes me displeasure, and I would never be able to reign over Kajoor if it were to exist. If you continue to try to operate your ship anyway, it will only find jackals and hyenas, for we will all abandon Kajoor."

Such a move by Lat Joor and the people of Kajoor would defeat one of the purposes of the railroad—that is, to provide a means of transporting greater numbers of peanuts from the productive lands of Kajoor. After all, an empty country would produce no peanuts. The governor was also concerned about reports that Lat Joor had a visitor with him when he kicked the surveyors out: Albury Njaay, the leader of the neighboring Jolof kingdom to the east of Kajoor who also happened to be the damel's cousin. The new governor suspected Albury's presence augured a military alliance, one that could perhaps gather enough strength to march against the French.

Just a couple of weeks into de Lanneau's tenure, the signature program of his predecessor was at risk and the country was on the brink of war. He wrote the minister in Paris right away to please send reinforcements. The minister was reluctant; it was already May and the country was on the cusp of the bad season, when the rains would drench the sand, flood the rivers, and spread fevers that were especially dangerous for those new to the continent. The reinforcements would have to wait.

Instead, the governor expedited a delegation headed by the qadi on a path lined with hardy succulents across the sandy plains of Kajoor. They were to smooth over any disagreements, just as officials had when Lat Joor had been persuaded to sign the treaty authorizing the railroad in 1879. But the man who had brokered the original accord, Bou-el-Mogdad, had died about six months before this new crisis. When Lat Joor had received word about the cleric's death in late October of the previous year, he had sent his deepest condolences to the governor: "We are so devastated by this sorrowful news that we can no longer distinguish night from day, sky from earth, or elephant from ant," he wrote. "I swear, in the name of God, that I have lost my protector and my support. Who will look after our affairs after his death?" Who indeed? Brière had said that Bou-el-Mogdad's death was a "calamity" for the colony. The new qadi, although a respected merchant and learned man, did not and could not have the same influence as his legendary predecessor.

The new qadi's visit seemed to further convince Lat Joor of his decision, especially when a certain Yamar who was present at the talks—who may have been a canton chief from the long-colonized kingdom of Waalo—warned the nobles and leaders of Kajoor. "Look at me, I was once free like you," he said. "But now I am a French vassal. If you accept this proposal for a railway, you will become like me, a subject of the French, because you will no longer have any influence in Kajoor."

The only consolation that de Lanneau could take from the visit was that the qadi informed him that it was possible that Samba Lawbé Faal was not as opposed to the railroad project as he had given out in public. The governor soon wrote to the little damel, saying that he heard that the young noble would be ready to answer the call to serve his country, if his uncle Lat Joor should stumble. Whatever confidence the qadi had, Samba Lawbé's next letter did not bear this out. "As someone who will one day be called to reign over Kajoor, I only desire its prosperity and such peace as will contribute to it," Samba Lawbé wrote. "If you persist in this railroad idea, this is what will happen to us—either we will no longer be considered a free people, or we will desert our country, or we will defend it to the last mile, which will ruin trade and agriculture: three equally disastrous consequences for Kajoor."

32

A Colleague and a Partner

Georges Golaz. *Courtesy of Defap*

Georges Golaz thought the house was being robbed when a sharp sound cut through the deep silence of the night. He and his wife, Louise-Caroline, had finally arrived in Saint Louis about a week before, in early February, to aid Walter Taylor, who had been laboring alone for nearly three years. From the speeches Golaz made at his ordination, we know that he considered himself and his wife to be modern apostles of their faith who were going to spread the good news. They were assured, by their faith, of their success. But that night, Georges and Louise-Caroline were sure of nothing; they did not know what was happening in this strange house, in a rough city, on an island at the edge of the unknown.

He peeked through the slots of the shutters, where he saw something or someone emerge from the dark courtyard below. He grabbed a weapon—he forgot what exactly—to defend himself and crept out of his apartment into the stairwell, taking careful, quiet steps in the darkness. At the top of the stairs, Golaz found himself face to face with a "colossus" who was, it seems, looking for him.

"I shouted for him to stop and asked what he wanted," Golaz later wrote in a letter to the Missionary Society's director in Paris. The man lifted his face. Golaz breathed a sigh of relief; he recognized the man. It was Fadouba, a member of the mission's small church, a middle-aged man with a broad build and a jovial disposition. Fadouba had come to find Golaz in the middle of the night because the situation called for immediate action.

"He brought me a poor woman with a two-year-old child on her back, a runaway slave," wrote Golaz. Fadouba told him that the woman knew her master would be hard on her heels and she was desperate. "She was asking me," Golaz wrote, "for sanctuary."

Georges Golaz took one look at the pleading woman in front of him and decided that he could not send her away. He moved quickly and directed to her and the child to a cubbyhole to hide. The next day, he heard that her master was wandering the neighborhood in search of her. The woman's husband had escaped the month before and was currently staying hidden at Taylor's house. "It's a whole family pulled from slavery," said Golaz.

What a sensation of satisfaction Golaz must have felt, as a new missionary full of zeal and idealism! Before leaving for Senegal, he had addressed a crowd in Paris and spoken with gravity about the sacred task he was to undertake: "It is not my work that I am going to do; it is the work of the Lord himself, and my greatest ambition is to become a humble and docile instrument in His hand."

As God's instrument, he protected the woman and her child in his house. First one night, then two, then three. The next month, when he wrote to the director, she was still there.

His letters suggest that after the woman and her child left, there were others who came and took their places. He did this, despite the Paris board's admonitions to rein in the costs associated with runaway slaves. "When a poor slave, pursued by his master, takes refuge with us during the night, it is impossible for us to chase him away," wrote Golaz. "I declare myself incapable."

Georges Golaz was a prodigious correspondent, often scratching out twenty-page letters that spared no detail about his new life. It was his first time in Africa, and, having grown up in a tidy Swiss town full of watchmakers in the foothills of the Jura Mountains, the change must have been jarring. Saint Louis was an assault and an invitation in those earliest days of their discovery: the relentless sun; the horizon dominated by the blue ocean, whose waves crashed on the golden shores and sparkled like shattered glass; the whitewashed walls of the city's houses topped with burnt orange roof tiles; the green canopy of palmiers, cocotiers, and baobabs; the mix of people in the streets, from white men in familiar suits and uniforms to Wolof traders in majestic, flowing boubous in shining shades of the brightest white and the deepest indigo, to local women who smoked pipes stuffed with tobacco and twisted scarves in intricate designs around their heads; and the sounds of the tam-tam cutting through scorching days and thick nights. Far from the rocky, mountainous paths of his childhood, here he walked on "sand that flees from under our feet."

The Golaz couple's trip to Senegal at the end of January had been a difficult one, and Louise-Caroline had been sick most of the way. It had taken them only nine days to travel from Bordeaux to Dakar on an ocean liner. From Dakar to Saint Louis they transferred to a smaller, more nimble ship that could better handle the fearsome bar, the place where the Senegal River's flow confronted the ocean's currents. When a ship was lucky, it could do the trip in little more than half a day. Georges and Louise-Caroline boarded such a boat on a Saturday afternoon, hoping to arrive in Saint Louis on Sunday morning. But their captain missed the tide, and they had to wait until Monday. "On Monday morning, the pilots signaled to our vessel to approach, so they can help us pass, but the captain was in bed, and his second could not do anything without an express order," wrote Golaz. "We are stuck until Tuesday."

The captain had warned them before they boarded that he was not responsible for feeding passengers, but the Golazes had only had time to buy a bit of bread, a small can of food that turned out to be rotten, and a bottle of wine, certainly not enough to last several days. They were soon reduced to begging for bouillon from the captain; he would not oblige. It wasn't personal; when one of the African deckhands fell ill, Golaz reported that the captain likewise refused to help him. "Give him a few kicks, that will cure him," said the captain. And so the days passed. Tuesday, bar blocked. Wednesday, bar blocked. Golaz soon became agitated. It was not a good beginning. "For five days, we have been gripped by the anguish of hunger," he wrote. Louise-Caroline had been seasick since Bordeaux and now was weak from lack of sustenance. "Towards noon I go down to the cabin where I find my wife with a strange pallor, her eyes fixed and with a great fever. She could hardly speak. I go up on deck, resolved to try anything and I felt enough strength to lift a mountain. . . . I go to the captain and ask him for a boat to seek help elsewhere." Other boats were waiting for the bar to open, too. Golaz rowed out to a Maurel & Prom ship and came back loaded with food: soup, meat, biscuits, and more wine. But their situation with the ocean and river currents did not change. Thursday, Friday, Saturday, bar blocked. Finally, Sunday evening as the sun was setting, what must have seemed like a miracle: "We find the bar open and we pass. Five minutes later and it would have been too late."

An hour later, they arrived at the island of Ndar, the city of Saint Louis. Waiting at the quay was a gaggle of men, women, and children; they were members of the church and they had come to help. "In an instant, all our luggage was removed and, in great procession, we arrive at our abode," wrote Golaz.

The Golazes settled quickly into their new house. They got a dog to keep them company even though, Golaz reflected later, they should have gotten some cats to scare off the "enormous rats that threaten to weaken the house"; he set up an office in a small structure [pavilion] on the roof where he could look out over the village of Guet Ndar and, beyond it, the ocean; and they engaged a cook so that Louise-Caroline could rest more, especially as she found that some of her ill health wasn't a sickness at all, but a condition: she was pregnant with their first child.

Georges Golaz soon proved himself to be the partner and collaborator that Taylor needed. He got to work right away: teaching at the mission's growing school with Salimata, ministering to the sick, and getting to know his new parishioners by paying each family a visit. He and his wife soon met Fadouba, Samba Coumba, Illou Seck, and many others. Golaz notes that a few of the young men were laborers on an ambitious colonial infrastructure project to bring fresh water to Saint Louis from area about twenty kilometers away. Another member resisted such work, the one Taylor nicknamed "Samou le joyeux"—because of the smile that brightened his face and scrunched up the ritual scars on his cheeks. Once freed from servitude, Samou refused "to bend over backwards to work for others," preferring to depend on himself, working mostly as a woodcutter.

Golaz also undertook a round of official visits to local dignitaries, including the outgoing governor, Brière de l'Isle. "He spoke to me about Mr. Villéger in the most bitter terms," wrote Golaz, noting that once the military man had started on this subject, he went on at length. "I wish the committee had been there to hear it. What a humiliation for us to inherit such a legacy!" Not all was lost, because Golaz said that the governor "sang Mr. Taylor's praises," which suggests that the governor had radically changed his opinion of the mission and its director. The cause of this change of heart is not known, if, indeed, his words to Golaz reflected his true opinion. Perhaps he had recognized how

paranoid his assertions had been the year before. Or maybe some rap-
prochement had been reached through their mutual friend Gaspard
Devès, who also sang Taylor's praises to Golaz. "He [Devès] said to me,
with deep conviction: 'It is this man [Mr. Taylor] who will transform
our colony.' "

Golaz felt the weight of Villéger's actions everywhere he went
in Saint Louis, as a lingering scent of suspicion followed him on his
walks and visits. Every couple of letters, Golaz would rant about his
predecessor: "I have promised myself twenty times never to talk about
Mr. V. and even never to think about him, but I can't help it and I always stumble," he wrote to the deputy director. "There ought to be
proceedings against this wretch. Poor man! If his conscience ever
wakes up from its long sleep, I think he will die!" Golaz soon discovered another reason to be angry with Villéger. One day, Golaz was
reading dispatches Villéger had sent about the Saint Louis mission to
the society's *Journal des Missions Evangéliques*. When he showed them
to Taylor—who had never seen those issues before—Taylor was upset.
"He told me that from end to end, it's all a bunch of lies," wrote Golaz.
It seemed that Villéger had made up "edifying stories" about the work
he was doing and the people he was evangelizing, with only strands
of truth.

Golaz himself was overwhelmed with this knowledge, and, when
Taylor left, he burst into tears of grief and shame for Taylor, for the
church members, and for the reputation of the Protestant mission in
Senegal.

Long before Golaz's arrival, Taylor had begun to think of a solution to
the flagging reputation of the mission, one that would also solve the
problem of the runaway slaves. In 1879, he decided that he wanted to
establish a village of Protestant Christians who were also freed slaves,
and had already gotten enthusiastic feedback from then-Mayor Devès.
Soon, he drew up a more formal request to the committee for funding
to create a village where the liberated and converted could create their
own community where there would be "strength in numbers."

Taylor would finally get authorization from the colonial government for the first piece of land in June of 1881—a concession of about twenty acres, situated across the river from Saint Louis proper.

When Golaz arrived, he also started to share Taylor's dream, noting that in their own village, the new Protestants could avoid the worldly temptations of Saint Louis, strengthen their faith, and support them-selves through farming. Golaz planned to petition the government for another piece of land so their members could support themselves. After all, their congregation was growing. "I want to try to establish members of our Church there to grow peanuts," Golaz noted. "It is the future of the colony, according to those who have studied the issue closely and who have lived here for a long time."

33

Since the Invention of the Peanut

When Senegal's administrative body, the Conseil General, had considered a report about the railroad project proposal in 1879, both career politicians and representatives of French trading houses were in agreement with the report's conclusion: "This railroad will become, inevitably, the most useful means of generating prosperity and wealth for the oldest and most backward of the French colonies."

It seemed like it would be an advantage for everyone: the military would have easy access into the interior; merchants would be able to draw crops from deeper into Kajoor and Bawol; farmers would no longer have to pay camel caravans or donkey drivers high fees to transport their peanuts long distances across sandbur-strewn trails and crumbling dunes to Gandiole, Saint Louis, or Rufisque, but could target any one of the stations between those major ports; and productive peanut farming could expand in all directions. The future looked like a ray of light, and most people were inclined to believe the governor when he assured the council that no one and no place would be left behind: "Railroads spread fertility everywhere."

They thought it would be that simple, since they felt that Senegalese farmers had taken to peanut production so quickly and, thus, the peanut must have been an easy plant to grow. "Nothing is simpler and more appropriate for the indolent ways of the natives than this crop," wrote one contemporaneous French naturalist, and his opinion was shared by the majority. Over the years, the pervasive European perception of African farmers, workers, and leaders as lazy only seemed to flourish. This banal prejudice was so common that it's difficult to read any book about Africa written by a European without encountering such *beaux mots*. Doctor Laurent Bérenger-Féraud, who for decades studied yellow fever in West Africa and collected local folklore, included a whole section in one of his books about "Negro intelligence," or, in his estimation, their lack of it: "Negroes are extremely lazy physically, as we know. Well! They are even lazier in spirit. They don't think much, they are incapable even of sustained focus. As soon as they are told something a little complicated, they no longer understand; they then give in to their natural apathy."

The truth is that, looking through the records, most European merchants and colonial officials did not seem to know much about the agricultural techniques of Africans, or even, for that matter, know much about the peanut's growth cycle. The peanut trade was extractive; most merchants just wanted the nuts and did not much care how they were produced. Only a handful of forward-thinking people seemed to consider the actual fertility of the land and the crop on which they were basing their prospective prosperity. Most, however, persisted in thinking that the peanut had only to be spread on a piece of productive land for it to take root. In their estimation, if more land could be farmed in farther-flung reaches of their nascent empire, it would yield an indefinite increase in supply.

But some—very few—merchants and bureaucrats were paying attention to what was happening in the Southern Rivers and the Gambia, where the peanut shipments were full of empty pods and shriveled seeds. Some were wondering if such a malediction could befall farmers in Kajoor, the pearl of all peanut lands.

In 1880, a colonial official asked the council for 2,000 francs to encourage peanut agriculture in the north along the Senegal River. "The 2,000 francs requested is a modest sum when compared to our purpose, which is to increase the production in these countries that are beginning to grow peanuts by teaching them how to grow crops efficiently and profitably." He suggested, above all, training farmers to use the ox-driven plow, a foreign instrument for Senegambian farmers who mostly used a butterfly-shaped hoe and a lot of human labor to work the earth.

Émile Maurel, the Bordeaux-based director of one of the largest trading houses, Maurel et Prom, was also a booster of the plow: "Since the invention of the peanut, Senegal has become an agricultural colony but there is no agriculture without the use of the plow," he wrote to his agents in Senegal in 1881. He was convinced that it was the solution to the problems that had appeared in regions to the south and which had so ruined their commerce, although neither he nor the aforementioned officer had ever extensively studied the peanut-cropping practices of peasant farmers up and down the coast. Still, he was convinced: "The use of this machine would double the production of each individual and put an end to the degeneration of the peanuts and the depletion of the soil," he insisted in yet another letter to a different subordinate.

It does not seem that any of the Maurel et Prom agents took his advice, though. And the Conseil General rejected the official's request, citing other, more pressing priorities. Why invest in helping people farm better when they could just farm more land and push into new territory? The new railroad would help them do just that. The peanuts of Kajoor were some of the best in the world, and there was no reason to believe that would change.

34

Special Seeds

In March 1881, just about a month after the arrival of the Golazes, Elizabeth Taylor left with the children to go to Sierra Leone, and she planned to be gone for the better part of the year. The children would stay behind with their grandparents; Walter Jr., Samuel, and Sally Margaret would attend school in Hastings or in Freetown.

In the meantime, the Golazes promised to keep Taylor company, and he was to take his meals with them. Taylor was happy with the addition of the Golazes to their spiritual community, of course, but his own ill health, both mental and physical, had not much abated. In June, seeing how well the Golazes had adapted to Senegal, Taylor wrote the committee to ask for six months of leave to recover his health in Sierra Leone. He had been working alone, doing the jobs of at least two or three missionaries, for years with no vacations. "I'm increasingly tired and unwell," he wrote. The doctor prescribed a trip for Taylor, to reestablish his health in a more temperate place, such as the Portuguese island Madeira. "My doctor believes that a change would do me good; I need distractions, travel, rather than medications. Because of the climate, he would prefer that I go to Madeira rather than Sierra Leone. But Sierra Leone is my homeland. If I were to get sick and die, I'd like to die in Senegal or Sierra Leone and not in Madeira."

The committee members did not feel that they could say no, recognizing all of Taylor's hard work and his struggles in the intervening years. They did ask him to go to Gorée first, to see if that island's bracing sea air could restore his strength.

But Taylor would not get a chance to go to Sierra Leone; in early July yellow fever broke out in Senegal, and the English liners that would normally take on passengers at Gorée or Dakar refused to stop at the ports for fear of contagion. He would not go to Gorée either, not wanting to abandon his congregants or the Golazes during a time of crisis.

Yellow fever was "a gnawing canker," according to one doctor, a pulsing ulceration that developed across the body of the Atlantic for centuries, flaring up not just in lands closer to the equator but also in North American cities like New Orleans, Memphis, and even, on occasion, Philadelphia and New York City. It seemed to arrive at ports of call from dank ships that spread their "special seeds" of contagion, or sometimes emerged after the summer rains unbidden.

The beginnings of the disease were routine enough and reminiscent of many tropical illnesses: a sudden fever, chills, body aches, and excessive weakness. The lucky could recover after a few days, but the unlucky would only seem to recover. They would relapse some hours or even a day later, falling into delirium, their skin turning yellow, bleeding from their eyes and mouths, and their stomachs churning so that they would vomit up black grains of partially digested blood.

Nineteenth-century theories of disease scapegoated dank, malodorous air for the sickness, the miasmas. "The common mischievous agent is septic exhalations, formed from alluvial marshy soil," wrote one Louisiana doctor in a slim 1878 book on yellow fever facts at the time. Once the sickness started, they believed that it could be spread on surfaces or objects or through contact with infected people.

In 1881, a Cuban doctor would hypothesize that the culprits causing yellow fever to emerge and spread weren't miasmas from swamps, but something that often lived in those water-logged lands: the mosquito. At the time, few scientists and doctors would have even imagined the role that this wily flying insect could play, and it would take another two decades before the doctor's hypothesis would be validated.

Public health officials in Senegal during the 1881 epidemic had no access to this knowledge and no real idea about what caused yellow fever, so they also had no notion of how to prevent it. The conventional wisdom of the day in urban areas held that surfaces should be disinfected using compounds like carbolic acid to prevent yellow fever contagion, which was not particularly effective since it didn't hit at the source. Many cities also tried to avoid miasmas by draining areas of standing water, an approach that *was* effective since it limited breeding areas for mosquitoes. But Saint Louis was a series of low-lying islands in the middle of a river, on the edge of the ocean, and no amount of nineteenth-century engineering could help officials drain the sea. For treatment, doctors would prescribe purgatives, enemas, poultices, and tinctures. None of it was particularly effective.

Golaz reacted to the yellow fever outbreak with a mix of anxiety and bravado, according to Taylor who wrote that young Mr. Golaz was taking unnecessary risks: "He'd expose himself to the sun and rain, visit infected houses saying he was unafraid of fever, while he washed himself with carbolic acid." But Golaz was also obsessed with understanding how the sickness was enveloping the city. "More than once he had the doctor come to his home, although the illness was only in his imagination. Seeing that his mind was troubled, I did everything in my power to calm him down. . . . I went further—I begged all his friends not to tell him much about what was going on in town, but he always found a way to know more than I did and to tell me and his wife about it."

A month into the outbreak, the toll was growing and the epidemic seemed to have mercy on no one. "Our poor governor, Monsieur de Lanneau, died the day before yesterday," Golaz wrote in early August. The governor's death at such a sensitive moment would surely throw the colony into disarray. But the virus wasn't done. "Several senior officers, the senior commander of the troops may be dead by now," wrote Golaz. "In ten days, there have been sixty deaths!"

But he had other concerns and other joys to consider, too. Some days after writing that letter, Louise-Caroline went into labor and delivered a healthy boy. "I cannot tell you how enthusiastic and joyful Mr. Golaz was!" Taylor wrote. "He said that if it were not for the birth of his child on that day, he would have been afflicted with yellow fever."

Golaz was wrong, though. At that moment, the virus was probably already incubating within his body, preparing itself to emerge.

Georges Golaz would start to feel feverish and weak a few days after his son was born. Some days later, his wife started feeling sick, too.

While long-suffering schoolteacher Salimata nursed Louise-Caroline, Taylor attended Golaz day and night using the treatments of the day. "I followed the doctor's orders scrupulously," he wrote, "administering the medicines and enemas myself at the indicated times." After a few days, Golaz started feeling better and said he was almost fit enough to leave his bed. "He was full of excitement—he talked about the many things he would do after his convalescence," Taylor wrote. But Golaz wasn't cured; this was one of the cruelest hallmarks of the disease. The next day, his fever was back and so severe that the doctor—who knew that when the disease took such a turn, the patient was not likely to recover—told him to put his affairs in order. The delirium was taking Golaz, though, and Taylor was instead charged to read to him from the scriptures. Taylor sobbed through his reading of the seventy-seventh Psalm:

I cried unto God with my voice,
Even unto God with my voice; and He gave ear unto me.
In the day of my trouble I sought the Lord:
My sore ran in the night, and ceased not:
My soul refused to be comforted.
I remembered God, and was troubled:
I complained, and my spirit was overwhelmed.

Georges Golaz died soon after; Louise-Caroline followed her husband to oblivion two hours later. They were both buried by nightfall; it was an epidemic after all, and the bodies of the sick were thought to be capable of contaminating other people and so were buried with all expedience. Following the public health protocol, too, their house was shut up until it could be decontaminated, and most of their affairs would be burnt.

A week later, their infant would die, too.

Taylor was shattered by his grief; he looked through his old letters from Golaz to gain solace from his friend's words. Golaz had written

Taylor in late 1879, after declaring his interest in the Senegal mission. "I pray every day for you, for your family," Golaz wrote, "and for the converted members of your flock. Also pray for me; ask the Lord himself to prepare me and my fiancée for the battle, to grant us a long life in his service in Senegal, and if he should recall us early, that he will give us a rewarding death for his glory and for the good of this small part of Africa, which is the object of our tender youthful affections."

It had been a deadly summer; by mid-November, the city registered more than five hundred deaths from the disease, most of them Europeans. The military and colonial administration was in disarray, with not more than fifty European survivors left to work in the colony. The bells that announced the dead must have rarely gone silent, forming a desperate din to accompany Taylor's days and nights.

Soon the rains stopped, the puddles dried up, the morning and evening air turned cool, and the fevers drifted away. In December, the epidemic had receded enough for Taylor to reopen the school. He was back to doing the work of two or three men again, overworked and overwhelmed, moving through his duties with a heavy heart.

The new village project, he decided, would have to wait a little longer yet.

35

Interregnums

After Governor Louis Ferdinand de Lanneau's sudden death from yellow fever, an interim governor was sworn in for a couple of months and then followed by a series of appointees who would have to be replaced at an alarming frequency. They would be carried off as much by politics as by sickness. Over the next two years, six men would occupy the office in Saint Louis and assume the title as the constantly shifting Emir of Ndar.

Throughout the personnel changes, the passions in Kajoor seemed to cool and the equilibrium of the country appeared to return to normal. In late 1881 and the first half of 1882, Lat Joor and his influential compatriots still sent plenty of letters to each governor, but they were related to routine disputes over cows and camels; requests for medical help for friends and family, including for Lat Joor's cousin, whose ailment was a painful venereal disease; offers from sundry minor nobles to betray Lat Joor and support the French; the damel's endless desire to invade Bawol; a couple of inheritance issues; a murder; and of course, many runaway slaves.

In early 1882, Lat Joor had written to the newest Emir of Ndar a warning about the latter issue: "Such things [the freeing of captives] can break alliances. I cannot live without captives or without being able to send them to Saint Louis."

That governor, who had been posted to the colony in various roles for more than three decades and who had been beaten by Lat Joor on at least one or two battlefields, recognized the subtext of the message: Lat

Joor was calling his treaties with the French into question. The governor was concerned and readied a military column to send into Kajoor in case it became necessary—only a small one since yellow fever had struck the military with force. The minister wrote back reminding him to avoid any display of aggression and to placate Lat Joor on the runaway slave issue: "I would like to draw your special attention to the importance I place on our continued good relations with this chief, who needs to be reassured of our intentions with respect to his captives. Lat Joor's friendship is indispensable to us in order to finalize our Dakar to Saint Louis railroad plans."

The minister hoped that through some cajoling Lat Joor would change his mind again about the project. In a letter a couple of months later, he reiterated this point to the governor, that cracking down on the slave trade "would alienate us from them [the leaders of Kajoor] and gravely damage our commerce."

The commerce, though, was already suffering. The situation reports about trade that colonial officials sent from outposts on the margins of Kajoor were pessimistic that year, as farmers picked up on the more subtle threats of war that were spreading throughout the country in the spring of 1882:

4 March 1882

Rufisque: Agriculture—None. There is almost no trade in peanuts. The shipments from Diander seem to be finished, and those from Kajoor and Bawol are starting but do not look promising. As a result, exports hurt, despite the high prices the traders are offering; in 1878 peanuts were 20 francs per 100 kilos, today they have increased to 25 or 26 francs and have reached 28 francs per 100 kilos.

Diander: Agriculture—none. The rumors of warriors gathering in Kajoor and Bawol cause the caravans to dwindle by the day.

What's more, the rains were poor that year; in October, just as most farmers were bringing in their harvests, the commandants noticed that the crop season was a failure for peanuts:

20 October 1882

Diander: Bad harvest; almost everywhere plants dried up before flowering, the peanuts have very small seeds and don't seem to promise anything worthwhile.

Famine would be inevitable, they said, in the areas that stretched between Dakar and Saint Louis, and so risked affecting those cities, too.

During all this time, the railroad project itself had stalled, pending its authorization by the French parliament and negotiations about how to finance the construction, with costs estimated at close to 18 million francs—a huge sum for the central government that was often in budgetary distress. By the end of June 1882, the vote came through in the affirmative and the French company that had received the contract readied itself to start construction by the end of the year.

Lat Joor, however, remained steadfast in his opposition.

"For as long as I live, know this well, I will oppose the building of this railroad with all my might," he wrote to the governor. "That's why every time I receive a letter from you about the railroad, I will always give you the same answer, 'no, no,' and I will never respond any other way, even when I'm asleep. Even my horse Maalaw would give you the same answer."

Spies infiltrated the cities and villages in and around Kajoor, listening behind palaver trees and in village squares, sending word about Lat Joor's movements, the people with whom he met, his purchases and conversations. They were district chiefs, wives of nobles or of religious leaders, petty traders, and many others who were not described in the records for fear of retribution.

After the harvest, the police commissioner in Saint Louis said he had heard from an informant that Lat Joor had warned his subjects to not supply the city with millet or he would fine them and confiscate their livestock. The commander in Thiès soon received intelligence: "Lat Joor is only trying to get his former captives back so that he can sell them, in order to raise enough money to buy horses and guns." And another report suggested that partisans of Lat Joor had recently bought a chemical in Saint Louis that they might use to poison Kajoor's wells if the damel were ever to retreat, leaving his country empty for the jackals and the hyenas, as he had threatened.

The French already knew of Lat Joor's alliance with Albury Njaay from Jolof and with Abdul Bubakar in Fuuta Tooro to the north. But there was a rumor that the damel was attempting to make amends to the Emir of Trarza, a kingdom on the other side of the Senegal River, whose forces were considerable. Lat Joor was even said to be making overtures to the ruler of Bawol, a person whom he had been threatening with war for the better part of his reign. That attempt was not successful.

In early August, news came that Lat Joor had assembled 1,200 cavalrymen and about 3,000 foot soldiers in his village, while the colonial government had only approximately 400 men in Saint Louis, 200 in Dakar, and a handful at the bases on Kajoor's edges.

The governor sent a flurry of letters to likely allies inside and outside of Kajoor, sending them with his fastest horsemen, who raced across searing sands and acacia forests to areas far and wide. Some of these leaders would claim to stand with Lat Joor in public only to repudiate him in their letters to the French. In this way, the French were able to neutralize some of Lat Joor's efforts to recruit neighbors and notable subjects in support of his cause. Lat Joor also had his ways of getting information, or so he said. Writing to the governor, he revealed: "I must warn you that I have read the letters you have been sending to the people of Kajoor because every time you write to one of my subjects, the letter is read out loud in front of me."

The first railroad construction workers arrived from France in November and December and started working on French-controlled land in Dakar and the outskirts of Saint Louis. When he learned that construction had started, Lat Joor saw it as a provocation, saying that, by traditional rights, even parts of Kajoor that had long been ceded to the French through treaties were still his. "The suburbs as well as Kajoor belong to me; they come from my ancestors," he wrote that November just as the first workers were arriving. "If I have left this suburb to you, it's because of the good relations we've always had."

Lat Joor reiterated his refusal to allow the railroad to pass.

As 1882 drew to a close, the conflict that had been averted the year
before now seemed inevitable. In one neighborhood of Saint Louis, the
griots were singing songs about war, belting out, "the gunpowder will
do the talking."

Reinforcements were requested again from the ministry, like the previous year, and this time they were authorized and sent from France.
In late December, hundreds of foot soldiers and cavalry mounted on
horses and camels marched into Kajoor with a singular goal. According to the governor's explicit instructions to the senior commander,
"The purpose of this offensive is to expel the King of Kajoor Lat Joor."

36

The Propagation of French Culture?

"You are all aware of the devastating catastrophe that befell our mission last year," Walter Taylor wrote in the annual letter to his subscribers in Bordeaux in early 1882. The loss of the Golaz couple had affected the congregation in Saint Louis, as well as the whole mission society, a cruel tragedy that compounded all of the mission's other losses and struggles.

But one bright spot remained, Taylor said. The runaway woman and child—the ones who Georges Golaz had hidden away—well, they had obtained their freedom and were still counted among those affiliated with the mission. The child was a boy of about five years old, and Golaz had given him a nickname, calling him Jacques Golaz. After Golaz's death, the boy's parents decided to keep it. "I hope that in memory of our dearly departed comrades," he wrote to his subscribers, "that you will remember Birama and Awa Dhiajaté and their child Jacques Golaz Dhiajaté in your prayers."

The young Jacques Golaz was a sharp little boy, according to Taylor, and was soon attending the mission's school. The school had always been one of the main ways that the mission conducted its outreach to the people of Saint Louis, teaching local boys and girls to read French and do their sums.

Most colonial schools at the time were run by Catholic missions that were so heavy on religious education that many Muslim residents remained reluctant to enroll their children. Instead, they would send their children to learn the Koran with a knowledgeable holy man. As the French increased their territorial ambitions in Africa, the colonial government started paying more attention to the role that French-language education could play in the cities and territories it controlled, seeing schools as a means to disseminate French habits, traditions, and values. It was an idea that transcended political orientation, creed, and confession, and the idea of "civilizing" Africans by exposing them to French culture was a palatable one to most French officials of the time.

Some Muslim parents must have ceded, as Taylor reports in 1882, "A good number of native families, while holding onto their religion, are also interested in providing their children with a good French education so they can cope with the current situation." That situation was the ever-expanding maw of French domination in their territories as part of a global empire. At the time, Taylor said he had at least two Muslim children, the sons of a rich trader, boarding with him and attending the school.

The Protestant mission's school was much smaller than those run in Saint Louis by three separate Catholic orders, but it soon drew the government's attention as a possible vehicle for the propagation of French culture. As for its curriculum, French Protestants were a religious minority and tended to support policies of secularism since they were aware of the dangers of using the state to sponsor religion. Muslim parents in Saint Louis could send their children there for primary instruction without any Bible or catechism classes.

In mid-1882, Taylor received a proposition from the government to take in twenty newly freed boys and to educate them, for which the mission would be given a subsidy. Such children often were handed over to the Catholic missions or the military, or were confided to some local notable or craftsman or housewife as wards. The proposition was a sign that the mission was gaining ground as an institution in the city, and Taylor could not help being pleased with the recognition and show of confidence in his abilities. His tense relations with the authorities, which had so burdened him in previous years, seemed to be a thing of the past. "Another source of encouragement that God has provided for us," he wrote in another letter from the period, "is the increasing ease of our dealings with the government on the one hand,

and the public in general. The few complaints I have had to make over the past year have been listened to with sympathy and settled in a most satisfactory manner."

But the same problem posed itself that had the year before and the year before that. Taylor needed help. "I have had many plans go through my mind," he wrote to the director, "but what will I be able to do on my own?" Into the breach had stepped Samba Coumba and Moussa Sidibé to help with pastoral visits, evangelization, and some work in the school. "Our two friends were pleased to be asked to come to my aid," and, probably, with the prospect of the small salaries they would receive for their time. But they couldn't replace a trained and ordained minister who could also write sermons and take care of administrative issues. Taylor described his schedule to the committee to give them an idea of his frenetic pace:

"I teach school every day, except Thursday, from 8 a.m. to 11 a.m., and 2 p.m. to 6 p.m., unless I am forced to go out to visit the ill or to deal with some procedures in government offices. Every Thursday I hold two meetings: one for the children from 8 to 9 in the morning, and the other for the men who are members of the church from 7 to 8 in the evening. . . . On Sundays we have two worship services from 8 to 9.30 in the morning and from 4 to 5.30 in the evening. Sunday school is held at 3 to 4 o'clock and is presided over by my wife and Miss Salimata."

Walter Taylor, alone in Saint Louis and facing so many obligations, weighed the proposal of taking in twenty young boys with a pessimistic eye: "Twenty boys! Where can I house them? How can I alone shoulder such a heavy responsibility in an adequate manner?" After a few months of deliberation, he had to turn down the opportunity. Who knows what happened to those boys?

Earlier in the year, the governor split some recently liberated children between a Catholic mission, the army, and the colony's public works office. It was a moral gray area. Was giving children to the army or to a part of the government to work any better than keeping them enslaved in Mauritania or Kajoor?

In Paris, some members of the committee hesitated to send a

replacement for Golaz, concerned that they could be said to be sending another young missionary to his death. Taylor even asked if they
might look in the British colonies like Sierra Leone and the Gambia or
even as far afield as Lesotho, where the French Protestants had long
ago established a mission.

But the atmosphere in Saint Louis was changing. Taylor wrote some
months later, "After much thought, I have finally given up on such a
plan for the following local reasons." He explained that the local government and the governor and the French merchants, and all the people in power, were having conversations and debates about the "native
question." Their concern was how, in these small cities that they saw
as African outposts of the French Empire, the French could maintain
their authority and influence even as Africans gained more demographic weight and clamored for more political power. Runaways and
refugees from unrest in the areas outside of Saint Louis or Dakar—
unrest often created by French forces—fled to the cities run by the
French in a demographic explosion. They would soon influence those
colonial towns and forts with their customs and religions. "In such a
state of affairs," Taylor explained, "the colonists are anxiously wondering: 'What should we do?' "

Taylor summarized the different ideological camps as he saw them.
"For some, emancipation is a mistake whose consequences have un-
dermined the country's prosperity and the well-being of the natives
themselves," he wrote. Those people wanted to allow open domestic
slavery to continue in the colony. "Others recommended the use of
force to compel the natives to adopt the habits and customs of civilization," which is to say to make laws forcing Africans to speak French,
dress like the French, and think like the French or else be expelled
from the colony. Many others subscribed to the idea that influence
could be applied to Africans indirectly through capitalism. "To create in them [the African population] those thousand needs of civilized
life . . . whose satisfaction would require a greater amount of labor."

It's difficult to know whether Taylor's own thoughts had changed on
the issue of Europeans spreading their "civilization" along with their
religion, since his letters from this period are more formal and do not

express many of his personal opinions. After all, his correspondence is calibrated to his readers, groups of bourgeois French Protestants, most of whom believed in the spirit of these ideas about civilization, and it is possible and even probable that he often avoided telling them things that they did not want to hear. It was clear that the stance Taylor had articulated so eloquently during his stay in Paris, the one that took exception to this European preoccupation with "civilizing" Africans, was no longer an idea that was favored in the metropole. Civilization had become the stated raison d'être of colonialism. Soon, it would be a complete European takeover, cloaking imperialism in the language of humanitarianism.

All that Taylor wrote after explaining the "native question" debate was: "The poor Negro is truly to be pitied. How he's being bullied! It's shocking!"

But Walter Taylor was also a man whose specific social context may have led him eventually to embrace parts of the ideology of "civilizing" Africans. After all, he had grown up in Sierra Leone getting a classical education, wearing close-buttoned suits and starched collars in the tropical heat, reading European philosophy, and generally aspiring to that elite class who dominated the political and cultural life of his country to the exclusion of the mass of people in the interior who had few rights. Taylor believed that Black men could and should rule themselves, an idea that put him in direct conflict with the prevailing anxieties of the day found among the leaders in Saint Louis—anxieties about a change in demographics. Maybe he, too, embraced a kind of paternalism, an idea that a capable African elite should rule over all the others, and perhaps that point of view gave him a kind of sympathy for the "civilizing" movement. It's impossible to know from his surviving writings. If we look at his life, though, his own work with the mission, where he evangelized about Christianity, marriage, work ethic, and electoral participation, can be seen as serving the cause of assimilation. But it can also be seen as Taylor harnessing his own experiences within a series of institutions to help people who lived on the margins. Maybe both interpretations are true?

The "native question" had created another problem for Taylor, too.

"As a result, an active crusade against the Wolof language is now un-
derway in the colony," he wrote. Soon, he told the committee that he
had felt it prudent to stop using Wolof or Bambara in his Sunday services, "to guarantee the continuation of our mission in the principal
town and to shut the mouths of our enemies who, on the lookout for
targets to criticize, have tried to portray us as promoting the Wolof in
our mission too much." Taylor confided, though, that, in their private
meetings, he still used all the languages in his arsenal and that his parishioners spoke Wolof, Bambara, and English.

It seems illogical, but the same imperialist "civilization" lobby
started advancing the idea of creating "native villages" for the swell-
ing numbers of freed slaves. It was the very thing Taylor had been
trying to do for the liberated affiliated with his mission. In fact, one
booster of the idea was the colonial minister, Admiral Jauréguiberry,
whose interest in the project may have been planted by Taylor's many
letters to the committee on the topic. A memo from the minister in
late 1882 suggested grouping newly liberated people in the areas near
Saint Louis or Dakar and giving them land to be "used for crops specific to the climate, such as peanuts. They would provide regular supply for our exports."

And in January 1883, a publication whose imperialist stance was
evident in its name, L'Afrique Explorée et Civilisée, published a column
advocating for such villages: "By creating native villages, and by ac-
customing these freedmen, under intelligent guidance, to regular
work that would be rewarding for them, a sense of solidarity would
be fostered among them, and they would be capable of being a good
influence on the other natives."

The idea of Taylor's village was one whose time had come. In early
1883, Taylor announced that the village project was finally taking
shape, the land occupied, the people building residences—three adults
and a child, to be precise. "As a first step, the spouses Birama and Awa
Dhiajaté with an old Bambara man are living there at the moment,"
he wrote. Taylor wrote to his subscribers in France, saying that if the
mission had some assurances about security and the necessary funds,

they would welcome "all runaways seeking freedom, to settle down on our land and place themselves under our protection."

Other pieces of land contiguous to this first one would be sought and received over the years. The government's records would refer to it as the Bambara village near the Khor bridge, but Taylor would call it Bethesda, like the place in the Bible whose waters could heal the sick and on whose shores the wretched could find mercy.

Part VI

37

The Damel

The stories about how kingdoms are born are almost as varied as the stories of how they die. This story of how Kajoor became independent is just one in a multiplicity, blending two oral histories, both versions probably distorted in their own ways. This is legend and epic poem as history. The truth is here, somewhere, in its rhythm.

In the nineteenth century, Jolof was a kingdom, but in the fourteenth century it had been an empire, and Kajoor was one of its subordinate states. The bourba, or emperor, of Jolof ruled over much of what we now know as Senegal and dominated several kingdoms in the region. It controlled its vassal states by force, and every year Kajoor, Bawol, Waalo, Siin, and Saalum had to pay an honorary tribute to the emperor, carried on donkeys or on the heads of their subjects to the Jolof capital, or else be raided and pillaged by the emperor's army.

From Saalum, the emperor demanded his tax be paid in baobab fruit; from Siin, he demanded cotton; from Waalo, he demanded fish; and from Kajoor, he demanded the very ground upon which they walked, the fine, bright sand from their dunes, which he used to decorate his court.

In the fifteenth or sixteenth century, a Kajoor laman—a head chief— had a son whom he had named Amary Ngooné Sobel Faal. The young man one day asked his father why the people of Kajoor should be obliged to pay another master, and in such a way as to underscore their subservience. He asked his father: "Why do you accept so readily

this humiliating burden that I have seen you perform for so long?"
Was the emperor, he asked, more knowledgeable than them, was he
more noble?

When Amary Ngooné Sobel was older, he gathered together the
leaders from every region of Kajoor, along with his friends, his advisers, and marabouts. He asked them, "What should a man do when he's
in chains and humiliated? Should he simply resign himself and wait
for the death that will deliver him, or should he try to break his chains
and set himself free with dignity?" They all agreed that they should
rise up and that they would stand behind him in battle.

Amary Ngooné Sobel sent a messenger to the emperor to let him
know "that I will give him a fair fight with the firm determination to
free my country." The emperor responded with haughtiness: "What a
presumptuous young man! To attack me?" He told the young man to
meet him on the battlefield, and "he'll find out who I am."

Amary Ngooné Sobel ordered the drums of war to be beaten and
rode with his army to meet the emperor. This was a time before there
were many guns, so they used lances and leather lashes to attack their
enemy.

In some versions of the story, Amary's warriors were outnumbered
by the emperor's army on the battlefield and the fight was bloody. In
others, Amary used a few tricky ruses to bring his cause into the emperor's palace. But all the songs tell us that Amary Ngooné Sobel and
his warriors emerged victorious.

Kajoor was free. It was an independent kingdom, and no one outside
of its borders could control its destiny.

Amary Ngooné Sobel's father became Kajoor's first leader as an independent nation, but the older man died only days after taking the
throne. The people then demanded that their liberator be their ruler;
they would accept none other than Amary Ngooné Sobel. He would
not be called by any of the traditional rulers' names—not a laman like
his father had been, not a bourba like the ruler of Jolof. The new leader
of their independent kingdom would have a new name: the damel,
which means "the one who broke the staff," the staff of servitude.

38

Bethesda

SÉNÉGAL — Famille Bambara du Pont de Khor

Bambara family at the Khor Bridge. *Courtesy of Archives du Sénégal*

To get to Bethesda from the mission house in Saint Louis, Walter Taylor would ride his horse across the pontoon bridge to the other side of the river; traverse the Sor neighborhood where workers were building the train station; take a sandy path out of town, bordered, as another visitor wrote, "on either side by immense ponds where forests of rushes and reeds grow, and from whence all manner of amphibians greet us with their croaks." Maybe he would pass a winding caravan of tired porters, camels, and donkeys from Waalo or Fuuta, pushing to walk the last few kilometers to their terminus in Sor. Or maybe he would come across some military men patrolling the area, for the enemies of the French were many and could come from any direction. After about twenty minutes at full gallop, or an hour of walking on foot, he would arrive at the village, which in the 1880s and even 1890s hardly merited the term. There was just a handful of huts made from sticks and reeds and topped with conical roofs of hay.

Soon after they moved to Bethesda, Awa and Birama Dhiajaté had been joined by another man and woman and then others. Although the land was owned by the mission, the people who later found their way there were not always members of the church. They were friends, cousins, and countrymen—all people who spoke similar languages and kept similar customs.

Colonial officials were glad to see the initiative, wrote Taylor in 1883. "Birama told me a few weeks ago that the governor visited Khor Bridge and he expressed his hearty approval of the choice Birama had made for his home, outside of the already overcrowded Saint Louis." Taylor also constructed a little hut for himself on the concession, where he could take a break from the dust and sun on his visits and rest if necessary, prone, as he was, to terrible migraines and spells caused by his asthma. "I will go to monitor the construction work and encourage our people," he said.

In 1884, a young lady called Coumba Sidibé, who had been living with the Taylors for a year and whom they considered almost a daughter, married a man from Bethesda and moved there. "She was in white with a large shawl, on her head a handkerchief of green and yellow silk artfully arranged," a wedding guest wrote. With Coumba on Taylor's arm and a whole procession of spectators, they stopped off at the photographer's studio for a wedding day photo, then went to city hall for the civil marriage, and finally arrived at the chapel, where Taylor presided over the religious marriage ceremony.

Most of the inhabitants of Bethesda lived by their agriculture, growing peanuts, of course, as well as potatoes, beans, and even a bit of
cotton. Birama Dhiajaté did well for himself there, and managed to acquire a couple of cows and a few sheep; they were big investments
in the future from a man who had been, until recently, enslaved. By
1884, Taylor reported that sixteen adults were living in Bethesda and
access to land for planting was becoming a contentious issue. "I had
to go and demarcate everyone's land to put an end to the grievances
and complaints that had become all too frequent lately." The limited
amount of land, Taylor said, restricted "the growth of our agricultural
population."

Even after the mission asked for and received other concessions, the
land could not permit everyone to live by farming. The population of
Bethesda would swell and then shrink, as the newly liberated moved
on to find other places to live, up and down the coast and into the interior. They would follow word of mouth about someone's cousin or
friend, about opportunities here and there.

The situation of the Bethesda enclave, a little distant from the main
town and with a concentration of people from one ethnic group, must
have reminded Taylor of his own childhood village in Sierra Leone,
where most of his neighbors had also been united by a common language and a history of trauma. The topographies couldn't have been
more different: one was nestled in the green mountains, an equatorial
sun coloring the vegetation in tones so vivid they were almost gaudy;
and the other was a low-lying hamlet in brown, tan, and beige drylands, bordered by dark green mangroves. As a man who had grown
up in a place settled by the liberated, he must have known what a
balm it was for people who had been displaced to meet neighbors
who spoke the same languages and followed similar customs; but as
a missionary, he also must have known that such a grouping could
help them keep alive the very thing he was trying to change—their
spiritual allegiances. Even determined converts, when faced with
challenges, might find solace in the ways they had learned from their
parents.

In Bethesda, masquerade groups called *komo* societies would occupy the streets on certain nights to administer justice. The leader was not decked out in layers of robes like the Egungun masqueraders of Walter Taylor's youth, but a cotton tunic, "covered with a number of small, shimmering mirrors," holding a cowrie-studded horsetail in one hand and wearing on his head "a cap featuring an animal's head adorned with real horns." The leader sang along with the other komo initiates: "I am the chameleon/My headdress is the sky/My shoes are the earth."

Members of the society were sometimes pure animists, but more often they were also Muslims or Protestants, too. Was Taylor reminded of his childhood glimpses of the Egungun masqueraders dancing in the Hastings village square, as they brought blessings and judgment in equal measure?

Taylor never wrote about the komo or any of the customs he must have witnessed. But even if he did not approve, Taylor never wielded the gospel as a weapon; you would never find him flogging the komo leader as that old missionary had back in Hastings.

In his letters, Taylor and the missionaries who soon joined the mission often wrote about parishioners who were backsliding. One woman who had married a drunk soon left him to marry *à la mode musulman*, which is to say, a polygamous union. A male member of the church was excluded for the vague reason that he "could not withstand the drives of debauchery." And, saddest of all, when Birama Dhiajaté decided to marry a second wife in 1886, he would be kicked out of the church for engaging in polygamy. In retaliation, he took young Jacques Golaz out of the Protestant mission's school for boys and placed him in a Catholic school.

Did Birama Dhiajaté stay in Bethesda with his wives, his sheep, and his cows? It is possible, because the village near Khor Bridge had become more than just a Protestant settlement; it was also a place where people with shared language and a shared experience of servitude could create new lives for themselves.

39

Poor Lat Joor

The military offensive against Lat Joor was over even sooner than anyone in Saint Louis or in France could have hoped. In early January 1883, ten days after the troops left on their march, the governor sent a telegram to the minister in Paris: "Stunning impression on the people. Unconditional surrender of entire Kajoor arranged. Railroad project secured."

"Poor Lat-Joor!" wrote Walter Taylor in Saint Louis, sharing the latest political news with the director in Paris. He had soon heard, as indeed had all of Saint Louis, that, faced with the military column that was on its way to fight him, Lat Joor had abandoned Kajoor, taking with him a contingent of wives, warriors, marabouts, and some of his subjects, although not as many of the latter as he had threatened. The French rounded up the livestock near Lat Joor's village—reputed to be more than 2,000 cows, steers, horses, sheep, donkeys, and goats—and sold them at auction in Saint Louis to a public looking for deals. Lat Joor's land was gone, his homes destroyed, his fields razed, and his wealth sold for bargain prices to his former friends and current enemies. "His stubbornness has cost him dearly," Taylor wrote.

As the military spread out across the kingdom, they posted and read out a decree in each village:

People of Kajoor,
French troops have entered the territory of Kajoor. They have come to carry out a great work of civilization among you: the

construction of a railroad between Dakar and Saint Louis. Your oppressor Lat Joor had promised to let the railroad pass through your country and spread prosperity, abundance and wealth by facilitating trade. Lat Joor has betrayed his promises. He opposes the construction of the railroad; he has tried to deceive us; he has defied France; he will receive his punishment. Let the people be reassured! Let them stay in their fields; let them cultivate their crops and trade in peace. Honest, peaceful, hard-working men have nothing to fear from our soldiers. Far from disturbing your activities, we are protecting them. We will respect your property, your morals, your customs, your institutions. We come to you as liberators. Welcome us as friends.

After all, the instructions from the governor to the commanding officer of the column were to do all that was possible to maintain good relations in Kajoor and to help trade restart as soon as possible. It was prime selling season, and the farmers needed to send their peanuts to port.

But the reality was that the military campaign in Kajoor, or rather, the conquest of Kajoor, was violent. Many towns that are mentioned in the commanding officer's reports no longer appear on any maps, because they were destroyed and their people scattered. A handful followed Lat Joor, but others went wherever they could, settling in other kingdoms or on the outskirts of Saint Louis. Some notables offered their unconditional surrender, including one who hastened to write to the governor, addressing him as the "the master of Saint Louis who is like the angel of death."

A certain Captain Dupré led the light cavalry at the head of the column, arriving in each village before the rest of the forces. At most stops, he found time to write letters to his mother about his experiences, which were later published in a slim volume. They are a casual rendering of the conflict; he took in the beauty of the landscape and vegetation so riotous after the rainy season, its forests of baobab and gum trees, towering cailcedrats, brilliant green tamarinds with clusters of rusty-colored drooping fruits, and the flaming blooms of flamboyant trees and described his more troubling interactions with the people of Kajoor with insouciance. A taste: "Today, good, short and interesting stopover. In the village of N'Dackouck we found traces of enemy cavalry, I had the chief taken, who was brought to Louga, to be interrogated by the colonel commanding the column. The poor devil has just been shot with his secretary [cleric] in the front of the camp. A tirailleur burned his brains out with his rifle. It wasn't very pleasant, I confess, but what can you do about it?"

When Dupré reached Lat Joor's capital, he found the damel and his people long gone. Samba Lawbé was also in the wind. The soldiers set fire to everything, burning down the whole village. Dupré proceeded to burn down most villages in the area with a speed that became reckless. "When we set fire to a village this morning," Dupré wrote to his mother, "we roasted a poor old Black man who had been forgotten by his people; it was my batman [orderly] who pulled him out of the fire, but a little late, I think."

Lest the reader think this was acceptable behavior, some time later Dupré wrote that he was reprimanded about his tactics. "The colonel has just woken me up in the middle of my siesta," he lamented, "to tell me not to charge on horseback any of the Blacks I might encounter, as they are all coming to surrender."

The minister and the governor had decided to replace Lat Joor as damel with another person with the right pedigree, a young man called Samba Yaya Faal, Lat Joor's cousin, who had recently offered his services as a pro-French partisan in a secret letter. Samba Yaya took a different name as damel, calling himself Amary Ngooné Faal II after the man who had led Kajoor to independence in the sixteenth century. Was the bitter irony lost on the people of Kajoor? They must have known that Kajoor would be less than it was—less physically, since the French annexed a couple of provinces to rule them directly, and less metaphorically, since all sovereignty would now be a pretense. The damel would be a figurehead, and Kajoor would be a puppet state, independent only in name.

In February of 1883, Amary Ngooné Faal II and his warriors accompanied the military to Saint Louis, where there was a parade in the

streets of the capital to celebrate the French victory. Taylor went out to
witness it:

> If I am not mistaken, his [Amary Ngooné Faal II] arrival was
> greeted by a twelve-gun salute. He was escorted by musicians
> with their drums, and a cavalry of nearly one hundred and fifty
> men armed with muskets and sabres. You had to see them! . . .
> The king himself, mounted on a magnificent saddle that was a gift
> from the governor, seemed pleased with himself.

Taylor wondered, like many others in the colony, if this new damel
would be able to maintain a lasting peace. He speculated, "Will Lat
Joor give up his rights so easily? It is to be feared that he won't."

40

Go East!

In early 1883, Walter Taylor again took up his pen to write to his sub-scribers, this time to share some good news about the mission. "Since my last report," he wrote, "the law dealing with the fate of runaways in Senegal has undergone a welcome change."

After François Villéger had written about the colony's dirty secret of the way it expelled runaway captives, there were some reports that the policy had changed and that runaways could obtain their freedom papers in eight days instead of ninety. But in early 1880, Taylor said, that did not seem to be the case, adding: "To date, the situation of these unfortunate people has not changed." He said he spoke to a member of the administration, who said "it would be dangerous to declare a complete abolition." Dangerous for whom? Taylor does not say, but it seems likely that the official was considering the danger to the colonial administration, which always felt like the slavery issue alienated their allies.

For the next few years, Taylor was still frequently obliged to help hide the men, women, and children who came to him for protection. "Sometimes, to thwart the vigilance of their masters who were lurking in the vicinity of our house, we had to transport four or five runaways in the middle of the night to a hastily rented room," he told the sub-scribers. "Other times, it was at the political office that we had to go and plead the cause of discovered runaways, and convince their masters to relinquish their rights by paying them either in money or in merchandise," a price determined by the runaway's condition, health, beauty, strength, and age.

But in early 1883, the then-governor would take a step that would make life a bit easier for Taylor. The colonial administration would eliminate all delays in delivering freedom certificates. The governor's rationale, according to a later memo attributed to him, stated that on French land "there can and must be only free men here, and no one has the right to come and claim or take a captive. This is the law." And they had decided to implement that law nearly forty years after the abolition of slavery.

Taylor informed his readers about these encouraging developments. "As soon as they arrive in Saint Louis they only have to report to the political office to obtain, without any further formalities, their freedom certificate." Now, there would be no more cases like Awa Dhiajaté's, who, with a child on her back, had been given refuge for months by Georges Golaz. The small amount of protection afforded by their freedom papers would be available to them immediately.

"I will never forget all the setbacks that I was exposed to in sheltering runaways under the law that required them to be declared to the government and hidden for three months in order to be freed," he wrote. "What a tremendous relief for me that I am no longer called upon to perform similar acts to continue my work."

Taylor reminded his readers, though, that even once the liberated had gotten their papers, they were still sometimes at risk. In 1882, a representative of Trarza's emir, accompanied by the Sor village chief, had even knocked on Taylor's door to reclaim some runaways; Taylor not only refused but even later testified in court proceedings against the chief. In his letter, he recounted the travails of newly liberated people who had been tricked back into servitude or mistreated upon returning to the villages where they had once been enslaved.

Taylor told them about a tirailleur named Amady who had been enslaved in Fuuta and, after completing the requisite number of tours of duty, went back to his village with a sizable fortune: "Proud of his assets, our man occupied the same rank in the social hierarchy as his former master by placing himself side by side with his former master in the place where they prayed, instead of keeping behind him at a distance prescribed by Muslim customs." But one day, after praying, "someone approached him from behind and unexpectedly knocked him down; then all the assistants who had just recited their prayers were upon him, bound him and gave him a barrage of kicks and blows and delivered him to his former master." Amady was destined to be sold back into slavery, Taylor explained, but through "skillful and timely blows" he managed to escape and make his way back to Saint Louis.

The lives of the newly freed *were* tenuous, but Taylor probably had another motivation for mentioning these challenges in his letter: to stave off potential fundraising losses, since this work among runaway slaves was supported by donations. Maybe Taylor realized that his readers would think of the new policy as a definitive solution to the runaway slave issue, even though it very much was not. He was likely afraid that his donors would start longing for a new cause to support far from the mission in Saint Louis.

In fact, the events happening about 1,000 kilometers away in the area between the Senegal and Niger Rivers were diverting France's attention from Saint Louis, too. Early 1883 saw French military forces sweeping through that area and establishing their first fort on the shores of the wide, gracious Niger River in a town called Bamako, a traditional Bambara stronghold. They hoped to eventually build a railroad from Dakar to Bamako and, by so doing, to ensure their domination of much of the Upper Niger River's course.

On placing the first brick of the Bamako fort, Colonel Gustave Borgnis-Desbordes's speech to those there articulated a rationale for this expansion in humanitarian terms, saying that by extending French influence they were attacking slavery: "You have examined the social structure of these peoples and you have seen the slavery that is an integral part of their morals," he declared. "France and England spent more than six hundred million [francs] to ensure the abolition of the slave trade. Republican France can spend a few million to modify, little by little, with wisdom and prudence, the vicious, unproductive, immoral system which is so beloved of all these peoples." He was connecting the conquest and the new rail project directly to a fight against slavery.

Speeches like this would only get more common, as would-be conquerors constructed a humanitarian rationale for their impulsion to
carve Africa up between European powers. Slavery would serve that
purpose both at the Berlin Conference convened the following year,
which formalized the division of the African continent into spheres
of European domination, and at the Brussels Conference a few years
later, at which most European monarchs and presidents, the Persian
shah, the Ottoman emperor, the sultan of Zanzibar, and the government of the United States pledged to fight slavery within Africa.

Perhaps some of these powers truly believed that European territorial expansion would save Africans from themselves. But no one who
had been involved in the French military conquest of Kajoor—where
the French were still performing elaborate administrative pirouettes to
avoid freeing the enslaved—could have seen it as anything but a convenient way to cloak imperialist ambitions.

Taylor, though, saw Borgnis-Desbordes's speech as a sign, and sent
the committee the latest edition of the *Moniteur*, where the speech was
included. "What should we do in the presence of this fine path that is
opening before us to bring the Gospel to the Sudan [Mali]?"

The missionary society had been actively looking for opportunities
for their missionaries to respond to that call and go east to the Niger
and beyond. Taylor, always astute, noted that since large swaths of this
promised land in the Western Sudan had been part of the Bambara
states, and the Protestant Mission of Saint Louis was currently groom-
ing several newly liberated and converted Bambara men and women,
they were aptly placed to answer this call. And, in this way, he underscored for donors the importance of the work they were supporting in
Senegal. "Abandoning our work in the capital city, of course, would
be out of the question.—I would even say that it is imperative that we
build it up so that we can be more effective in those distant lands."

The budget proved to be a problem, and the Western Sudan was not
yet as settled as that French colonel had wanted to project. But this
evangelical excitement and taste for expansion influenced the missionary society's next steps. If the time wasn't exactly right to go all the
way east to the Western Sudan, maybe they'd go part of the way.

Two years after the death of the Golazes, the committee finally dispatched not one but two new missionaries to serve in Senegal with Taylor: Louis Jaques, the man who had founded the first Senegal mission in the early 1860s and whose resistance to the African fevers had been proven when he survived the Casamance swamps; and Jean Morin, a young man just out of medical school whose grandfather, Adolphe Monod, had been one of the most influential Protestant ministers in France.

The two arrived at the end of 1883. Director Eugène Casalis had retired the year before, but Jaques wrote a personal letter to the new director, Alfred Boegner, in which he extolled Taylor's work: "My growing personal impression—and it is also Morin's—is that the mission has in our brother Taylor one of those men whose presence is the work of providence." He said it was evident that Taylor had been, on some level, abandoned in Senegal without help and without many human or financial resources, but had nonetheless found the strength to continue his work.

"He is so well known, loved, respected: authorities, Muslim notables, as well as shopkeepers hold him in high esteem," wrote Jaques, impressed by Taylor's good reputation in Saint Louis. "People come to him with a sense of trust, as a man who knows how to enforce the rights of the unfortunate. For example, a poor laborer who has been unable to get paid will come to him, entrust him with his case, and it is rare that the man is not satisfied."

The committee hoped that eventually Morin would be able to open a clinic for the mission. But for the old hand Jaques, who must have been Taylor's senior by at least a few years and was probably in his mid-to-late forties, a bigger project was envisioned. The mission would finally expand into the interior of Senegal.

The place Taylor and Jaques decided upon was Waalo, the first Senegambian kingdom to have been conquered by the French in 1855 after they defeated the army of its last queen, Ndaté Yalla, whose opulent court included five hundred ladies-in-waiting and scores of soldiers.

Taylor had been interested in expanding there for a decade, ever since he had met Sidya Joob, Waalo's superior chief, who happened to be Ndaté Yalla's son, in the 1870s. Taylor had spoken to Sidya and excited the young man's interest about opening a school in Waalo. But Sidya was long gone by the 1880s; after rebelling against the French in 1874, he was betrayed by his cousin Lat Joor and sent to the French penal colony in Gabon, where he later died.

As some still slept away on the first day of 1884, Taylor and Jaques left to visit Dagana, a large town in Waalo, taking a small and slow steamboat up the Senegal River. "This sluggish pace did not suit me and my impatience to arrive," wrote Taylor, "but it gave me the pleasure of getting more than a quick glance at the two shores of Senegal River that I was sailing up for the first time." Taylor was struck by the difference between the sides of the river: on the right bank, camps of Trarza Moors in the seeming desert, and on the left bank, the green fields of Waalo, made fertile by annual floods that deposited the river's rich silt. But he wasn't much impressed by the natural environment they traversed, describing it as a vista of reeds and mangroves with the occasional mango tree, nor was he a fan of the ravenous mosquitoes. "But what a torment! Mr. Jaques fled at the first flare-up; after a desperate struggle I was forced to follow his example and abandon the cabin to those unpleasant guests."

They told the commandant at Dagana that they intended to establish a school, a plan that quickly won the support of the commandant and Dagana's traditional chief. They strolled the city, got into some discussions with some of the town's leaders, and at some point they were told that there was a village with many Bambara inhabitants not far away. The next day they decided to explore and walked the ninety-minute trail to the village. "When we arrived in 'Kerbala,' the name of this village of 300 inhabitants, what was my astonishment when I found a number of our freedmen there whom I had completely lost track of," wrote Taylor. "Their desertion, which had afflicted me at the time, now seems to me to be a providential direction inviting us to work among these people who know us and are waiting for us."

The joy of their discovery was mitigated by some somber news.

"Some days earlier," wrote Taylor, "some women and children, who had been enslaved in Dagana before their liberation, were recaptured by their former masters using armed force, and the whole village was in turmoil."

The reason why so many Bambara had settled in Kerbala is not clear. This area was part of a larger designation called Galodjina, north of the Ferlo desert and east of the Lac de Guiers, which was the home of many semi-sedentary Fulbe herders and some Wolof. *Kër* means "home" in Wolof, so the village literally means "the home of Bala." Although Taylor and Jaques mentioned the eponymous Bala, they don't share any details about him, except that he was accommodating to them and had at least three wives.

Some Bambara may have settled there from other areas because the region had been placed under direct rule by the colonial government in 1882, which meant that, as in Saint Louis, there should be no enslaved people living within its boundaries.

The Bambara who lived in Kerbala seemed to look out for slave traffickers and runaways, maybe because they knew that even in their own village they weren't safe. On at least one occasion about a year before Taylor and Jaques made this trip, the people of Kerbala stopped a man who was leading a group of children through the area, recognizing the band for what it was—a caravan of child slaves. They brought the man and the children to the commandant in Dagana.

Although Dagana was a major transshipment point for enslaved people from the upper river, it was customary for the French to turn a blind eye to the traffic, and they rarely intervened. On this uncommon occasion, though, the commandant was forced to investigate. His report on the subject is almost apologetic as he tried to justify the case as an exception: "I had to detain these captives because they were brought to me by people with no government ties and in the midst of a large competition among the people; in the presence of these Bambara, former captives who had served as tirailleurs, and many people from Dagana, it was impossible for me to send these children away without questioning them," he wrote. "I could not foresee that by proceeding in this way that I would be working against the interests of the government." In the end, they found a solution that was prone to other kinds of exploitation; the twelve children were duly liberated and, as they were all minors, given over to the care of some Dagana notables as wards, where some were, undoubtedly, treated as laborers.

Taylor wrote about the turmoil in Kerbala only briefly, saying they used the occasion to announce the Gospel to villagers. He was, after all, writing this travel narrative, knowing it would be published in the society's journal. Perhaps he excluded that information on purpose.

Jaques's impressions on the subject, though, were included in a letter to the director that he marked as "personal" in large letters at the top so he could be sure that it wouldn't be shared with the public. He confided that he was horrified not just by the raid on Kerbala that they had narrowly missed, the taking back of the formerly enslaved women, but also by the governor's response. "When I was telling the governor about this incident—and we had it from the people of Kerbala themselves—the governor smiled in disbelief and told me that it was an exaggeration and finally asked me if I had been there and if I had seen it with my own eyes."

What's more, the governor warned them away from becoming too involved with runaway issues in the area. Despite these constraints, Taylor and Jaques decided that Kerbala was the natural extension for the mission while waiting for the right time to expand farther into the interior. By the end of 1884, Jaques would draw up a plan and send an estimate to the committee for the cost of building a station, some 15,000 francs, a staggering cost equivalent to three years of a married missionary's salary. Jaques would himself soon enjoy that status; he married a Swiss woman, Thérèse, in church on New Year's Day of 1885, the day after she arrived. Jaques would get the authorization to move to Dagana, and Thérèse was thrilled with the opportunity to have their own mission field. They would make plans to start construction on a house and a chapel in Kerbala as soon as it could be arranged.

41

The Dawn of a New Era

On the morning of July 27, 1883, the interim governor of Senegal and a procession of colonial notables arrived at a Dakar hangar that was decorated for a special occasion. Yet another governor had died the month before, and the new temporary official, a certain Adolphe Le Boucher, stood to say a few a words: "Gentlemen, this is a solemn moment, and it will be the most poignant memory of my administrative career to have been called upon to preside over the inauguration of the first section of the railway from Dakar to Saint Louis."

The first handful of railroad construction company agents who arrived in November of 1882 had almost all died of yellow fever over the course of a month, causing many skilled workers from Europe to change their minds about sailing to Senegal. Still, hundreds of others soon embarked on the voyage from Italy, France, and Spain, lured by the promise of cash in an economic atmosphere still marked by the Long Depression. Once in Senegal, they worked with hundreds of African laborers to cut down the elephantine baobab trees in their way, grade the land, and lay mile after mile of tracks. Every delay cost the company more money, so they were urged to work faster.

"In a few moments, when this locomotive, decorated with the national colors, will set off on the tracks shuddering, shall we not believe, indeed, that we are witnessing the fatherland itself, its genius, its civilization taking possession of these lands that are still victims of banditry," Le Boucher intoned with emotion to the crowd's applause. The train, he said, would "bring peace and security and thus lead to more production and more wealth, the fruits of which will be reaped by our nation's trade."

Officials boarded this vehicle, their "messenger of progress," along with so many inhabitants of Dakar and Gorée that the correspondent who reported on the event for the *Moniteur du Sénégal* said there wasn't a free seat on the whole train. There is no information about the composition of the riders. Were they mostly European merchants and métis notables? Or did Africans from Dakar's main communities board as well?

The apostolic prefect blessed the engine, the train cars, and the tracks, and then it was time: the machine let out a high-pitched gasp, a whistle, the walls and floors shook as the engine rumbled, and then the locomotive crept forward, building up to a "vertiginous" speed, according to our enthusiastic correspondent. "Everyone felt as though they were at the dawn of a new era," he wrote.

The trip did not last long. All of this ceremony was for a section of track that ran from Dakar to the neighboring town of Rufisque, a distance of just thirty kilometers. The authorities must have felt that it was, nonetheless, an achievement, however small. After so much trouble—the coerced treaties, the wars, the fields that had been left to rot or go to seed, the burnt villages and villagers—the colonial administrators celebrated this tiny new segment with a bit of pomp, the better to gain advantage in the war they would always struggle to win, that of public opinion.

"July 27," wrote the *Moniteur* correspondent, "a date that will go down in the history of Senegal."

After Lat Joor fled, he retreated in the direction of Saalum and then the region near the Gambia River valley, just where he had gone after the French chased him from Kajoor the first time. Some of Lat Joor's warriors followed him this time, too, but not Demba Waar. All those years ago, it was Demba Waar's political acumen that had ensured Lat Joor a welcome at Maba's court, despite his youth. This time, the series of betrayals that the damel often left in his wake limited his options. In

one of the versions of the epic poem about Lat Joor's life, the bards sing
about the damel's dilemma:

Lat-Joor, why don't you go into exile?
Why don't you go to Siin? He was told.
He replied:
—Have you forgotten my day spent with Ndame Sanou and Wala
  Sanou,
When I burned Tioupane and Diakhaw?
—Why don't you go to Bawol?
—Have you forgotten my meeting with Tialaw Ndoup Koumba Diarigne
  Ngoné Siin
Between Sambèye Guent and Sambèye Tousel?
I can't go there! . . .
Go visit Trarza?
—Have you forgotten my meeting with Sidya Ndaté Yalla in Bangoye?
I can't go there!

Even if those leaders had been sympathetic to him—and most of
them were not—some also had agreements with the French that prohibited them from offering refuge to Lat Joor. But Albury Njaay in Jolof
remained one of Lat Joor's reluctant allies. His own antipathy toward
foreign rule made him sympathetic to Lat Joor's position, and, after
all, they were cousins and had grown up together in Kajoor. Together,
they launched attacks against Kajoor's eastern borders and made occasional raids on French-controlled territories to the north; all were
unsuccessful.

And so a couple of years passed. Albury suffered both for his loyalty to Lat Joor and for his own antipathy toward the colonial government in Saint Louis. The administrators attempted to ban the sale of
goods destined for Jolof, and although not all traders obeyed the policy, it was applied in many places to the detriment of Albury's subjects. In 1884, a year when the millet crop failed on Jolof's drylands,
the people suffered grievously from this policy, and there was famine.

Albury was also facing an incursion from Kajoor's new ruler on one hand and a challenger to his throne on the other: his own brother, backed by the French. Eventually, he, too, negotiated a treaty. One of its key terms was that Jolof should no longer provide safe harbor to any of France's enemies: "Since the presence of armed men creates a bad effect on peaceful populations, Albury Njaay, to prevent Jolof from being viewed as a refuge for bandits, commits himself to drive from his country on order from the governor any individual who takes refuge there with the purpose of harming the security of the inhabitants of the suburbs of Saint Louis, Njambur, Kajoor, or Bawol." This was clearly a provision aimed at Albury's most infamous guest. Lat Joor, former damel of Kajoor, was pushed out of Albury's kingdom, landing in a series of no-man's-lands between Jolof, Bawol, and Kajoor, where he ruled over only the sand and the trees, over the birds, gazelles, and wild dogs. He would have to watch the changes happening to his country from the periphery.

Amary Ngooné Faal II did not last long as damel. Kajoor was always a difficult country to manage, and he had not been chosen through the country's traditional deliberative process; he and the colonial government soon found he lacked the authority to rule this obstreperous kingdom. Right away after he took the throne, skirmishes here and there targeted the new damel's interests, all provoked by Samba Lawbé and Lat Joor. That was only to be expected, but most concerning to the colonial administrators and the merchants was that Amary Ngooné Faal II was unable to stop the exodus of Kajoor's people who followed Lat Joor and Samba Lawbé at the beginning of the military offensive and who continued to flee the unrest; the country was emptying, and Amary Ngooné Faal II could not persuade them to come back. What's more, few farmers were planning to grow their annual peanut crops because of the uncertainty. How could anyone plant seeds that would take three or four months to bear fruit, if war could whisk an entire village away in an instant?

By May 1883, merchants in the coastal cities were fed up. It was the cusp of the rainy season and Kajoor was not settled enough for

farmers to produce their annual peanut and millet crops. Many merchants signed a letter to the governor, asserting that the new damel
was not able "to establish the tranquility necessary for the return of
the emigrants and the sincere and cordial resumption of peaceful agriculture." They asked that Kajoor be allowed to choose its own leader,
as they always had, a person who could settle the country and bring
back its stability.

Of course, the people had already chosen a damel when they had
selected Lat Joor's successor a few years before, Samba Lawbé, and
would choose him again if given the chance.

At the beginning of May 1883, Samba Lawbé had surrendered his
sword, literally laying down his arms, along with several of his warriors, near the Khor bridge where members of Taylor's flock had established themselves; Demba Waar surrendered soon after. By August
1883, the French administration formally backed Samba Lawbé as the
new damel—a real and full damel, no longer the petit.

Samba Lawbé and his entourage had already called for the people of
Kajoor to come back and tend to their fields, and the merchants were
pleased; one of them crowed that the government would "with this
appointment, ensure the peanut and millet harvest." In the governor's
political situation report to the minister, he went even further by saying, "The millet and peanut harvest will produce excellent results this
year. Never, if the traders and the natives are to be believed, has Kajoor
had as many fields being farmed as this year." His boosterish confidence was wrong, though. According to one historian, the 1883 peanut
harvest in Kajoor was "disastrous." In 1882, Senegal exported 83,000
metric tons of peanuts, but in 1884, the exports were less than half of
that at just 36,790 metric tons.

Samba Lawbé's association with his uncle had always been strategic,
and now he seemed ready to leave it behind. The brand-new damel
was so pleased with his new position that he wrote to the "Grand Emir
of France," the president of France, in gratitude "of the great honors
and benefits you have given me by returning my ancestral heritage
to me, which is to say the territory of Kajoor. Know that I am noble,
and that the benefits that I receive are to my heart what a clear and

sweet-tasting water is to the person who is consumed by an intense thirst. I will never forget the behavior of the French towards me and I will never violate the treaty we signed together."

The terms of that treaty, though, were the same ones that Amary Ngooné had accepted: the French annexation of some strategic areas, the diminished powers of the damel, and, of course, the peanut train. Did he hesitate over any of the provisions? The record does not say. He signed it and agreed to all the terms, even the one that said, "Lat Joor is banned from Kajoor forever," and provided that Samba Lawbé and his warriors should "strictly prohibit him from entering" ever again.

Part of the Dakar-to-Rufisque section that the government had so celebrated washed out a few weeks after the inauguration, falling prey to the driving rains of Senegal's seasonal monsoon. The workers repaired it a few months later, at least well enough to continue construction, after the rains ended. Smaller and less congratulatory openings of railroad segments followed over the next two years. In January 1884, the company reported that it had finished the first Saint Louis segment, a 33-km tranche to the village of Mpal. By May 1884, they said the Rufisque-to-Pout line could be opened. The crews worked in two teams, one moving from Saint Louis and the other from Dakar, and each day they crept closer to one another, making as much progress as was possible during the dry season. It was impractical to work much when the rains would turn the sand to mud, and the European workers needed to return home every season to escape the fevers—at great expense to the company and the colony. When they were there, the construction workers were urged to proceed with speed, if not with care.

One tricky section of the line caused delays because of repeated derailment attempts from their restive neighbors. If the government thought the train would solve the banditry problems they had near the ravin des voleurs, they were wrong. During the summer of 1884, a letter from the company to the Minister of the Navy and the Colonies reported that there had been some armed attacks and attempted derailments: "It is to be feared that these acts of hostility will become more frequent and even more serious if the military authorities, who are on the ground, are reluctant to intervene in a forceful manner." Reports followed about a station chief who was assaulted by a member of a camel caravan, about a local man who was found putting stones on the track, a conductor who was fired upon, and of workers who were set upon by a group of armed men. Some of the attacks may well have been pure banditry as the railroad company suggested, but others, it was certain, were in retaliation for injustices. The European construction workers were a rowdy and undisciplined bunch; they indiscriminately barred herders from using their wells, got into street fights in Saint Louis, including one that cost a local man his life, and, at least on one occasion, claimed to be victims of a surprise attack by at least eight armed men when they were really beaten up by just two locals because the workers had skipped out on a bill for palm wine. Still, the construction continued, if sometimes under armed patrol.

Finally, on May 12, 1885, the two teams met on a stretch of track about midway between the two major cities, near a village called Ndande, whose deep wells were reliable sources of water. There, the current governor would drive in the last ceremonial spike made from silver. A proper inauguration of the full route from Dakar to Saint Louis would take place about two months later with the requisite amount of pomp.

Although there is no record that this happened, imagine for a minute that Samba Lawbé Faal attended this final inauguration of the railway. Would he have come in with a procession of his warriors? Would he have sat in his own section or taken a place at the front along with the railroad company director and the governor? Would he have marveled at the train's belching and bellicose engine like other spectators? Would train company officials have used the occasion to give him the card they had prepared that would allow him to ride the train for free along with some members of his entourage? Did it look the way they had envisaged, a card in French and in Wolof with Arabic characters to be stored in "a kind of finely crafted and ornate leather pouch, similar in shape to a gris-gris"? And, of greatest import for our purposes, as Samba Lawbé Faal listened to all of the speeches, each ending with a vigorous exclamation to the crowd—"Vive la France! Vive la République!"—did he start to wonder, if the railroad that ran like a scar through the middle of his country was part of France, what would happen to Kajoor?

Just as his uncle had, Samba Lawbé, after coming to power, had started asking for the annexed provinces to be returned to his control and direct leadership. "I let your railway pass and I protect it, I do everything that could contribute to our common happiness," he wrote in 1884. "Know that I have abandoned my relatives for the kingship of Kajoor. If this country does not belong to me in its entirety, what confidence can my subjects have in me?" But the terms would not be renegotiated.

The train soon started taking passengers and, most important, the precious cargo for which it was built. The peanut train was now in service.

The peanut train. *Courtesy of Archives du Sénégal*

42

We Have Already Proven
That the Negro Is Capable

In early 1885, with Jean Morin in place in Saint Louis, and Louis and
Thérèse Jaques bound for Dagana and Kerbala, Walter Taylor decided
he would finally take the vacation that he had been obliged to postpone when Georges Golaz had fallen ill and died four years earlier.
In March, he and Elizabeth caught an English ocean liner from Gorée
and sailed down the coast to Freetown.

The trip only took about five days, and Elizabeth got her sea legs
right away, walking around on deck and eating regular meals, but
Walter was sick in their cabin throughout their voyage. "I only got up
when I was told that Freetown was before us," he wrote to the director. It had been over a decade since he had last stepped a foot on the
rocky, red laterite soil of his home country, so different from the sandy
lanes around Saint Louis. He had longed for it during those days of
heartache and ill health. Queasy stomach be damned, he must have
thought, as he climbed gingerly to the deck. "At the sight of the coast
rising gradually to hillsides that measure about 1,500 feet above sea
level, the 'Sugar-Loaf,' standing proudly above the other mountains, of
the crests of churches and other buildings that can be seen from afar,
my heart jumps with joy, and a host of thoughts and emotions rush
through my mind."

Some friends met the Taylors at the port, and Walter spent a couple
of days visiting other friends who hadn't expected to see him; he was a

revenant, a specter from their younger days. Notice of Taylor's arrival would appear in one of the country's main papers, *The Sierra Leone Weekly News*, which reported that he and his wife had been "labouring for many years" in Senegal's only Protestant church.

The most meaningful moment, though, was when he and Elizabeth finally made their way to Hastings, where Walter Jr., Sally Margaret, and Samuel had been told of their parents' arrival. "Our first encounter with our children was a mixture of joy and pain," wrote Taylor. "They responded to our effusions with hesitation and looks of astonishment." It was only after several days that the children could feel at ease with the parents they hadn't seen for about four years.

Walter and Elizabeth Taylor would spend almost eight months reacquainting themselves with their children, their relatives, and their friends. Taylor was supposed to rest, but he was swept up into a whirl of activity in short order. He would attend meetings with the scions of Sierra Leonean politics and trade; guest preach at a handful of churches; make inquiries about enrolling young Walter Jr. and Samuel at the Freetown prep school he himself had attended. He made the unhappy discovery that, unlike the Anglican missionaries, he would not receive a discount for their schooling. Taylor also got a chance to visit his brother Samuel, who was an Anglican missionary at a post in Port Loko. Taylor would discuss many of these details and much more in a series of dispatches about his country published in the missionary society's journal.

"It is true that we are far from having reached perfection;" he wrote. "But, in any case, Sierra Leone is a living apologetic of the divine power of the religion of the Crucified One. The liberated, who arrived in the colony in a state that was hard to see, now own large and beautiful houses. They lead public opinion, are members of the jury and have seats on the Legislative Council and are addressed with the title of honorable. Their children have distinguished themselves as pastors, lawyers and doctors, and have occupied the most important positions in government offices. Hatreds and rivalries among members of various tribes have barely survived. To work for the emancipation of the race is the great motto of everyone."

The success of Sierra Leone's liberated people, after all their trials and triumphs, he suggested, could be replicated in Senegal, if only they could find the right way to proceed.

One method, as had been common in the early days of Sierra Leone, was to send promising young people to attend vocational and professional schools in Europe. That was how early Sierra Leonean luminaries like Bishop Crowther and Rev. George Nicol had been educated. Salimata, too, had spent several years as a child in France, studying so she could later be of service to the Protestant mission. Children, unlike their parents or grandparents, had not been practicing other spiritual beliefs and so were not attached to the old ways and gods of their forefathers. Child converts who had been taught from an early age to mistrust the processions, fetishes, and rituals so common in their communities, and to believe that truth was only to be found in the pages of the Bible, would be a valuable evangelical tool whether as members of the clergy or as laypeople.

Taylor's Bordeaux collaborators wrote as much two years before in 1883, just as the regulations regarding fugitive slaves had loosened. The annual report written by Taylor that year included a tantalizing suggestion: "Our other desire is to provide Senegal with hardworking and Christian workers. We can imagine what a strength it would be for the small Church of Saint Louis if in a few years' time it would have 4 or 5 young men skilled in their trades of shoemaker, tailor, carpenter, and perhaps a teacher, all eager to do good for their fellow countrymen. Around them, the young neophytes would follow and they would be eager to live in a Christian environment."

The following year, it was done; three boys had arrived in Bordeaux, the two youngest to go to school, and the third, a sixteen-year-old from the Bambara countries, was to learn a skilled trade. The teen, one Moussa Tarawaré, had splashed into history, like so many of his compatriots, on the freedom rolls listed in the *Moniteur du Sénégal*. His own liberation happened on May 8, 1883, when he was about fifteen years old. He was still a child, and so the paper says he was entrusted to the care of a M. Gilbert-Desvallons, the colony's public prosecutor. We can only assume, since there aren't any records about it, that this man enrolled young Moussa in the Protestant school, where he must have somehow impressed Walter Taylor.

By 1885, Moussa was also impressing his Bordeaux patrons and mentors: "Moussa Tarawaré is a strong and robust lad. He finished his apprenticeship in a watchmaking workshop and now he is working and earning some money. You might say that he has become a very skilled worker; thanks to his desire to do well, he has learned more in less than two years [than] what his white comrades barely learn after three years of apprenticeship."

The project of turning the formerly enslaved into model citizens had taken another step forward. Could they soon become like Sierra Leoneans? Taylor reflected. His compatriots, he said, were a people who "have already proved that the Negro is capable of something." The return to Sierra Leone had imbued Taylor with a sense of optimism for both his home country and his adopted one: "Thus, we must anticipate that there will be better days for an oppressed race."

Part VII

43

Lost and Found (Ephemera)

CHEMIN DE FER DE DAKAR A SAINT-LOUIS

MARCHE DES TRAINS DE VOYAGEURS

Service au 15 novembre 1892.

PRIX DES PLACES AU DÉPART DE DAKAR (Trajets simples)				DE DAKAR A SAINT-LOUIS	TRAIN N° 1	TRAIN N° 23	PRIX DES PLACES AU DÉPART DE St-LOUIS (Trajets simples)				DE SAINT-LOUIS A DAKAR	TRAIN N° 9	TRAINS N°s 100 et 102
1re CLASSE	2e CLASSE	3e CLASSE		GARES, STATIONS, HALTES			1re CLASSE	2e CLASSE	3e CLASSE		GARES, STATIONS, HALTES		
fr. c.	fr. c.	fr. c.			matin. h. m.	soir. h. m.	fr. c.	fr. c.	fr. c.			matin. h. m.	matin. h. m.
»	»	»	»	DAKAR............départ.	6 30	3 30	»	»	»	»	SAINT-LOUIS.........départ	6 40	
1 70	1 10	» 75	14	Tia: oye................	7 06	3 56	2 15	1 45	1 »	5	Leybar.. ....halte	6 54	
3 60	2 40	1 65	22	M'Baou.............halte.	7 24	4 12	3 15	1 45	1 »	18	R'o Poundioun........ ..	7 24	
3 60	2 40	1 65	30	RUFISQUE.........{arrivée.	7 43	4 20	3 85	2 55	1 75	32	M'Pal...............	8 01	
				{départ.	7 52	4 40	5 40	3 60	2 50	45	N'Gui k-Sakal.........	8 30	
5 60	3 70	2 55	46	Sébikotane.............	8 31	5 19	8 50	5 70	3 90	71	LOUGA.........{arrivée.	9 26	
6 70	4 50	3 10	56	Pout................	8 54	5 43					{départ.	9 33	
8 50	5 70	3 90	71	THIÈS..........{arrivée.	9 28	6 16	11 »	7 30	5 »	91	Goumbo-Guéoul........	10 17	
				{départ.	9 36	6 24	13 05	8 65	5 95	106	Kébémer............	10 52	
11 25	7 45	5 10	93	TIVAOUANE........{arrivée.	10 22	7 10	14 60	9 70	6 65	121	N'DANDE.........{arrivée.	11 23	
				{départ.	10 57	soir.					{départ.	12 02	
12 70	8 40	5 80	105	Pire-Goureye............	11 31		16 35	10 75	7 30	133	Kelle. :..........	12 31	
14 60	9 70	6 65	121	N'Gaye-Mékhé........	12 08		17 25	11 55	7 85	143	N'Gaye-Mékhé......	12 54	
15 80	10 60	7 20	131	Kelle..............	12 33		19 20	12 80	8 75	159	Pire-Goureye..	1 29	
17 25	11 55	7 85	143	N'DANDE.........{arrivée.	12 59		20 60	13 80	9 40	171	TIVAOUANE.......{arrivée.	2 01	matin. h. m.
				{départ.	1 11						{départ.	2 07	»
18 80	12 60	8 60	156	Kébémer......	1 44		22 25	15 55	10 70	193	THIÈS..........{arrivée.	3 03	5 46
20 85	13 95	9 50	173	Goumbo-Guéoul........	2 20						{départ.	3 03	5 57
23 35	15 55	10 70	193	LOUGA..........{arrivée.	3 03		23 05	16 75	11 85	208	Pout...............	3 38	6 32
				{départ.	3 13		23 25	17 55	12 10	218	Sébikotane............	4 01	6 56
26 40	17 60	12 15	219	N'Guick-Sakal.......	4 10		28 20	18 80	12 95	234	RUFISQUE..... {arri-ée.	4 39	7 34
27 95	18 65	12 85	232	M'Pal...............	4 46						{départ.	4 46	7 46
29 60	19 80	13 65	246	Rao-Poundioun........	5 18		30 10	20 10	13 85	242	M'Baou..............halte.	5 06	8 06
31 65	21 15	14 55	259	Leybar..............halte.	5 47		30 10	20 10	13 85	250	Tiaroye................	5 25	8 25
31 65	21 15	14 55	263	SAINT-LOUIS.........arrivée.	6 » soir.		31 65	21 15	14 55	263	DAKAR.............arrivée.	6 » soir.	9 » matin.

Dakar–Saint Louis train schedule in 1892 as printed in the *Journal Officiel du Sénégal*

September 27, 1886

To Mr. Under Secretary of State in the Ministry of the Navy and Colonies

Our head of operations, in Senegal, has just sent us a list, a copy of which is attached, of objects found in stations and trains, asking us what to do with them.

State of the objects registered and found existing for more than six months

Lost and Found
An old birdcage
One packet spun cotton 0 K, 800 g.
A small trunk, old, containing dirty linen
A small black trunk, new, containing dirty linen
A trestle for a saddle
An empty earthenware jar with a capacity of about 100 liters
An old suitcase containing dirty laundry
An old empty suitcase
Two irons
An old black rifle
A box containing crimping irons and old-fashioned items
One case of unroasted coffee 14K . . .
An old cast iron pot and its lid
A small white wooden box containing a decameter roll, and a
    lighter for a smoker
A bag of monkey bread—10 K
A white wooden frame with broken glass

44

Why Have the Peanuts Degenerated?

Between Christmas Eve and New Year's Day, the people of Saint Louis often gathered in the streets for a joyous event weeks and months in the making. Starting at dusk, people paraded with bright lanterns, a floating procession accompanied by the beat of the tam-tam, and thus, much song and dance. These were not regular lanterns with oil wicks that could be held in one hand, but rather were handcrafted model-scale edifices made from wood and crepe paper that took several people to maneuver, representing ornate houses and cathedrals, mosques with intricate tiles, ships complete with masts and sails, and soon, a new addition, locomotives in tribute of the new railroad. In 1886, a columnist from *Le Réveil du Sénégal,* the colony's first independent newspaper, joked that it was "the trans-Saharan train intended to link Senegal to its big sister in Algeria," just like the one that Paul Soleillet had lobbied for in the years before the Dakar-Saint Louis train took shape. Each float was illuminated by scores of candles that made the structures come alive, as if at any minute a model-scale person could enter that mosque, hop on the deck of the ship, or peer out the window of the locomotive.

As the Dakar–Saint Louis railroad construction had progressed bit by bit over the years, traders of every stripe had established auxiliary posts at train stations along the route, from the representatives of the largest European commercial houses to the small brokers who bought peanuts to resell. Merchants came "to do business there and thus encourage the natives to farm more land." Soon, they would cut down

more of the primary forests and use its wood to build shelters and ki-
osks. In Thiès, where the train from Dakar had started functioning in
1884, the population had exploded, from just 260 people in 1878 to over
1,000 in 1885. Nearby Tivaouane, a market town where people from
Bawol and Southern Kajoor came to do business, had twice as many
inhabitants in 1885 as it did in 1878.

But almost as soon as the peanut train started running the full
length of its route, there were rumblings of trouble in the peanut trade.
The new newspaper Le Réveil du Sénégal soon took up an old subject.
Just over a month after the final inauguration of the railroad, the paper
published an article aptly titled "Why Senegambia's Peanuts Have
Degenerated."

By "Senegambia" the author mostly meant points south, those
waterlogged, riverine communities from the Gambia to Sierra Leone.
"People who have seen peanuts from Casamance, Gambia or Bolama
must have noticed that these seeds are blackish on the outside; inside
the shell lining is rough," the columnist wrote. "The two kernels are
dirty red, with brown and black stripes: the shell is not full. What are
the causes of this unfortunate degeneration?"

The unstated question in that 1885 article was whether Kajoor
or Bawol or the new lands in Saalum could escape the fate that had
befallen the Southern Rivers and caused peanut cultivation to be
abandoned.

The author posited some possible reasons for the degeneration, all
focusing on the practices of "les naturels": the native farmers were too
hasty and did not let the peanuts develop fully; they did not rotate
their crops or use enough fertilizer; or they did not till the land enough
for the peanuts to grow well. In another article, the same writer advo-
cated: "What will always make farming difficult in Senegal is the lack
of money and not, as it has always been said, the laziness of the inhabitants." He prescribed intervention from the commandants at each post
to the village chiefs. "It is necessary to restore the peanut's good reputation, so that it can compete effectively with its competitors."

In fact, the competition was brisk. Farmers in Pondicherry, France's
colony in southeastern India, had expanded their acreage and their

exports. In 1877, they exported just 11,400 metric tons of peanuts to France, but by 1884, they were sending 60,000 metric tons. Indian peanuts were of lower quality; they often arrived with pockets of rot or a little bit rancid, but came in such quantities and were to be had for such low prices that they were an unavoidable tidal wave at the ports of Marseille and Bordeaux. The overall price of peanuts at those French ports soon retreated from 36 francs for 100 kilograms in 1884 to just 24 francs for the same amount in 1886. The prices offered to Senegalese farmers also went down in those years; in fact, the pattern over the following twenty years shows a persistent downward trend for African farmers, even as the market fluctuated in France. In 1883, farmers could make 20 francs per 100 kilograms of peanuts, but a decade later they were making only 15 francs for the same amount, and by 1903 that price dipped to a low of 10 francs.

The train had come at exactly the right time to help the peanut trade in Kajoor and part of Bawol, but only in the areas with easiest access to the stations. Those farmers at least could still derive some small benefit, even with the low prices, since they were paying less to the camel and donkey caravans that had traditionally taken harvests from the interior to coastal markets.

Many Kajoor farmers expanded into lands adjacent to the stations. Soon after the railroad opened, farmers cleared thickets, cut down trees, and planted more fields. One observer in 1890 noted that along the railway, "in Kajoor, we find large villages spread out." At one station, Mpal, he noted the village was "surrounded by peanut fields."

In early 1886, when merchants complained that Senegalese farmers were holding back their peanuts because of the low prices, the governor asked Samba Lawbé to intervene and "use his influence to make trading easier." It seemed to work because the governor observed later that the trade had picked up a bit.

Soon, though, Samba Lawbé would fall out of favor and the French would find other ways of persuading Senegalese farmers to sell their peanuts at any price.

45

Kerbala

During the rainy season, the river near Dagana turns from muddy blue to an opaque yellow, a gift of silt gathered from the river's winding path. Louis Jaques experienced the phenomenon in August of 1885 as the river's annual flood deposited these rich waters on the plains around the city. "In the place where, two months ago, tall stems of the millet were swaying with their bunches wrapped in rags, leaves or dry grass to keep them away from birds, we now travel via pirogue and catch fish between 80 centimeters and one meter long." Even though the river water was unappealing, he still collected it to drink: "After solidifying the earthy matter with alum, I pass the water through a carbon filter of my own making and from there through an English filter, which gives me water as pure as one can get it, but still with a distinctly unpleasant taste."

Was it this river water—even before it had turned the color of dirty honey—that led to Thérèse Jaques's illness? Soon after arriving in Dagana, she came down with a case of dysentery, a kind of bloody diarrhea caused by unsanitary water or food. Thérèse recovered for a bit, only to get worse. Jean Morin, who had been called from Saint Louis to attend her, but arrived when her condition was already critical, said that dysentery rarely resulted in death among Europeans. Thérèse was just unlucky, because she died about a month after first falling ill; she had only been in the country for five months.

Her husband was devastated. His acquaintances in Dagana soon came to visit and condole with him; the Muslims always said, "It was

God's will." Although Jaques always railed against Islam as blinding people from what he saw as the true path, he couldn't help but feel comforted by this phrase. "Sometimes they are more Christian than many Christians," he wrote. Jaques's own letters sometimes included a phrase that was close in sentiment as he kept reminding himself and others: "The ways of God are not our ways."

Instead of heading back to Europe after his loss, Jaques stayed in Dagana and moved forward with his plans for Kerbala. Was it his own sense of loss that motivated him, so that her sacrifice would not be in vain?

As the rains ended, he found in his work a kind of balm for his grief: "The task that the Lord has entrusted to me here is fraught with difficulties, complications of all kinds, which cannot be contained in a letter. . . . It is true that, in the end, the Lord provides for everything, often in ways I would not have expected."

There was much to do and several structures to build: a main house for the principal missionary (him), a meeting house that could also serve as a schoolroom, a house for Samba Coumba, who would work as a translator and evangelist for the Kerbala station along with his wife, Lissa, and children, and at least two outdoor kitchens and a stable.

Jaques had requested a good mule from France or Algeria and a cart to move supplies from Dagana, but a much larger donation emerged from a charity—a Decauville rail system, a wagon that could run on mobile rails that workers could reposition as it moved forward. But in order to use the system, Jaques needed a flat and straight surface to lay the rails down. So he first had to clear a road.

"I limited myself to removing grass, rushes, bushes, thorny shrubs, over a 3 meter breadth. In a few places I had to dig trenches to flatten the slopes and remove many termite mounds." All of that effort and more would come. The wood for the house came from Bordeaux, the bricks for the foundation had to come from Saint Louis. For the bricks alone, "with the Decauville loaded with 2,746 bricks loaded in twos, it takes six days to travel there and back and requires 18 to 20 men."

From all the justifications that Jaques wrote about laborers and bricks and master carpenters who had to be brought from Saint Louis at great expense, it was obvious that he was over budget. "Rest assured," he wrote in December of 1885, "that I am doing everything in my power to accomplish everything as simply and economically as possible, and that I am putting myself to work, doing the possible and the impossible, getting up at four o'clock in the morning and, after an

The mission house in Kerbala on the occasion of Director Alfred Boegner's visit and that of a carpenter from Saint Louis, circa 1890. *Courtesy of Defap*

hour's walk and more, arriving at the train (near which the workmen camped) at six o'clock in the morning and staying with them, pushing the car from the shoulder when there is some kind of ascent, cheering them on, encouraging them, pushing them; then coming home at half past six in the evening, so exhausted that you can scarcely imagine it."

By mid-February of 1886, most of the major work was finished and Jaques could finally move into his new home. He said he was eager to turn his focus from constructing buildings to building up what he called "the spiritual work."

Now that he was finally installed as the full-time missionary of the Kerbala station, Jaques began to notice a few problems. For one, he discovered the people in and around Kerbala were more mobile than he had thought. "Indeed, the entire male population and even a few women were forced to look for work elsewhere, mainly in Saint-Louis," he wrote. Jaques thought it was because the previous year's harvest was poor, but would learn later that it was just the way things were. People always left half the year to work—some in Dagana and some further afield, only coming back in June or July as the first rains fell.

The other revelation was just as discouraging. He discovered that the area in which Kerbala was situated was in the midst of demographic upheaval. While many of the Bambara went west to Saint Louis for a season, the Fulbe of Waalo were going east, not just for a season, but for good. They were emigrating to Nioro, the main stronghold of a state founded by a Fulbe cleric from the neighboring Fuuta Tooro kingdom a generation before. In the 1880s, that cleric's son sent emissaries to recruit more followers, and many Fulbe answered the call, thousands more every year. For some, it was a considered migration to a promised land, but for others it may have been opportunity to protest against colonial rule with their feet.

Their grievances were many: taxes and fees, and changes to their customs and traditions. When the area near Dagana had come under direct administration in 1882, many of the Fulbe herders and Wolof farmers living there were subjected to a yearly livestock tax and a head tax—a per-person price for living. And then there was the question of their slaves. The new rules said that there were not supposed to be any enslaved people in directly administered territories. These regulations were rarely enforced and many resorted to a simple linguistic subterfuge of calling the enslaved by a different name. They were servants, instead. Still, many Fulbe and Wolof farmers and herders perceived the specter of full slave abolition as a threat.

The area around Dagana would start hemorrhaging herders and farmers in short order. Each year, after the rains ended, more people would sell their livestock and buy tickets on the riverboats that transported people and goods to the upper river, where they could then continue the rest of the way overland to Nioro. Presumably, most of the able-bodied enslaved were forced to accompany their masters, but the weak and infirm were left behind to deal with life and taxes in the colony on their own and as best they could. Jaques said in June 1886 he took in an injured enslaved woman who had been abandoned by her master. "He went to Nioro," wrote Jaques. The man had given as his reason for going that "his slaves were fleeing one after the other."

Those enslaved men and women most likely fled all the way to Saint Louis, as there was little protection to be found in Dagana. In 1884, when Jaques and Taylor first approached the governor about setting up a station near Dagana, the governor had been clear in his warnings about doing the work they were becoming known for in Saint Louis. "He advised us to be extremely cautious regarding these matters concerning the freed Blacks, given that the situation was quite strained," Jaques recounted in a letter to the director. "He also informed us that outside the suburbs of Saint Louis and the grounds of certain official posts, he would in no way commit to providing protection for freed slaves."

Even after all this emigration, the French administrator in Dagana in 1904 estimated that enslaved people made up half of the region's population.

Jaques reported that his evangelical efforts were slow, but they must have been moribund, moving at the pace of a wounded, aged snail.

The truth was that the missionary enterprise without the refuge for runaway slaves did not work. What use was it to evangelize in an area where slavery was still an active open secret?

46

On the Run

When the train had been completed in 1885, Samba Lawbé had found that despite his cooperation with the French and his support for the peanut trade, he was still unable to reclaim Kajoor's lost provinces. His yearning for those lost territories was about more than just ego and ambition; the damel needed land to distribute to his partisans and patronage to convey upon those who served him and who, in turn, maintained him on the throne. If he could not recover the old parts of Kajoor, he decided he would invade another kingdom.

Jolof was Samba Lawbé's chosen quarry. In late May 1886, he rode out with more than 3,000 warriors, but by early June he was retreating in panic, for the kingdom's ruler, Albury Njaay, was hard on his heels. Albury had won and said that he could, by rights, claim Kajoor as the spoils of war. Instead, Albury allowed the French to broker an agreement whose terms included a few things for themselves: cession of a larger perimeter around the rail line and each station; and a French supervisor to reside in Kajoor. They also agreed upon a heavy indemnity to be paid by Samba Lawbé to Albury without delay. The price of the damel's foolishness was fixed at a sum of 20,000 francs.

But Samba Lawbé did not have the money. What's more, it was the beginning of the summer, not an ideal time to raise such a formidable sum from his subjects since peanut trading was over and people had already spent most of the money they had made. No more would come in until at least December or January, and then only if the harvest was good.

Samba Lawbé said he refused to pay, but, according to reports, he was desperate to find the money. His honor, his freedom, and his kingdom were at stake. Young merchant Joseph du Sorbiers de la Tourrasse wrote in his memoir that he first met the damel during this time as his procession came to his outpost. "Five griots led the way, playing ckralam [xalam] and singing the praises of the damel, while two others accompanied them by beating the tam-tam. The group split at the fence and entered my house in two ranks. In the center walked the damel surrounded by his command staff. The damel was recognizable by his very tall stature, green turban, and gris-gris." He was followed by a few hundred infantrymen, armed with rifles that they had decorated with shells.

The French merchant served some refreshments and spoke with the damel at length, finally putting a few apt questions to the young leader. "How will you pay the fine of twenty thousand francs that the government has imposed on you?" he asked. "Samba Lawbé's face darkened; his features contracted. With an abrupt gesture he put his hand to his sword: 'I will provide,' he said, 'and Allah is with me!'"

Soon, it seems Samba Lawbé did find a way, with or without a higher power; he established a new policy requiring traders who were settling in booming market towns like Tivaouane to pay an "extraordinary fee" directly to his emissaries or be expelled, even though they were established, mostly, on French land. Of course, none of this sat well with the French. The newest merchant fees were a direct violation of his 1883 treaty, which specified where the damel could collect duties on Kajoor-grown products. There were rumors of violent confrontations between traders and the damel's men.

The kingdom was tense, dry kindling for a bright fire, and anything could have been the spark.

The trains ran once a day from each terminus, leaving around six in the morning just as the sun started to move over the horizon and race up into the atmosphere. Once the locomotive had warmed itself and crept out of the station, it would gather speed, building up to an impressive twenty-three or sometimes twenty-five kilometers per hour.

At this pace, it could take more than twelve hours to traverse the 264 kilometers of track that separated Saint Louis and Dakar, so passengers would spend the better part of their daylight hours sleeping or fidgeting in their seats, talking with their neighbors, or staring out the windows as the landscape changed from bogs, bulrushes, and birds to sand dunes and camel caravans to flat stretches of fields planted with peanuts.

The train had ticket prices to meet most pocketbooks; in the first and second classes were administrators, prosperous merchants, the military, and the clergy, while in third class rode most local people who might hop on for short trips to destinations one or two stations away. Such short-distance passengers soon made up the majority of people using the train.

On August 31, 1886, a family arrived at the Tivaouane train station. The documents don't say if the family arrived on that day's train, but it is possible, for they had only recently come from Saint Louis. The telegram that the civilian stationmaster wrote to the military commandant at the fort in Thiès said that they arrived at around six in the evening; it does not include any details about how many people were in the family or if there were children as well as adults. It just said: "A Kajoor family living in Tivaouane, slaves duly freed, came to take refuge at the station to avoid being taken captive again by the man named Demba Waar, the so-called Prime Minister of Samba Lawbe. I gave shelter to this family. Demba Waar himself came to claim them, along with 50 armed men. I refused to hand them over and after a few threats he left, telling us that if these freed slaves left the station he would have them seized by force. Please give me instructions."

With its 264 kilometers of French land through the heart of Kajoor, the new railway had exacerbated the old problem for French administrators: what should they do with the people who came in search of their freedom on land that was supposed to liberate all who entered? The train stations were, after all, French land by treaty. Would administrators apply the hard-won rules now in force in places like Saint Louis and allow French soil to free the people who touched it? Or would they continue the pattern established along the Senegal River at forts like Dagana, where the authorities did all they could to ignore the traffic in humans happening in front of their eyes?

Soon after the first telegram, the stationmaster sent another. He said that Samba Lawbé himself had arrived at the station and made the same demand that Demba Waar had. Never mind that the members of this family already had their freedom papers; he wanted them to be returned to their former master.

The commandant recognized the situation was tenuous and would only escalate. So he dashed off a response to the stationmaster right away: "Return the family."

It is not clear why Demba Waar, always so strategic, launched this bold attack on the station. Could there have been a more diplomatic way to proceed? This action by Demba Waar and similar offensives by members of his family were seen as provocations in the eyes of the French, and perhaps they were meant to be.

The interim governor wrote to the minister a couple weeks after the incident, saying: "Putting aside the more or less keen concern that the situation of these captives elicits, I believed that such a reckless violation of the French land and buildings was a violation of the utmost gravity, and if I manage to get my hands on the person of Demba Waar, I reserve the right to make an example of him that will remind his peers of the respect due to us."

In early October, about a month after the capture of the runaway family in Tivaouane, the governor sent one of his officers along with a contingent of cavalry to that village to speak not with Demba Waar, but with Samba Lawbé himself.

What happened after is the subject of some dispute, but most sources agree that Samba Lawbé refused to parley with the envoy and refused to leave Tivaouane. The French officer continued to insist. Then, suddenly, a shot rang out. It had come from somewhere on the damel's side, although some people at the time speculated that it may have been fired by a spy sent by the French to provoke conflict and provide cover for everything that would follow. Whatever the origin of the shot, the French forces returned fire and a fight broke out in a confusion of guns and swords, horsemen and foot soldiers.

The commanding officer relentlessly pursued Samba Lawbé in a fight, both at first mounted on their horses with guns, and then on the ground with sabres, racing along the railroad's tracks, now obscured in a haze of gun smoke. Samba Lawbé must have faltered for a moment and was shot and then stabbed or stabbed and then shot, but either way, at the end, the bloody corpse of the damel of Kajoor, Samba Lawbé Faal, was lying in the dirt.

According to de la Tourrasse, the soldiers left his body in the town square for some hours "so that everyone could recognize him. He is there, lying in the middle of a pool of blood, and, while on the horizon the sun disappears in a trail of purple, men, women and children, who had believed until then that their damel was unbeatable because of his many gris-gris, slowly approach and utter a lamentable 'bissimilay'— in the name of God." The young merchant claimed that the French collected the damel's body in the middle of the night and sewed him up in a sack of peanuts. They would bury him inside their fort in Thiès. Or so it was said.

The whole colony was in shock when they heard of it—and frightened. A Kajoor without a damel would always be at war, and would threaten the stability of territories around it. The governor hastened to Tivaouane himself, called up reinforcements, and deployed two special trains outfitted with Hotchkiss machine guns to secure and protect the railroad.

When he wrote to Paris, the governor tried to manage any appearance of impropriety. "This affair did not have the effect that was feared," he wrote less than a week after the damel's death. He claimed that "the people of Kajoor say in loud voices: The damel picked a fight with the French, and he shot at them first; he deserved his punishment." This last comment does seem doubtful since the facts of Samba Lawbé's death were contested and everyone in Senegal knew it. Did Samba Lawbé's camp really shoot first? And was the point of the military column really to just speak with Samba Lawbé or was it, as the independent newspaper *Le Réveil du Sénégal* suggested, simply an ambush and an execution? The paper's argument was persuasive; but then the governor attempted to remind people that the newspaper was backed by one Mr. Gaspard Devès, to whom, it was said, Samba Lawbé was deeply indebted. As such, Devès had much to lose with the damel's death. Could anyone really believe the news coming from a source so biased? These speculations and innuendos swirled around the colony.

Passing on the train the day after Samba Lawbé's death, the missionary Louis Jaques wrote that Kajoor was *"en pleine fermentation."* He was headed to Gorée for a much-needed break from Kerbala, its harsh climate, and his own failures; a friend, the American consul Peter Strickland, had offered him a room for a couple of weeks so that Jaques could regain his strength. They must have discussed Kajoor's political climate over dinners full of foods Jaques could not get in the bush: proper bread, plentiful fruit, fresh seafood, and wine. Strickland penned a cable to Washington, D.C., some days later, sent along with a clipping of the *Réveil* column about the damel's death. "This unfortunate affair has a commercial importance on account of its liability to affect adversely the peanut trade," he wrote. "It is now the beginning of harvest time and should war ensue, a large proportion of the year's crop would unavoidably be lost. Great efforts will doubtless be made to preserve peace and it is hoped they will prove successful."

47

Your Civilization Has Not
Dazzled Him

The writer who depends on voices from the archives is often disappointed, and that was the case here, when the collection of Walter Taylor's correspondence yielded no comments on the fate of Samba Lawbé or the other events of that October in Kajoor. That Taylor had an opinion on this unrest is probable, for how could someone who had written with so much passion about Zulu sovereignty and the British conquest thousands of miles away not have a point of view on a conquest happening in his backyard? But when Louis Jaques and Jean Morin arrived in 1883, Taylor started to take a bit of a backseat when it came to correspondence with the director and the committee in Paris. His French-language letters, always full of awkward turns of phrase that show a mind translating its thoughts from English, must have been a chore to him, and he would have been glad to leave it to the native francophones. When Taylor and his colleagues had differences of opinion, which they increasingly did, he would pen a letter about the mission's work and his own perspective. But gone were those little snapshots about the world of Saint Louis, its holidays, triumphs, and conflicts, as well as the current affairs of the colony.

So, in October of 1886, all we know is that Taylor had another cause of excitement that interested him, one that would vindicate the work he had been doing for the past decade.

Moussa Tarawaré, the freed Bambara teenager who had been sent to Bordeaux years before, was coming back. Moussa had finished his watchmaking apprenticeship and then studied with a goldsmith to refine his skills; he had been devoted in his readings of the Bible and had been baptized in Bordeaux, taking on the middle name of Nathanaël. The reports of him in Bordeaux were all glowing, enthusiastic in their estimations of his goodness, his forthright nature, and his piety.

Moussa finally arrived near the end of October. Taylor wrote to his collaborators in Bordeaux, "How he has changed! He's no longer the Moussa of 1883." Moussa returned to the Protestant school where he had once been a student and regaled the children with stories of his experiences, a shining example and "a duly Frenchified spokesperson."

The young man, now nineteen or twenty years old, took out an ad in *Le Réveil du Sénégal* announcing his services in a shop near the courts.

And he would help Taylor out with Sunday school, working as a lay evangelist, a kind of deacon, among the Bambara of Saint Louis and Bethesda.

The gambit had worked. More children would follow in his wake, attending Protestant schools in rural parts of France and returning with trades or degrees, including, eventually, Jacques Golaz Dhiajaté, the young boy whose family had been the first settlers in Bethesda. Whatever dispute the mission had with the boy's father, Jacques Golaz was welcomed back into the church with open arms and sent to France to study in the 1890s. The story behind his return is also lost in the archives, but the name is too unique to refer to anyone else.

A couple of weeks after Moussa's arrival, Taylor wrote to his collaborators about how pleased he was for the step toward progress and respectability for the freed slaves of Senegal. "Dear friends, allow me to thank you once again. You have taken good care of Moussa's education, especially from a moral perspective," he wrote. "He does not believe that he is an extraordinary individual, for having lived in France, or too high above his compatriots to associate with them or speak their language. I rejoice in this." Moussa was the culmination of Taylor's hopes and dreams for the freed slaves of Senegal. He was a model of

Taylor's ideal: educated with European texts and ideas, but still embracing the values of his forefathers, if not their religion.

"Your civilization has not dazzled him," Taylor wrote. "He did not get dizzy." Moussa was walking that fine line between assimilation and autonomy that Taylor himself tread with caution. In the long run, though, could either of them maintain their balance?

48

This Land of My Ancestors

Sometime in 1885, Lat Joor quietly crept back into Kajoor and settled in a village close to his last capital, the one from which he was chased in 1883. There was, it seems, a tacit agreement between him and his nephew, and he had promised to pass his time by cultivating his fields of millet and peanuts and studying Islam. And by all accounts that's what he did.

Still, when he heard the news about Samba Lawbé's death, Lat Joor wrote to Saint Louis right away. He reassured the governor that the killing of his nephew had not angered him. On the contrary, he said, "You can be sure that Samba Lawbé's death is sweeter to me than honey, for it was known to everyone that this man was my greatest enemy."

Lat Joor said that many of Kajoor's people had come to consult with him about what to do. Should they emigrate like the Fulbe in Waalo? Should they fight back? Should they stay and accept what was happening? "In short, your flocks of sheep have declared that they no longer have a shepherd—and yet a shepherd is required to lead that flock, and a shepherd is simply an employee. I am one who could be employed." This was probably false modesty, meant to reassure the French of his biddability, which was always of short duration.

The former damel wrote again to French officials a few days later and a few days after that. Lat Joor was about forty-four years old, a man still in his prime, and after almost four years of exile, maybe he felt it was finally the right time to make his comeback.

The editorial board of *Le Réveil du Sénégal* seemed to be pushing for Lat Joor's return, too. After all, Lat Joor was heavily in debt to the newspaper's backer, Taylor's old acquaintance Gaspard Devès. In a *Le Réveil du Sénégal* article that retraced the history of French interaction with the damels of Kajoor, the author concluded that Lat Joor "is the designated damel" for this moment, the right man to restore tranquility to this strategic kingdom.

Officials in Saint Louis and Paris, though, were already considering a new radical action. What if, they wondered, they could avoid the choice between either installing a malleable puppet damel who would not be able to rule or dealing with a strong leader whose stratagems would always, eventually, conflict with the French? What if they could eliminate this damel business altogether?

But what could they put in its place? Annexation was out of the question because it would call for too much in direct administrative costs and mean that they would have to enforce their own laws on slavery. Besides, they were afraid that annexation would provoke more emigration, as it had in Waalo and in parts of Fuuta Tooro, where groups of herders were leaving after the annual rains and not coming back.

The governor and the minister in Paris hit upon a different solution: Kajoor could be transformed from a single kingdom with a damel into a confederation of provinces with multiple chiefs. The French had meddled with the appointments and elections of customary rulers all over Senegambia for years, but this was far more extreme; they would be changing the very political structure of the country, all in the name of peace and stability.

The colonial government quickly started talks with some possible candidates, people whose influence had been so useful to the French in the past. Talks were conducted, conditions were imposed, compromises were made on both sides, and sooner than anyone could have imagined, six such chiefs swore on a Koran that they would remain loyal to France.

Lat Joor would hear of this along with the whole colony and kingdom when it was already a *fait accompli*. In fact, the governor sent a contingent of soldiers directly to Lat Joor's village with a messenger to read out the proclamation. If this sounds like solicitous deference, it wasn't. The last section of the proclamation contained a direct message for Lat Joor. It said: "Lat Joor, who, despite the treaty of August 23, 1883, is in Kajoor, will leave it immediately. The chiefs of the provinces are responsible for enforcing this treaty like the others."

The message, brought under military escort, wasn't a courtesy—it was a warning.

The decision must have stung Lat Joor all the more since the appointed chiefs who would rule over Kajoor were many of his former friends, including Ibra Fatim Saar and, of course, Demba Waar.

"Upon the reading of this proclamation (October 25) Lat Joor fell into a violent rage," the governor later wrote to officials in Paris. The former damel, however, did not lash out. Instead, he gathered his family and the few warriors he had left and traveled east during the night toward the border with Bawol, stopping in a town called Dekkélé.

A contingent of French cavalry and the forces of Demba Waar and the other chiefs followed Lat Joor's party "to prevent looting and all offensive counterattacks." He seemed to be proceeding willingly back into exile. But even as the French received information that his group had crossed the border the next day, Lat Joor, on his favorite horse Maalaw, silently doubled back toward the west, accompanied by some 250–300 of his men. They hid in the tall grasses and overgrown bushes while the cavalry started to water their horses at the wells of Dekkélé, and they started shooting.

"No one saw this move coming," the governor wrote. "When the shooting broke out at the wells of Dekkélé, the spahis [cavalrymen], who thought they had no one in front of them, were almost completely surprised."

Three horses were struck immediately and fell to the ground. The captain of the unit rallied his men, only to be attacked by gunfire coming from a different direction.

"They waged a fierce battle against us. For a quarter of an hour we shot each other so close that many of our enemies had their clothes burned by gunpowder," wrote the captain of the spahis.

Finally, he was able to maneuver about twenty cavalrymen out of the snare and push Lat Joor's men back until more soldiers arrived. Now more in control of the situation, they were able to counter the former damel's assault.

In the epic poems about Lat Joor, the griots say that Demba Waar and his allies prepared two magic bullets to shoot Lat Joor, made from "a bit of gold, a bit of silver, a bit of copper, a bit of iron, all wrapped in an unclean cloth, buried for eight days in the toilet of an unclean woman; all given to an uncircumcised person."

The griots sing that the first bullet caught Maalaw, slicing through the white spot on his forehead. It was the second magic bullet that attained its true mark; it struck Lat Joor's head and tore out his right eye. He fell, dead, along two of his sons, many followers, and his loyal steed Maalaw.

"The enemy was totally defeated," the captain reported. Victory came at a price, though. "During this short battle, the spahis had suffered huge losses: a third of the troops, both men and horses, had been put out of action."

Word soon spread that Lat Joor was dead, and many, merchants mostly, were quick to rejoice. A telegram came from the mayor of Rufisque and made its way to the governor the day after these events: "Kajoor news affirms Lat Joor killed," he wrote. "What's true? Commerce Rufisque very interested to know. Please inform me. This brilliant success secures lasting peace."

Many people of Kajoor, though, refused to believe it. After all, few had seen his body. For months, *Le Réveil du Sénégal* reported on rumors of Lat Joor sightings here and there in Kajoor, a development that frustrated the governor. "The Blacks are gullible and besides they are convinced that Lat Joor could only be killed by a canon," he wrote to the minister. "I had a note inserted in the *Moniteur* declaring that: 'the individuals who spread this noise were lying.' "

The American consul, Peter Strickland, soon sent a report of this development to Washington. It was good news for the trade and economy and yet, his letter is almost melancholy. Something, to his mind, was also lost. "The crops will be harvested us usual, and rushed to the sea coast by the iron wheels of civilization, while the patriotic deeds of brave Wallace-like heroes are being jested at and forgotten," comparing Lat Joor to the Scottish hero William Wallace, who had fought the British for independence and was killed and dismembered for his trouble. Lat Joor, Strickland noted, was also killed while "trying to defend himself from being exiled by foreigners, on the border of his own country."

Perhaps Lat Joor never expected to win the battle at Dekkélé, at least according to the oral histories that survive. Maybe he knew this would be his last stand. In the poems and songs the griots still sing, before Lat Joor and Maalaw rode off, he gathered his family and devoted members of his court together for a final declaration: "Here in Kajoor and Bawol," he said, "I have savored every pleasure and every honor; I have also tasted all of life's bitterness. Today, before the sun sets, I shall be dead, after my body has bled profusely upon this land, the land of my ancestors."

Part VIII

49

A Peanut Fable

Contrary to the epic poems, which were the exclusive domain of griots attached to great families or noble men, a story could be told by anyone, from any strata of society. In the evenings, a storyteller could gather the children with the telltale phrase: *"Léeboon!"* which roughly translates as, "There was a tale!" The children would respond, *"Leepoon,"* an alliterative complement, a nonsense word but that here means something like, "Tell it." And so it continues, a formula for telling myths, legends, and fables.

Sometimes the stories were tales with moral lessons that were easy to understand, exhortations to be honest or respectful or resourceful. Others were reverse morals: the clever hare who would win out through deceptive stratagems, the irreverent child whose perspicacity reveals the truth about the sorcerer or the forest. And many other stories were a kind of exacting mirror through which the truths of society could be perceived. This tale about how peanut agriculture came to spread within Senegal is one of the latter. It was collected in a volume of myths and legends first published in the 1980s, but must have been circulating for some years or even decades. It goes like this:

Léeboon!
Leepoon!
Amoon na fi. (Once upon a time)
Daan na am. (It happened)
Ba mu amee yeen a fekke? (Were you there when it happened?)

Yaa wax nu dégg! (You're talking and we're listening!)
A long time ago,
There was an imam who called for a palaver at the mosque
And all the villagers came. He said:
"I had a dream where I saw the Creator. He told me it wasn't
    going to rain this year."
There was a heavy silence in the audience
Another man stood up and asked for the floor.
It was granted to him and he told them:
"I was born in this village."
"Yes, yes," replied the audience.
He said to them:
"My ancestors were born in this village.
I dreamt it won't rain this year. I would like us to save our seeds."
But one farmer told them:
"I will not save my seeds. I will plant them."
That's how everyone ate their seeds, but this farmer sowed his.
The imam went to look for him and said to him:
"Did you not hear what I said? You are stubborn!"
The farmer said to him:
"I am not farming for you."
At these words the sky was filled with black clouds and it rained
    for three days.
The farmer's field was so green that through the blowing winds
    the peanuts spoke:
"Borrow, we will pay (the debts)."
The farmer stood in his field and looked at the monkeys there. He
    spoke to them:
"Kor Koumba Korkor! Will I buy one slave this year?"
The monkeys replied:
"Not just one!"
He asked them:
"Will anyone else be able to buy a slave?"
The monkeys answered him:
"We don't think so!"

The peanuts grew to maturity and the imam came to the farmer
and said:

"You, you were right."

Then the villagers elected the farmer as the new imam of the
mosque.

The authority that the imam represented, the one by which all villagers had abided in the past, was undercut by the seductive economic
wiles of the peanut. In this tale, we could substitute imam with a chief
or even a damel; the peanut had subverted the order. It had allowed
the farmer, through the promise of a good peanut harvest, to borrow
money and invest in slaves, of course, but also probably many other
things like tools, gold, cloth, and maybe even the price of a dowry for a
new wife for himself. If the tale were to continue, maybe the enslaved
people the farmer bought would eventually be able, in turn, to overthrow the authority of the farmer turned imam, and so on and so on.
The peanut, which had, in many cases, helped enslave so many, was
now giving those same people new options for their own futures.

It would be a social revolution.

50

One of the Most Delicate Questions

The griots of Kajoor, the ones who had been preserving worlds in words for hundreds of years with their stories of the damels, must have quickly added sections about Lat Joor after his death, about his heroics, his horse, and the tragic and magical circumstances of his death. Maybe some moved from village to village, singing a murder ballad about their lost damel? Perhaps they sang the whole saga, starting with Amary Ngooné Sobel, lest the people forget, sharing the stories of a succession of damels, emphasizing their cleverness, their courage, their generosity, and their nobility. But the damels of Kajoor were gone, and they would never return.

In the years after the demise of the damels, the daily lives of Kajoor's citizens did not change much in the new Kajoor Confederation. This was by design. The Confederation had, according to an official in Paris, "the same advantages as annexation, without the disadvantages." It was a kind of soft occupation; Kajoor still had its own customs, commerce, and courts, and it wasn't considered French land like Saint Louis, but there was a French official who resided in their midst, watching and directing when the occasion called for it. The new president of the Confederation was Demba Waar Sall, and the other chiefs were mostly members of his own family. They had already wielded administrative power under the damels, and they would continue to rule the country with a firm hand. It was hoped that they would provide enough social continuity to keep people quiescent and stem the worst possibility—that the people would migrate to other territories and abandon Kajoor.

Many determined peasants and nobles still left, hoping to escape the creeping control of the French. Some moved into the drylands of Jolof or into neighboring Bawol, which were both governed by traditional rulers and were still somewhat independent, if only just. Some of the semi-nomadic Fulbe, who spent part of the year in Kajoor, continued to head east to the Fulbe state on the Niger River, where they were still fighting against French aggression. Soon, Lat Joor's cousin and sometime ally Albury Njaay, the ruler of Jolof, would join them. In 1890, when he felt the web of French imperialism surrounding him, he would emigrate to that last bastion of anti-colonial hope. But the Fulbe state where he took refuge fell to French conquest in 1891. So he moved even farther into the interior, fleeing French control again and again until his death in 1901.

For those who stayed, there was eventually a head tax to pay—the per-person price for the honor of being governed. It was a small amount, at first just 1.50 francs, to be paid in cash, but most people could only obtain cash by selling something, and most people did not have much to sell except for peanuts. When the going price for peanuts was 20 or 25 francs per 100 kilograms, that wasn't so much to pay, even for a large family, but when the peanut prices started to fall, it became much more of a burden.

The head tax was one incentive for small farmers to expand their acreage, but many historians have noted that it was not the only one. The subsequent expansion of peanut agriculture in these parts of Senegal far outpaced their individual tax burdens. Another incentive could have been the allure of cash itself. Cash was useful for so many things: to invest in cows, sheep, donkeys, and goats; to save for bridal dowries; and to purchase enslaved people from the interior so that the farmer could work more land.

Reports from French officials in Kajoor started noting that a bit more land was being cleared to grow peanuts every year.

January 1895: In some regions the natives prepare new fields to increase their cultivation.

July 1897: The peanuts having been sold at a good price during the last trading season, the natives planted more peanuts this year.

May 1898: The acreage under peanut cultivation this year will be
much larger than last year.

Even though the peanut export increases weren't linear, they showed
a long-term upward trend: from 25,100 tons in 1887, the year after Lat
Joor and Samba Lawbé were killed, to 51,600 tons in 1895, and, finally,
at the dawn of the twentieth century, 140,921 tons.

By the 1880s, slavery was nearly gone in the New World, but one of
the main provisions of the 1886 French treaty with the Kajoor Confederation was that the country would be able to keep its traditions
and customs—a measure designed to protect slavery and, in some
measure, the slave trade. In the peanut-growing regions, this was
fortuitous since this expansion in acreage, of course, required more
laborers, and the demand for new enslaved people from the interior
increased proportionately.

In 1893, another treaty restricted the sale of slaves inside areas that
were under French protection like Kajoor, but left giant loopholes allowing them to import slaves from unconquered areas. At the same
time, the treaty declared that the enslaved should be considered "domestics" or "servants," a linguistic sleight of hand that was meant to
muddy the waters about their condition.

Even as slavery was disappearing on the other side of the Atlantic,
members of the commercial communities in the colonial cities along
the coast of Senegal still wanted to protect the rights of the farmers to
keep their slaves. A note in 1895 from the president of the Saint Louis
Chamber of Commerce about the "delicate question of captives" show-
cases some of their main arguments: "All farm workers in both Sudan
and Senegal are captives," he wrote. "It is the immigration of Blacks
from the interior, brought to the places of cultivation by the Juula
[traders], which maintained the production of the colony and brought
it to the point where it is today. If you suppress the supply of these
captives to the colonies, you will destroy farming everywhere and in
short order." He underscored that, in any case, most of the enslaved
were "voluntary captives" or had been brought from areas where famine and war reigned. "Under these conditions," he wrote, "it would

be inhumane to impede, under the pretext of humanitarianism, the movement of the Juula."

Neither the Chamber of Commerce president, nor its members who sent the president's memo along to Paris, were outliers. These ideas are reflected in confidential correspondence between top officials in the colonial administration and bureaucrats in the regions, in notes and directives that continued to insist upon looking the other way when it came to the traffic in enslaved people. In 1899, the director of native affairs in Saint Louis sent such a note to the administrator of Kajoor, saying: "You should already know that this question is one of the most delicate, in regions where farming and herding are done on a large scale and require a large number of workers. . . . Subjects of protectorate countries retain the right to buy slaves to raise them to be servants, who should be freed only in the event of serious and duly noted abuses. . . ."

A legal traffic in slaves from unconquered territories did become more difficult as more territory was conquered, although such distinctions were not always heeded. By a few years into the twentieth century, the traffic in people from the interior had become more rare and more risky for traders. And the colonial administration, which had now been restructured so that the central government in Dakar ruled over a 4,650,000-square-kilometer [1,800,000-square-mile] expanse of Africa from Mauritania to Cotonou, moved to establish a coherent policy on the slavery issue. In 1905, the French president signed a decree that said that no person would be allowed to "alienate" the freedom of any other person anywhere in French West Africa or the French Congo. It was a timid measure, and many people disregarded it, but it did allow those who wanted freedom and had the will to claim it to leave and find their own way in the world.

For those who did not head to a big city, access to land was their first hurdle. In some cases, the formerly enslaved could claim land by clearing a forest, borrowing a few years of fertility from hundreds of years of tree growth, to create fields, houses, and villages of their own. Land that had reliably nourished multiple species of trees, shrubs, birds, and bees for generations could fall victim to the desperate wind, the angry rains, and the relentless sun once the trees were cleared and the fields worked for some time. If these new farmers did not manage the land well, they might have to move on again, eventually.

The colonial administration had established a number of what they called "freedom villages" near French forts, first in the area between the Senegal and Niger Rivers, starting in the late 1880s, and later all over French West Africa. They were more of a political strategy than a humanitarian effort, draining fleeing slaves from areas the French military hoped to conquer. These villages were not like Bethesda, the Bambara village established by Walter Taylor, where people were able to farm and build a new life for themselves. The freedom villages were not places most people wanted to stay since land was scarce, food resources were limited, and inhabitants were often forced to work in the nearby French forts for little or no pay. Their condition was so little changed that people who took refuge in the freedom villages started to be called "captives of the whites."

At the turn of the century many other freed slaves would start to join the religious movements sweeping Senegal, led by Sufi mystics, scholars, and teachers. Many former slaves gathered on collective farms where they studied spiritual matters and worked the fields for their teachers. After a certain period of something like indenture, a man could acquire his own fields and marry. Different clerics led such groups, including Cheikh Bou Kunta in Ndiassane in the heart of Kajoor and El-Hajj Malick Sy in Tivaouane, among others. But no group was more involved than the Sufi tariqa, the Muridiyya, led by Cheikh Ahmadou Bamba. His followers took to peanut farming with such zeal that for many years they would be synonymous with that crop as they helped the peanut expand into new frontiers to the east and south.

Many other formerly enslaved people probably addressed the key problem of freedom—that of limited access to land and thus limited ability to support themselves—by melting into the population of nawetaans, those seasonal migrant sharecroppers who arrived with the rains. Sharecropping and similar types of labor schemes have been a common transitional economic system since ancient times, something that exists between slavery and full freedom over one's own labor. It was in frequent use in the post-slavery eras across the Atlantic. In Senegal, the nawetaans would offer their labor to land owners and, in return, receive food, lodging, seeds, and plots of land to work on their own time. The nature of the agreements varied from region to region and changed over time, so sometimes the nawetaans owed rent at the end of the season, or a portion of the harvest, and sometimes they were free to go after just reimbursing the owner's seeds. In this way, they could build up capital slowly so they could have more choices in life. In 1903, a French administrator in the northern town of Podor said: "All the freed slaves left for Kajoor and Bawol, attracted there by relatives who are already living in this area where millet is abundant, and where the possibility of acquiring money by cultivating peanuts exists."

51

A Child from the Dark Continent

"LATEST NEWS: Happy arrival of Mr. Taylor.—Mr. Taylor, arriving from Senegal, docked in Bordeaux on March 18. We ask that churches wishing to receive a visit from him give notice now to the Director of the Maison des Missions, 102 Boulevard Arago."

When Walter Taylor had come to France the first time in 1878, it was as an unknown man from a faraway land; he was sent to study Protestant thought and, when he was determined to be knowledgeable enough, to be ordained. By 1888, much had changed. Taylor's arrival was a big event because, in this small milieu of the Paris Evangelical Missionary Society, he was now a star, and would conduct a speaking tour across France and Switzerland. It was a fundraising campaign—not to raise money for Senegal's Shelter for Runaway Slaves as one might have assumed, but mostly for the missionary society's general fund. Certain special collections were also to be earmarked for the construction of a new church in Saint Louis.

The trip came at just the right time for Taylor. Conflicts were brewing in the mission again. Jaques had quit and returned to France in mid-1887, citing his own difficulties learning Bambara and a general feeling of discouragement and isolation in Kerbala. Jaques also had clashed with his young colleague Dr. Jean Morin, as both of them were locked into a silent war over who had precedence over whom.

Now with Jaques gone, the station at Kerbala was without a worker, and the obvious choice to replace him was Morin. But Morin's immediate family and in-laws included some of the most influential Protestants in France and Switzerland, so the question was complicated by their reluctance to send him to rusticate in the bush. They preferred that Morin develop his medical practice in the colony, even when it ran counter to the needs of the mission. When the colonial government had named Morin to a temporary medical post a few years before this, his family members on the committee had supported him, even though it had taken him away from his missionary duties in Saint Louis for months at a time—during which he did not teach at the school, evangelize among the people of Saint Louis, or give sermons on Sundays.

Soon, Taylor's own uneasy peace with Morin seemed to break down for reasons that are not clear from the documents, although there were a few signs of trouble. In 1886, while Morin went upriver with the navy's medical service, the young man he had recruited to replace him at the school killed himself in Morin's quarters—which were in the same building as the school. And in 1887, Taylor wrote that Morin wanted him to stop using the Anglican liturgy in his monthly English-language service for his Sierra Leonean compatriots, since it included prayers for the Queen, and Morin thought it was "anti-French."

Another incident, a bit more subtle, seems to have had a strong impact in late 1887. Taylor wrote that "Mr. Morin in a fit of anger once said to our proteges at Khor Bridge: 'this plot of land is owned by white people and you must respect them wherever you see them. It is true that the one who placed you and did the most for you is a Black man, but he, too, owes everything to the whites; without them he would be nothing.'"

Some months later, Morin discussed his "unfortunate words" with the director in a letter, and at first said Taylor had misunderstood. He insisted that he had said, "That our people were indebted to the Europeans for, among other things, the blessing of Taylor's presence." But Morin didn't seem to completely understand what Taylor found offensive in either version of the events. "Was I wrong to tell Taylor that in this work he was like a European, and that without the Europeans he could not have done all the good he has done for them? I was dismayed at how he took it, and repeatedly asked him to accept my explanation, and to understand that I had no intention of offending him."

Apparently, though, the damage was done. Letters sailed back and forth between Saint Louis and Paris; Morin complained of Taylor's lack of organization, of his outsized influence among the Bambara, of this and that. Taylor soon started writing that he couldn't work with Morin anymore and, in a moment of desperation, offered to transfer to Kerbala himself. This offer was not accepted. Instead, a trip to the French provincial villages of the Midi, Alsace, and the Swiss Jura Mountains beckoned to him, along with his daughter Sally Margaret (Marguerite to the French), who, as a fresh-faced thirteen-year-old, would attend school in Southern France. Marguerite went despite the worries of her mother, who was reportedly against the move and suffered anguish at the idea of sending her only daughter to a place so far from those who loved her.

Taylor himself spent eight months crisscrossing the region, drawing spirals and concentric circles in his train and carriage tracks. The only check on his constant movement was his ill health. As the *Journal des Missions Évangéliques* explained: "A long-standing ailment and a state of fatigue, which makes it difficult for Mr. Taylor to speak too much, slowed his progress more than we would have liked." They organized it so that he would visit the coldest areas in the north of France and in the mountains during the hottest months of the year. Still, Taylor complained about the cold on the road in Switzerland in July. "I'm forced to pad myself with flannel vests," he wrote to the director.

That visit to Switzerland was cold in spirit, too, since Morin's wife was from a prominent family of Swiss pastors, and Taylor was often questioned about the causes of their strife in personal interviews. The young doctor's family had so much influence within the missionary society's committee that the director pleaded with Morin to call them off: "Do you know one of the great difficulties I am struggling with? It is the attitude of a part of your family," he wrote. "The fact [is] that having to deal with a situation and solve it in a spirit of justice and fairness is much more difficult when you are constantly confronted with a very strong, very sure opinion, which however cannot be absolutely fair, precisely because it represents the way of thinking of a family, of the family of the person concerned."

To the general public, though, such rifts were likely imperceptible. In advance of Taylor's visit to one Swiss town, not far from where Georges Golaz had grown up, the local newspaper ran an item announcing his speech: "Mr. Taylor, a missionary in Senegal, will give a lecture on Wednesday in Chaux-de-Fonds. Mr. Taylor, who serves the Paris Evangelical Missionary Society, belongs to the Negro race. It will be interesting to hear a child from the dark continent talk about his brothers, the Negroes."

The paper didn't review his speech after, but included an ad selling his photo to those who wanted a souvenir: "The photograph of Mr. TAYLOR, Negro missionary, is on sale at the studio of Mr. Rebmann, photographer." The proceeds here, at least the ad said, were to go to the Senegal mission.

We don't know what Taylor spoke about in Chaux-de-Fonds or in Lausanne, Rothau, Lyon, or Nîmes, but when he spoke during the missionary society's general assembly that year in April, his speech traced many of the same lines that his ordination address had outlined a decade earlier. In the fight that he, as a man of his time and vocation, perceived between Christianity and Islam in Africa, a fight between "the cross and the crescent moon," he suggested that it could be said that Christians were disadvantaging themselves through their own racism. While in Islam, the Black men who converted could eventually aspire to be religious leaders, he suggested, Christian churches often kept Africans in a persistent state of tutelage, underscoring the ways Africans didn't measure up in terms of piety and religious practice. Taylor suggested "that one seeks in Africa a perfection that is by no means achieved in Europe."

His biggest argument was about the lack of African Christian clergymen. "While the missions postpone the establishment of the native pastorate indefinitely, Muslim priests are penetrating into the interior of Africa, finding easy access among the pagans and converting them

to Islam," he said. "Christianity," they believe, "calls the Negro to salvation, but assigns him such a low place that, discouraged, he says to
himself, 'I have no part or portion in this matter.' " He said, in so many
words, that Christians needed to empower Africans to run their own
churches.

Audiences seemed eager to hear this message and to hold up Taylor
as a model of this unrealized perfect order. And they were also likely
interested to hear about his work among the formerly enslaved in Senegal and compare his discourse with the speeches of the French Car-
dinal Charles Martial Allemand Lavigerie, the Archbishop of Algiers
and Carthage and the founder of the "White Fathers" order of priests,
who also was on a tour across Europe in 1888. With slavery almost
eradicated in the Americas—Brazil, the last holdout for slavery in the
New World, would abolish the practice later that year—Lavigerie was
trying to gather support for a new "crusade" against slavery in Africa.
His efforts to influence European public opinion on this matter helped
create the political environment necessary for the convening of the
Brussels Conference on slavery the following year.

The missionary society was well placed to take advantage of this
political moment, but their commitment to Taylor and to the refuge he
had created for runaway slaves was wavering and would teeter even
more upon closer inspection.

52

Emaciated Lands

Even as more people cleared woodlands and expanded into new peanut lands in Kajoor and beyond, the price being offered for peanuts in the oil factories of Europe was falling throughout the end of the nineteenth century, a loss merchants passed on to farmers. If in 1880 peanut farmers in Senegal could get 25 francs for 100 kilos of their precious crop, by 1895 the going price was less than half that for the same quantity.

Émile Maurel, director of the large trading house Maurel et Prom, wrote that he was worried about the tumbling prices: "If it reaches its foreseeable threshold, it is feared that Senegalese farmers will be forced to abandon the cultivation of this product, as has already happened in part of the colonies on the coast of Africa."

The members of Senegal's Conseil General, themselves mostly merchants whose prosperity depended upon peanuts, were concerned enough that by 1895 they adopted, with alacrity, a proposal to hire an agricultural engineer for a special mission. The new agronomist's dual objectives would be to investigate how Senegalese farmers could pry more peanuts out of the soil without increasing their production costs, and, also, hedging their bets, to test out new cash crops like cotton, tobacco, and rubber to replace it if that became necessary.

Maurel, who had been advocating for more agricultural training in the colony since the 1880s, finally found fertile ground for his ideas and became one of the chairs of the commission that would pick the agronomist and guide his research. In his letter of instructions to the chosen candidate—a man named Lucien Enfantin who had experience in Colombia—the old industrialist made it clear what he expected from the study: "It is a question of training men and making them understand the advantages and to put at their disposal a model of plow that is light enough, simple and inexpensive enough to be within everyone's reach," he wrote. "This is the main goal of the mission entrusted to you. If you achieve it, I believe you will have rendered our colony an invaluable service."

The initial results of Enfantin's experiments with the ox-driven plow in parts of Kajoor and Bawol in 1897 were astounding and all that the merchants could have hoped for. He found that a regular peanut-growing farmer using his *iler*, a butterfly-shaped hoe, to work the land could expect to harvest, on average, 1,400 kilograms of peanuts per hectare, but with the plow, a farmer could harvest an average of 5,000 kilograms! The new governor-general of French West Africa crowed about the success in a speech later that year and predicted brighter days ahead. "Can one foresee the surprising results likely to be achieved in the country in a few years if, by the substitution of improved modes of cultivation to the primitive means currently employed, the native could manage to triple his peanut harvest without expending more effort."

But subsequent attempts to prove the plow's revolutionary worth did not replicate Enfantin's success. In fact, other studies in the years after showed only a modest increase in yields, and the agricultural experts speculated whether the small advantage was worth the expense of feeding and sheltering oxen throughout the year.

Another agronomist objected to using the plow in Kajoor for a reason that would seem prescient some decades later: "In addition, it is to be rejected as overly facilitating the movement of the easterly wind on the soil that is being cultivated." This was especially a concern in areas where the rains were often capricious and the lightweight, sandy soils, the famous joor, were at their most fragile.

Years of research then ensued on a new obsession for a new colonial agricultural service. Would a different kind of seed, a better seed imported from across the continent or across the ocean, work?

They carried out tests with seeds from Egypt, Mozambique, and

Java in 1905 and 1906 at five different sites, including in what they called the Bambara village near the Khor Bridge, which was certainly Bethesda. But here, too, the results were discouraging as the seeds that had seemed promising the first year underperformed in the second. A merchant's experiment with peanuts expedited from the United States was also a failure as the new peanut seeds planted in Kajoor only yielded a fifth of what was normal in Virginia. The reason why it failed would be obvious today to even the most casual gardener: a seed that thrived in the long, wet summers of Virginia might struggle in Kajoor's arid climate with its scant three months of rain.

At around the same time, the peanuts in the suburbs of Saint Louis and the most northern parts of Kajoor's traditional territory had started to show some worrisome signs of faltering, in both quantity and quality. When farmers pulled their peanut plants from the ground, they found many with empty shells or with shriveled-up nuts. And, worst of all for the industries that wanted to press them for oil—their primary use—they were becoming less oily and thus less valuable. In 1898, the peanuts from this area were rejected by the main factories in Bordeaux, which refused to buy them at any price.

By the early 1900s, there was a new railroad being built; it was a companion to the Dakar–Saint Louis train through the middle of Kajoor, but this one would run east–west, from Thiès to Kayes, and would traverse through multiple kingdoms. People came from across the region to settle along its tracks and grow peanuts, including people from Kajoor. "Since the creation of the Thiès–Kayes railway, many natives of Diambour, N'Guick and Northern Kajoor have been abandoning their local cultures to exploit the newer and more fertile lands of Bawol and Gambia," wrote another scientist in 1918. "This is a distinctly unfavorable symptom, and one can legitimately be concerned about the productivity of Senegal's oldest peanut lands."

The future that had been stalking Kajoor's peanut trade since the decline of the Southern Rivers two decades before had finally started to make itself known. These "emaciated lands" of the north were so worn out it was only a matter of time before they would have to be abandoned.

53

Drink My Cup to the Dregs

In late 1890, the Paris Evangelical Missionary Society's director, Alfred Boegner, visited Senegal to assess the mission's activities for himself. He sat in on classes at the school, listened to sermons, spoke to parishioners, visited Bethesda, and trekked to the still-empty Kerbala station. A hard look at the numbers revealed part of the problem. After years of evangelization and large sums of money spent, there were few converted souls to justify all the effort. He wrote in an after-visit report: "Since the beginning of the mission, 50 adults have been received into the Church by our missionaries. The first baptism took place on December 25, 1873, the last on June 9, 1889. Of these 50 converts, the first 6 were baptized by Mr. Villéger, 4 by Mr. Golaz, 1 by Mr. J. Morin; all the others, 39, by Mr. Taylor. Of this number, 22 are still members of the Church of Saint Louis: the 28 others were lost: 13 by expulsion or discipline, 10 by death, 5 by emigration." The twenty-two baptized members stood in contrast to the more than one hundred that the mission had given refuge to between 1878 and 1886, helping them obtain their freedom either through direct payments or by offering months of shelter. "Saved and rescued physically, these unfortunate runaways heard the message of salvation, and many accepted it," he continued. "It is to Mr. Taylor that we are indebted, in large part, for the work that now exists in Saint Louis."

Director Boegner, nonetheless, esteemed that although it had been a good strategy, somewhere along the way the two goals of charity and evangelization had diverged: "The mission inevitably became a work of protection at the same time as evangelization, and protection inevitably takes precedence over evangelization."

This was added to a series of concerns about Taylor that had already been identified by a commission: the Morin conflict, a history of a lack of fiscal rigor leading to overspending, a history of "a frequent state of depression, often leaving him in a state of semi-inaction," and the lax enforcement of some norms in church; Taylor had, it was said, defied such norms when he let a pregnant woman get married in a white dress. By the end of his trip, the director had made a decision. He wrote a letter to the committee, which they summarized in their minutes. "Mr. Boegner believes," it said, "that the committee will be forced to dispense with Mr. Taylor's services."

Maybe Walter Taylor saw the writing on the wall, because in early 1891 he gave a letter of resignation to the director: "It is with sorrow that I am forced to come and offer you my resignation as a missionary of the society in Senegal," he wrote, citing his ill health. "As a result of all the activities I have been engaged in for many years, where I have been alone in the wilderness, my health has become seriously compromised; and today I have become so overwhelmed by my fatigue that my retirement is in the interest of the mission itself."

Although this was exactly what the committee wanted, it wasn't how they wanted it. So they neither accepted nor rejected his letter of resignation, but rather held it in limbo for several months. At one of the committee's meetings, Director Boegner said that he wanted "the separation of Mr. Taylor from the Society be carried out with the kind of care to which Mr. Taylor's work, his popularity in France and Senegal, and the real services he has rendered to the Society, give him substantial claims." And he *was* popular in France, having showed himself to be a fundraising powerhouse during the 1888 trip to Europe.

A couple of months later, though, an allegation came from a new missionary that would change their kindly deliberations about Taylor's future. "The most serious suspicions about Mr. Taylor's conduct have to be raised," they noted in the meeting minutes in early May. Taylor, whose wife was away in Sierra Leone, had been seen to have other women sleep in his room, an allegation later corroborated by another staff member. The board increasingly believed the claim.

Taylor was devastated by the charges and at first even refused to respond to the allegations or to insist upon an investigation. "A serious investigation would turn out well for me," he eventually wrote. "I would come out of it triumphant in every way, but in the process it would upset the church and bring the mission into disrepute. Now, the line of conduct that I propose to follow all the way to the end has already been outlined: to drink my cup to the dregs, to erase myself completely, to sacrifice myself for the good of the church of Saint Louis, leaving it up to God to clarify everything at the time marked for him: 'God is His own interpreter and He will make it plain.' "

A week later, though, he decided to offer some explanations, not to defend himself, he said, but to make sure the truth was put into the record. Taylor did not deny the basic facts of the allegation; indeed, he had openly shared the information with many people, but he disputed the lewd conclusion that could be implied by those facts.

The causes were his old maladies: the asthma, migraines, and something he called "cerebral congestion," a nebulous diagnosis common in the nineteenth century taken to mean anything from apoplexy to headaches, depression, seizures, and diseases of the brain. "During my wife's absence in August of last year, one of these attacks occurred in the middle of the night. Alone in my room I made an effort by myself and crawled on the floor to call Jeanne and Fassal for help. They entered my room, perfectly dressed, quickly prepared a foot bath for me and stayed to give me my potassium bromide potion every half hour." Bromide of potassium is a strong sedative that was, we know now, also highly toxic. Even during his time, some doctors were raising concerns about the long-term effects of using it, but Taylor's episodes sound serious enough that, even if he knew of the problems, he may have been willing to take the risk. "After each illness, I myself highly praised their devotion without suspecting in the least that those who heard me talk like this could be led to believe that they usually spent the night in my room"

Whatever the truth, the committee, which opted to dispense with a formal investigation, seemed to proceed with presumption of Taylor's guilt. They altered their plans for a gentle separation from the mission after a year-long paid vacation. Instead, they decided that the man who had carried the mission on his back for so many years would, instead, be retired immediately with a pension that was a fraction of his salary.

In mid-December of 1891, Walter Taylor and his family would board a train to Dakar and then a boat to Gambia and, eventually, a steamer bound for Freetown. In the weeks leading up to Walter Taylor's departure, he preached his last few sermons with urgency, trying to impart all the wisdom he had. "More and more, I see how much he loved his work," a colleague observed. "These last days are sad for those who are leaving as well as for those that will remain."

No records tell us if some of the men and women Taylor had shepherded over the years—the Moussa Sidibés and Tarawarés, the Samba Coumba and Lissa Coulbarys and Jacques Golaz Dhiajatés— accompanied Taylor and his family to the Saint Louis train station to see them off. But how could they not? Some of his loyal parishioners must have wanted to walk the road with Taylor as he took leave of them for the last time. They must have shaken his hand or even embraced him before he boarded the train to Dakar and then waited at the platform, waving with vigor to bid Taylor a heartfelt adieu as the train belched black smoke and crept out of the station.

Taylor would have twelve hours or maybe more to look out the window as the train trundled through the flat lands of Kajoor, past its salt pans, its sandy dunes, its harvested fields, and its rail stations crowded with sacks of peanuts piled into domes as tall as cathedrals.

Peanut towers at the port of Dakar. *Courtesy of Archives du Sénégal*

54

The Crushing Supremacy of the Peanut

At the dawn of the new century, Paris once again hosted a World's Fair, this one far bigger than any that France had hosted before; it included more space, more exhibitors, more visitors, and more dioramas of native villages in the Trocadero garden featuring living "specimens," or a human zoo of real people doing their daily tasks. It was a triumphant vision of France's expanding empire.

For the occasion, the colonial government of Senegal created a book of useful facts about how it functioned, its budget, its schools and public works projects, its commerce and agriculture. Authorities were concerned about the state of peanut farming near Saint Louis and "the degeneration of the seeds that we are currently seeing." The report suggested that there were two causes: "It can be attributed to poor seed selection as well as soil depletion." For the tired soil, the report's authors recommended manure and a better technique for working it—they meant the plow—and as for the seeds, they suggested that local farmers needed to learn to pick out the biggest and best seeds to plant. "The thought of picking his seeds has never crossed the native's mind," they wrote. "However, it is the most practical and simple way to increase the yield of his crops and to improve the quality of his harvest."

Most Senegalese peanut farmers weren't planting their worst seeds because they did not know any better. Merchants regularly extended credit to farmers, offering them the chance to buy fabrics and tools, rice and sugar, knowing that when the harvest came in, the farmers would pay them back in corresponding amounts of peanuts, plus interest, for this convenience. Some proportion of farmers would become so overextended that they would be obligated to sell all that they had, even the best-looking peanuts they had wanted to save for seed. Now, when planting season came around again, they would be forced to borrow seeds from the merchant, a loan they would have to repay with interest, too, of sometimes 50 or even 100 percent.

The peanuts they bought from the merchants were rarely the best. "The seeds delivered to him [the borrowing farmer] are not chosen from among the most beautiful," wrote one agronomist. "And very often, he is even given more or less damaged batches, which would have been barely accepted by the European factories."

And just like that, many farmers would get caught in a system of credit that wove a web of dependence around them and would not soon let them go. The economic imperatives of the market itself were leading to what another agronomist called "a reverse selection." "Here's the real cause of peanut degeneration," he wrote. "You couldn't find a better one if you tried to systematically degrade the crop."

This was all the more tragic considering that, after the foreign seed trials had come to nothing, a new group of researchers had started to suggest something radical: that, in normal times, Senegal's seeds were just fine, better than fine, in fact. They said that peanut seeds in Senegal, through the ingenuity of generations of nameless African farmers, had been shaped and molded for their particular environments.

Whereas early merchants and colonial officials had often said that the peanut grew almost spontaneously, perfect, as they said, for the laziest of growers, one botanist in the early twentieth century tried to disabuse them of that notion. "One must be profoundly ignorant," he wrote, "or have a profoundly contemptuous attitude towards the Black race, to declare, as has so often been done, that the native of West Africa is a lazy man, unfit even to work the land. After having traveled in the rainy season through the great plains of Kajoor covered, on thousands and thousands of hectares in one piece, with peanut plantations. . . . We remain full of admiration for the Blacks who accomplished these agricultural works with rudimentary means." They had, every season, selected seeds from the most productive and most robust plants, gradually creating landraces, varieties that were adapted to each micro-region.

By the 1930s, agronomists working at a new field station in Bawol identified several different landraces, including the Ngouri, which was most popular in Kajoor and neighboring Jolof and was known for producing lots of small pods with thin shells that were nonetheless filled with heavy red-skinned peanuts; the Gerte Maka, which was

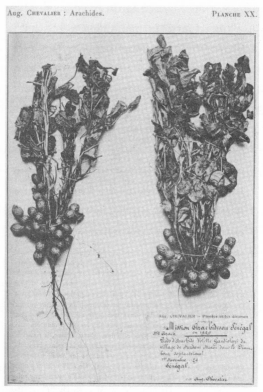

The fast-producing variety, volèté de Gandiole.
Image published in the *Revue de botanique appliquée et d'agriculture coloniale*, 1934.

like the Ngouri but had an off-white skin and was rumored to have been brought from Egypt by Muslim pilgrims; in Saalum another variety predominated, one that grew with fatter pods but whose shell was thicker and seeds smaller; and another variety thrived in the north in the suburbs of Saint Louis, the volèté de Gandiole, which was not prolific but could be harvested in a shorter amount of time than the others, only about three months compared to the four months required by most other landraces. If, by chance, a farmer missed the first rains, he could still plant the volèté de Gandiole and have a crop of peanuts to harvest. There was a peanut seed for every situation.

Had local farmers' debts and the need for vegetable oil and soap in Europe started to undo generations of painstaking choices and agricultural labor? As the demands of credit became more intense, some farmers would work lands that should have been fallowed, or forego millet on some plots in favor of peanuts, a move that deepened their reliance on merchant credit to buy millet or rice. It led people to move relentlessly, cutting down forests and woodlands to farm more new territories. Many consumed their fields from the inside out until the lightweight soils, bereft of trees and shrubs, flew up into the sky when a stiff wind blew. The poor harvests and dropping oil ratios were caused, as one geographer has put it, by "the crushing supremacy of peanuts in the minds of farmers and, consequently, in production systems."

Already in the years between the great wars of the early twentieth century, the prime peanut-growing region of Senegal started to move south to Saalum. If Kajoor was responsible for three-quarters of Senegal's peanut exports at the end of the nineteenth century, by 1920 it provided only a third of the country's total exports. Those parts of Kajoor that first gave the peanut its renown soon declined in economic importance and eventually in population, too. Siin-Saalum, with its plentiful land, became a migration destination for people from around the region. That area is still known as the Peanut Basin today, and Kajoor's former prowess with the peanut has been largely forgotten.

55

What Remained

Walter Taylor never went back to Senegal. Back in Freetown, he eventually started working as a French teacher at the Freetown prep school, The Grammar School, where he had studied as a youth. He must have missed preaching and leading a flock, but his ordination in the French Reformed Protestant Church had no analogue in Sierra Leone, so he had trouble making the case for his credentials in the sectarian religious atmosphere of the country that separated Protestants into different camps: here Anglicans, there Methodists, and over there, Baptists. At some point, he started the procedure to be ordained again so he could pastor a church, this time as a minister in the Anglican tradition like his brother Samuel, who was, by then, the pastor of a church in a hill town above Freetown.

Walter Taylor was set to be ordained in late 1897 or early 1898 when someone decided to mention a subject from his past at a public meeting, from the time before the Gambia and Senegal and a lifetime of religious service; the revelation threatened his ordination and even his job at the school. The principal reported the allegation to the school's governing committee, saying that "he felt it his duty to let them know that the French master Rev W. Taylor whose engagement in the school began in 1895 had been imprisoned in 1865 for three months, for 'petty theft,' connected with an affair of books stolen from the Fourah Bay College Library, by a student at the same time. That he knew of the circumstances only the other day, when Mr. Taylor was about to receive Episcopal ordination."

This objection about Taylor's past, raised at such a critical moment, is confounding; Taylor had spent years corresponding with some of the top Sierra Leoneans in the Anglican hierarchy, at least a few of whom had direct knowledge of the details of his case. Those people either didn't believe the charges or felt, as any good Christian might, that redemption was possible. As the memories of the newer Anglican decision makers were refreshed, though, they must have felt that ordination was out of the question. The school committee, however, operated with considerably more compassion, writing in the minutes: "The Committee were unanimous that Mr. Taylor's position in the school be not affected by the circumstance, that had occurred over 30 years ago."

The last piece of correspondence from Walter Taylor found in the Paris Evangelical Missionary Society's archive arrived in 1896. It was a note thanking Director Alfred Boegner for sending an update about the Senegal mission's activities, along with some photos. The director's letter was not found, so who knows what he wrote? Did he tell Taylor that Kerbala still did not have a full-time missionary and had never had one ever since Louis Jaques's departure in 1887? Each new missionary would visit Kerbala for a few weeks and say they had plans for it, but nothing seemed to come of these visits or these plans. Eventually, in 1900, a missionary would report that the mission house that Jaques had built in the crucible of his own grief was infested with termites from the inside out and would soon be completely uninhabitable.

For his part, Taylor reported that his own family was in good health and that his daughter Marguerite (Sally Margaret) had recently married in the Gambia.

There are, however, two letters in the archives from another Taylor a few years later. Walter's brother Reverend Samuel Taylor wrote saying that Walter's pension was overdue by several months in mid-1899, and that his brother was "laid up by illness" and beset with debts because of that late payment. Samuel said that Walter himself had written to the treasurer some months before with no response. "I humbly request that your committee will not treat him with neglect at this, his time of great need," Samuel Taylor wrote. A few weeks after that, Samuel picked up his pen again, this time to write that his brother Walter had died on September 8, 1899. He was just in his early fifties.

The society's *Journal des Missions Évangéliques* printed a glowing obituary about Walter Taylor, who, the author said, "played such an important role in the history of our mission in Senegal." We have no documentation about how Taylor's friends in Senegal felt when they heard the news, but it is easy to imagine that they felt aggrieved since they held their old pastor in such high esteem. Maybe they gathered together over a meal in Bethesda and shared stories about Taylor's life and about the many lives he had touched. Maybe some of them gossiped about the troubles Taylor had over the years or about how he had been treated after so many years of dedication. Maybe they prayed that, in spite of those troubles, their spiritual brother Taylor had found peace before he met his Creator.

The Refuge for Fugitive Slaves that Walter Taylor had founded and led would itself fold ten years later in 1909. In their annual letter that year, the Bordeaux-based organizers wrote that the 1905 banning of slavery by the colonial administration had removed the need for the "tragic and emotional side" of their work. Without the drama of helping fugitive slaves, the project had trouble finding its way. "This circumstance, together with the fact that the Paris committee was having great difficulty in balancing its budget," they noted, "prompted most of our collaborators to concentrate all their efforts in favor of the general organization."

Some years earlier, the lead missionary in Senegal had tried to reengage the waning interest of donors, writing: "If the old Bethesda, the charity among the freed slaves, need no longer take care of captives, since French law protects them better against their oppressors, it still has reason to attend to the slaves of sin, paganism, and bad heredity."

One must suppose that the donors and subscribers were not persuaded that slaves to sin and paganism were on par with people who were bodily enslaved.

The missionary was also wrong; slavery did continue to exist in Senegal for years to come as many people hesitated to take their freedom.

The transition to freedom took longer than it should have, and some people continued to live in the shadow of their servitude.

In the years after World War I, one man who had been born enslaved came home from Europe to a remote village in Saalum, not far from the Gambian border. He had been sent to war along with his brothers and cousins in lieu of his master's own sons. The man's father had been born free but was enslaved as a child, taken in a raid on his village. He had worked his whole life for this master, and he had provided much of the labor to cut down the forest when they had first come to this place so they could grow peanuts. He worked in the fields, and so did his sons. But this particular son, when he came back from fighting in the trenches of Europe for a country that was not his own, decided he would no longer be treated like a slave. "One day he got up and told his owners that he was not going to work for them anymore," his own son told me in 2015, for it's now a part of the family legend. "He said to the master, 'You're a man; I'm a man. You have two feet and I have two feet. We're the same.'"

Epilogue

The letters from the archive said the village of Kerbala was near another one called Galodjina, and about eight kilometers or a ninety-minute walk from the fort in Dagana. What the letters didn't say was in which direction. North was out, of course, because the old colonial fort with its thick earthen walls and arched windows, which was now the hotel where I was staying, was built flush with the Senegal River. On the other side of the river was a Mauritanian village whose mosque's powerful speakers startled me out of a deep sleep each morning. Otherwise, the river near Dagana was lonesome, sepulchral; the local fishermen, too poor to afford outboard motors, rowed with oars that made only a dull swish and thud. After they passed, all I could hear was the flow of the river, the water slapping the fort's walls.

The villages weren't to the west either, since that was the way we had come from Dakar, traveling on the highway past fields of rice and onions. To the east seemed unlikely, too, since it also stretched along the river, and the letters would have mentioned such a location, but there had not been a word about the river's benefits or its dangers— fresh fish or frequent floods. And anyway, just east of the fort stretched what was once a lively working quay, which then would have been full of warehouses and merchants who bought up millet, peanuts, and gum arabic and sold goods from Europe in return. Today most of the warehouses stand empty, crumbling a bit more with each rain, and seem to serve, mostly, as makeshift housing for goats and sheep; goods from abroad are still sold to locals, but are more likely to come from China than Europe.

As I sat under a tree to take a break from the midday sun, I felt that I had walked back in time. Some of the old photos that were hanging on the walls of the fort showed tableaux not unlike the one I was seeing before my eyes along the quay. At the boat landing, groups of women stood in the river with bright basins to wash their clothes, and bathe their children and themselves, just as they had in those old photos. I imagined that then, too, just as now, there were bands of children who took to the promenade and played endless cycles of stick and ball. Another group of children would have jumped in the river to play. Today, just as in the past, if they caught a snake, which they did, the more entrepreneurial among them would sell the snake's skin to the leather workers, and its flesh they would take to the medicine man.

But when we left the quay, the contemporary world intruded again. Televisions blasted Davido and Beyoncé music videos from the doors of corner stores, and motorcycle taxis zigged and zagged down narrow, sandy streets, beeping to get our attention. But we—I, a friend, and a gardener from the fort who acted as our guide—had another form of transportation that suited us better. Horse carts are still common in Dagana, acting as collective taxis with room for about three passengers, or, maybe four if they are slim. We hopped onto one; the sand was too hot to walk on anymore, the sun too strong.

Our first order of business when we arrived in Dagana was to visit an elder, one of the oldest men in town whose family, according to the stories, had always been there since before there was a town called Dagana. We found him sitting in the shade on a woven mat outside of his house, listening to kora music on the radio. We took off our sandals and sat there, too, greeting him and asking after his family. Someone would bring *attaya*—tiny glasses of strong, tooth-achingly sweet tea— to welcome us. The pleasantries and presentations always take some time, but we soon asked our questions. Had he ever heard of a village that in the nineteenth century was full of people who had been enslaved and then were liberated, a Bambara village called Kerbala or, perhaps, Galodjina?

He said that, according to his *dég-dég* [all that he has ever heard] and his *xam-xam* [knowledge], he had never heard of a village called Kerbala. Galodjina, though, sounded familiar. It was an area—not a single village but rather a group of them. And he *had* heard from his father or his father's father that there was once a Bambara village that way, and he gestured with his hand to the southwest, but the people had moved closer to the highway when it was built years ago. He remembered them because they used to make *thioup*, hand-dyed fabric with bright colors and patterns, a technique that is common in Mali. He thought they were of enslaved descent, but then again, it was not for him to say; he said that such things were not acceptable to speak out loud these days. The best detail that stood out in the old man's memory was that he had heard that there used to be a staircase near this village, one that rose from the earth but had no structure around it, a staircase to nowhere. But maybe that was a rumor?

The next day, we decided to try our luck and head south. We traveled like the people whose steps we were retracing might have in the nineteenth century, in our horse cart that clip-clopped on a dirt trail toward the horizon. Our brawny horse was so handsome that people called out for us to stop. Surely, they thought, such a hardy animal could take on more charges. But we refused; ours was a private rental.

At each conglomeration of thatched-roof houses, we stopped and asked, "Have you ever heard of Kerbala or Galodjina? Oh, I see. Where is Galodjina then?" They would gesture north, south, east, or west. No one had ever heard of Kerbala, but most thought Galodjina was this way or that. Three more villages to the right, they said, or, turn left and cross five cow enclosures, others called. When we got to each new place, another person would say, Galodjina is that way and gesture back to the way we had come.

At one village of Fulbe herders, we stopped and stepped inside. The young men had all migrated for the season with most of the cows, leaving behind only the old and the young, cows and humans. If it had been the rainy season, they would have offered us fresh milk from their cows, herder hospitality at its best; but it was February and since the rains were long gone, fresh milk was scarce. The man there told us, yes, he knew of a village where everyone spoke Pulaar like he did, but most of the people had Bambara surnames. He would show us.

He boarded our horse cart—a tight squeeze now—and guided us to another village that resembled all the others we had passed. We asked to meet the village chief and found him sitting under a kind of an open gazebo that offered shelter from the sun.

Daouda Camara was in his late eighties, with brown eyes that were turning blue. As we sat with him, on the ground, the whole village gathered around to hear his story. He said that, yes, his great-grandfather Sarri Camara was born near Segu and settled in Senegal in the nineteenth century. It was the time before they were Muslim and his great-grandfather worked with the spirits; his charms could make the wearers invisible, so that a slaver could walk right past them and not see them. Once, when Sarri was away, slavers came to raid his village and sold his family. That's why Sarri came to Senegal; he came in search of them. Had the original family been found or had Sarri started a new one? The old man did not know. But when Sarri settled here, other people with similar stories and experiences came from far and wide to buy his charms. Even in Senegal, they did not feel safe from the raiders and the slavers.

The original village, he told us, was that way, gesturing south again. He was too tired to come with us and the sun was too high in the sky for most living things to move around, so we thanked him, boarded our cart again, and headed toward the area he mentioned. It was not far, maybe a thirty-minute ride at a determined clip. When we arrived, all I saw was a mound, but then espied traces of a foundation along with some hard bricks and red clay shingles on the ground, just like the ones I had always noticed and admired on old colonial buildings in Dakar and Saint Louis. We had not been there long before a group of herders approached, alerted on that fastest of all networks—the village grapevine. They told us that there used to be a brick house nearby, but it fell long ago. They called the site *neegu toubab*, the white man's room. I asked, who was the white man? No one knew. They said that they had heard the last known occupant was a Bambara man who was a shaman; he would hide people in a secret room in the basement of the house that he protected with juju. He would save them from the slavers.

The stories had lasted, even if the house had not. The people had lasted, too. When we arrived, Daouda Camara had wanted to know why we wanted to hear these old stories. My Wolof was poor and so was his, so my friend tried to explain. She said I wanted to know more about the people who had been enslaved in Senegal, people whose histories were rarely recorded since they weren't warriors or princes or learned clerics. In a way, I wondered, by what twist of fate were my ancestors sold across the great ocean and theirs sold across the savanna?

The old man sympathized; he said a prayer for me that day, asking that Allah help me find my way. I held up my hands and listened to his prayer, touching my hands to my face and then my heart, as is customary, when he finished. –Jërëjëf, –Ajaaraama, I thanked him in the two languages he spoke, grateful for his time, for his stories, and for his memories of those who came before him. And then I continued along my way.

Acknowledgments

With gratitude:

To the many archivists and librarians in Dakar, Saint Louis, Paris, Aix-en-Provence, Marseille, Bordeaux, Lisbon, Freetown, Banjul, and Boston, who tracked down innumerable boxes of yellowing and crumbling documents for me. To the acquaintances and friends who suggested and ferreted out lost, obscure books, trekked to far-flung archival collections, and helped me with portions of the field research, including Rama Diagne, Moustapha Diop, Lafayette Gaston, Ayanna Lewis, Joshua Nicol, Paul Ouattara, Mamoudou Sy, and Carol Zall.

To my first readers, Ayesha Harruna Attah, Ciku Kimeria, Nansubuga Nagadya Isdahl, Autumn Spanne, and Ruxandra Guidi, thank you for your unflagging enthusiasm, as well as for your questions and eagle eyes that kept me honest. For boosting, support, and thoughtful reads, thank you to David Baron, Sharon Doorasamy, and Anna Badkhen.

To my agent Diane Stockwell, for years of encouragement, excitement, and suggestions that helped me give form to a shapeless thing. To Marc Favreau and the New Press team, whose tremendous patience, appreciation, and attention burnished the manuscript to a fine shine.

To the Institute of Current World Affairs, which sent me to Senegal in 2011 and let me follow my curiosity. To the Whiting Foundation and the Robert B. Silvers Foundation, whose generous support underwrote portions of my research, writing, and editing. To the Instituto Sacatar, for a room of my own on that island haven and the eternal inspiration of Bahia. And to the Ted Scripps Fellowship in Environmental Journalism, for the camaraderie and community that formed the background of some of my writing days.

To my parents, for always believing in my wildest projects and pushing me to achieve them, and to the rest of the Lewis family for their moral support. To Dara Lewis, especially, for her university library login and for the many hours she spent transcribing documents. To Gerard, for all that you are and all that you do. To the many other friends in Africa, Europe, and the Americas who spurred me on with countless discussions, occasional visits and vacations, virtual coffee dates, and real bowls of ceeb. And to all the other travelers who have accompanied me on parts of this long journey. *Sama xol sedd na.* My heart is full.

A Note on Sources

Each quotation in this book has been gathered from archival letters, contemporaneous accounts in newspapers, journals, or memoirs, and each scene has been pieced together from an assemblage of similar documents, along with photos, maps, academic histories, and works of naturalism and scientific inquiry.

This book, as a work of popular history, builds upon a substructure of generations of scholarly work on slavery in West Africa, on colonialism and imperialism, and, of course, on the peanut. I have depended on those scholars to understand the broader cultural, social, and economic context that forms the background of this narrative.

I have relied heavily on the collection of letters in the archives of the Paris Evangelical Missionary Society. Without that correspondence, I would not have been able to reconstruct the life and career of Walter Taylor and articulate so many of his struggles in his own voice. Likewise, the archives in Senegal and France were indispensable for the story of Lat Joor and Kajoor.

The following abbreviations are used in the notes for archival collections:

ANOM   Archives nationales d'outre-mer (French National Archives—Overseas Section)

ANS   Archives nationales du Sénégal (National Archives of Senegal)

Bostonian   Bostonian Society Archives

CMS   Church Missionary Society

Defap   Département évangélique français d'action apostolique (formerly the Paris Evangelical Missionary Society)

Gambia   Gambia National Archives

SLNA   Sierra Leone National Archives

Most of these primary sources were in French, and the translations from that language are largely my own.

The spellings of Wolof names and places in Senegal have long been influenced by a system of French orthography imposed on a language with its own logic and rules. These spellings, which are still the ones in predominant use today, are "Cayor" and "Lat-Dior Diop," instead of Kajoor and Lat Joor Joob. A movement that started after Senegal's independence began to codify how Wolof is written, eschewing such francophone conventions as "Di" for the "J" sound, and adding double vowels to draw out the pronunciation. I have opted to use this Wolof orthography for many names of leaders and critical places that appear in the book, although not exhaustively. In the cases where I have used it (Lat Joor, for example), for the sake of consistency and clarity, I have given myself the liberty of standardizing that spelling in most instances throughout book, even in direct quotations.

Notes

1. A Shelter for Runaway Slaves

3 **On May 27, 1879:** These details come from *Moniteur du Sénégal et Dépendances: Journal Officiel* (hereafter, *Moniteur*).

3 **But were any of these Moussa Sidibés:** The details about Moussa Sidibé and his journey, including all quotations attributed to him, are gleaned from an account published in the Senegal mission's *Rapport Annuel: Asile des esclaves fugitifs de Saint Louis (Sénégal)*, 1881–1882, (hereafter, *Asile*).

4 **France first abolished slavery:** An analysis of the first French abolition, the Haitian Revolution, and the broader context about the Age of Emancipation comes from: Robin Blackburn, *The American Crucible: Slavery, Emancipation and Human Rights* (New York: Verso, 2011), and two works by David Brion Davis: *The Problem of Slavery in the Age of Revolution, 1770–1823* (Ithaca, NY: Cornell University Press, 1975) and *The Problem of Slavery in the Age of Emancipation* (New York: Knopf, 2014).

4 **"Here all men are born":** Quoted in Blackburn, 174.

4 **This Haitian Revolution:** David Brion Davis poses many of these questions in *The Problem of Slavery in the Age of Emancipation*.

4 **France issued a second and more definitive emancipation:** Discussion about the events surrounding the 1848 emancipation come from: Anne Girollet, *Victor Schœlcher, républicain et franc-maçon* (Saint-Pierre-de-l'Isle: Éditions maçonniques de France, 2018); Seymour Drescher, "British Way, French Way: Opinion Building and Revolution in the Second French Slave Emancipation," *American Historical Review* 96, no. 3 (1991): 709–734; Lawrence Jennings, *French Reaction to British Slave Emancipation* (Baton Rouge: LSU Press, 1988); Lawrence Jennings, "French Anti-Slavery Under the Restoration: The Société de la Morale Chrétienne," *Revue française d'histoire d'outre-mer* 81, no. 3 (1994): 321.

5 **"Slavery can no longer exist on French land":** From the decree creating the abolition commission on 4 March 1848.

5 **France's holdings in Africa were limited to a handful of trading outposts:** Discussion about France's early colonial situation and ambitions emerged from a reading of John Hargreaves, *Prelude to the Partition of West Africa* (London: Macmillan, 1963); Boubacar Barry, *Senegambia and the Atlantic Slave Trade*, trans. Ayi Kwei Armah (New York: Cambridge University Press, 1998); G. Wesley Johnson, "Introduction: Reciprocal Influences Between French and Africans in the Age of Imperialism," in *Double Impact: France and Africa in the Age of Imperialism*, G. Wesley Johnson (ed.) (Westport, CT: Greenwood Press, 1985).

5 **Still, if any places in sub-Saharan Africa could be called "French land":** Discussion about Saint Louis, the administration, and the end of slavery in 1848 comes from Alain Sinou, *Comptoirs et villes coloniales du Sénégal: Saint-Louis, Gorée, et Dakar* (Paris: Karthala, 1993); Mbaye Guèye, "La fin de l'esclavage à Saint-Louis et à Gorée en 1848," *Bulletin IFAN*, série B, 28 (1966): 637; James Searing, *West African Slavery and Atlantic Commerce* (Cambridge: Cambridge University Press, 1993); Hilary Jones, *The Métis of Senegal: Urban Life and Politics in French West Africa* (Bloomington: Indiana University Press, 2013); Martin A. Klein, *Slavery and Colonial Rule in French West Africa* (Cambridge: Cambridge University Press, 1998).

6 **"the principle that French soil frees":** Article 7, *Décret d'abolition de l'esclavage dans les colonies françaises*, 27 April 1848.

7 **It would not have been more than a few days of walking:** Descriptions derived from Paul Soleillet and Gabriel Gravier, *Voyage à Ségou, 1878–1879* (Paris: Challamel aîné, 1887), 16; Benjamin Escande, *Souvenirs intimes: Extraits de son journal et de sa correspondance* (Genève, Switzerland: Jeheber, 1898), 62–65.

7 **Saint Louis is part of a riverine:** Edward J. Anthony, "Patterns of Sand Spit Development and Their Management Implications on Deltaic, Drift-Aligned Coasts: The Cases of the Senegal and Volta River Delta Spits, West Africa," *Sand and Gravel Spits*, Randazzo G., Jackson D., Cooper J. (eds.), (New York: Springer, 2015), 21–36.

8 **That was the fate of the area where the French:** Sinou, 30.

9 **The status of Saint Louis as a free city:** One of the best resources on this legal dance is François Renault, "L'abolition de l'esclavage au Sénégal: L'attitude de l'administration française (1848–1905)," *Revue française d'histoire d'outre-mer* 58, no. 210 (1971): 5–81; Bernard Moitt,

"Slavery, Flight and Redemption in Senegal, 1819–1905," *Slavery & Abolition* 14, no. 2 (1993): 70–86.

10 **Taylor was himself the son of enslaved:** Taylor's biography appears in the missionary periodical *Journal des Missions Évangeliques* (hereafter, *JME*), 1878, 247–251.

10 **"Woe unto me":** Taylor, 7 July 1879, Defap.

10 **"possess his own self":** The boilerplate language of the freedom papers said that the undersigned "pourra disposer de sa personne."

2. A Crossroads

12 **That river, unlike the Senegal River to:** Discussions about early Portuguese and British visitors to the Gambia River and the region's ecology come from Donald R. Wright, *The World and a Very Small Place in Africa: A History of Globalization in Niumi, the Gambia,* 4th ed. (Abingdon, Oxon, and New York: Routledge, an imprint of Taylor and Francis Group, 2018).

12 **They attacked the sailors:** Cited in John K. Thornton, *Africa and Africans in the Making of the Atlantic World, 1400–1800* (Cambridge: Cambridge University Press, 1998).

13 **Richard Jobson sailed up the Gambia River:** Richard Jobson, *The Golden Trade, Or, A Discovery of the River Gambra* (London: Nicholas Okes, 1623).

13 **"the houses whereof":** Ibid., 114.

13 **"We were a people, who did not deale":** Ibid., 112.

13 **By the end of the seventeenth century:** Good timelines of the entry and exit of European powers into the trans-Atlantic slave trade can be found in Paul Lovejoy, *Transformations in Slavery: A History of Slavery in Africa* (Cambridge: Cambridge University Press, 2000).

13 **The trans-Atlantic slave trade:** Using the Trans-Atlantic Slave Trade Database (https://slavevoyages.org/assessment/estimates, accessed 1 July 2021): From 1501 until 1866, an estimated 755,513 enslaved people left from Senegambian ports and offshore ports. Compare that with the 1,999,060 from the Bight of Benin or 5,694,575 from West Central Africa and St. Helena out of a total of 12,521,335 across Africa.

13 **But in 1807, Great Britain did what had been unimaginable:** Discussions of the British and American abolition of the slave trade, and the influence of early capitalist thinkers, are inspired by Eric Williams's *Capitalism & Slavery* (Chapel Hill: University of North Carolina Press, 1944), as well as David Brion Davis, *The Problem of Slavery*

in the Age of Revolution, 1770–1823 (Ithaca, NY: Cornell University Press, 1975), and Seymour Drescher, *Abolition: A History of Slavery and Anti-Slavery* (Cambridge: Cambridge University Press, 2009).
14 **"The products of a vast and fertile":** Robert M. Martin, *History of the British Colonies*, 4th vol. (London: J. Cochrane, 1834), viii.
14 **"It may add some interest to your chapter":** Ibid., 560.
14 **"pure golden coloured oil":** Ibid.

3. A Spark, a Solution, the Industrial Revolution

16 **because nineteenth-century Europe was starving:** Discussions about the run on oil in Europe come from Leo Waibel, "The Political Significance of Tropical Vegetable Fats for the Industrial Countries of Europe," *Annals of the Association of American Geographers* 33, no. 2 (1943): 118–128; Jonathan Robins, "Oil Boom: Agriculture, Chemistry, and the Rise of Global Plant Fat Industries, Ca. 1850–1920," *Journal of World History* 29, no. 3 (2018): 313–342.
16 **European slave traders had made grand fortunes:** This is the signature thesis of Eric Williams in *Capitalism & Slavery*, who notes: "The triangular trade made an enormous contribution to Britain's industrial development. The profits from this trade fertilized the entire production system of the country" (Chapel Hill: University of North Carolina Press, 1944), 105.
16 **One thing that all these machines needed:** Allan McPhee, *The Economic Revolution in British West Africa*, 2nd ed., vol. 106 (London: F. Cass, 1971), 81.
17 **The British railway system:** Ibid.
17 **British gold prospector:** Richard Jobson, *The Golden Trade, Or, A Discovery of the River Gambra* (London: Nicholas Okes, 1623), 45–46.
17 **That's because Europe:** Much of the discussion about hygiene habits and the plague in Europe comes from Katherine Ashenburg, *The Dirt on Clean: An Unsanitized History* (New York: North Point Press, 2008).
17 **And soap, which archaeologists:** Kristine L. Konkol and Seth C. Rasmussen, "An Ancient Cleanser: Soap Production and Use in Antiquity," in *Chemical Technology in Antiquity*, S. C. Rasmussen (ed.), (Washington, DC: American Chemical Society, 2015), 245–266.
17 **the bubonic plague or the Black Death:** Plague details come from Joseph P. Byrne, *Encyclopedia of the Black Death* (Santa Barbara, CA: ABC-CLIO, 2012).
17 **The theory of disease:** All details on miasmas are gleaned from Norman F. Cantor, *In the Wake of the Plague: The Black Death and the World*

It Made (New York: Simon and Schuster, 2001), 21; Marjorie A. Mac-Donald, "From Miasma to Fractals: The Epidemiology Revolution and Public Health Nursing," *Public Health Nursing (Boston, Mass.)* 21, no. 4 (2004): 380–391.

18 **"Steam-baths and bath-houses":** Ambroise Paré in *Traicté de la peste: De la petite verolle & rougeolle, avec une brève description de la lepre* (Paris: André Wechel, 1568), 51, quoted in Ashenburg, *The Dirt on Clean*, 94.

18 **Medical professionals:** See chapter 1 of Kathleen M. Brown, *Foul Bodies: Cleanliness in Early America* (New Haven, CT: Yale University Press, 2009).

18 **England's Elizabeth I:** Details about the hygiene habits of the royals is from Ashenburg, *The Dirt on Clean*, and chapter 4 of Olivia Remie Constable, "Cleanliness and Convivencia: Jewish Bathing Culture in Medieval Spain," in *Jews, Christians and Muslims in Medieval and Early Modern Times* (Boston, MA: Brill, 2014), 257–269.

18 **During the Spanish Inquisition:** See Ashenburg, *Dirt on Clean*, 111.

18 **In the mid-eighteenth century:** Ibid., ch. 5.

18 **The result was an explosion:** A.E. Musson, *Enterprise in Soap and Chemicals: Joseph Crosfield & Sons, Limited, 1815–1965* (Manchester: Manchester University Press, 1965), 63.

18 **In 1785:** Ibid., 22.

18 **Soap is made from:** Konkol and Rasmussen, "An Ancient Cleanser."

19 **In order to scale up production:** Jim Clifford, "London's Soap Industry and the Development of Global Ghost Acres in the Nineteenth Century," *Environment and History* 27, no. 3 (2021): 471–497; Martin Lynn, *Commerce and Economic Change in West Africa: The Palm Oil Trade in the Nineteenth Century* (Cambridge: Cambridge University Press, 1997); Robins, "Oil Boom."

19 **Soap industrialists had to:** Musson, 22.

19 **A scientific breakthrough:** See Charles Coulston Gillespie, "The Discovery of the Leblanc Process," *Transactions of the American Philosophical Society* 96, no. 5 (2006): 65–91.

19 **Whale fat was too expensive:** On global trade in oils: Robins, "Oil Boom"; Evridiki Sifneos, "On Entrepreneurs and Entrepreneurship of the Olive-Oil Economy in the Aegean: The Case of Lesvos Island," *The Historical Review* 1 (2005): 245–273.

19 **One of the first solutions:** Lynn, 28–30.

19 **"The first importation of palm oil":** Martin, 560.

19 **Former slave ship captains who were clever:** Lynn, 82–89.

19 **It is not surprising that slavers:** On legitimate commerce, see

George E. Brooks, *Yankee Traders, Old Coasters & African Middlemen: A History of American Legitimate Trade with West Africa in the Nineteenth Century*, vol. 11 (Brookline, MA: Boston University Press, 1970); Robin Law, *From Slave Trade to Legitimate Commerce: The Commercial Transition in Nineteenth Century West Africa* (Cambridge: Cambridge University Press, 1995); Christopher Leslie Brown, "The Origins of Legitimate Commerce," in *Commercial Agriculture, the Slave Trade and Slavery in Atlantic Africa*, Robin Law, Suzanne Schwarz, and Silke Strickrodt (eds.) (Woodbridge, Suffolk; Rochester, NY: Boydell & Brewer, 2013).

20 **Abolition campaigner Thomas Clarkson:** See Jane Webster, "Collecting for the Cabinet of Freedom: The Parliamentary History of Thomas Clarkson's Chest," *Slavery & Abolition* 38, no. 1 (2017): 135–154.

20 **"It would be much more":** Thomas Clarkson, "An Essay on the Impolicy of the African Slave Trade, in Two Parts" (J. Phillips, 1788), 24.

20 **One company that used palm oil:** See *Journal of Society Arts*, 1852–1853, advertisement in fly papers.

20 **Not all oils:** Musson, 24–28.

20 **A London soap-boiler:** Ibid., 14.

21 **French soap-makers:** Xavier Daumalin and Olivier Raveux, "Marseille (1831–1865). Une révolution industrielle entre Europe du Nord et Méditerranée," *Annales: Histoire, Sciences Sociales* 56, no. 1 (2001): 153–176; Sifneos, "On Entrepreneurs and Entrepreneurship."

21 **French industrialists:** Bernard Schnapper, *La politique et le commerce français dans le Golfe de Guinée, de 1838 à 1871* (Paris: Mouton, 1961), 125.

21 **So Marseille soap-makers:** Xavier Daumalin, "Commercial Presence, Colonial Penetration: Marseille Traders in West Africa in the Nineteenth Century," in *Slave Trade to Empire: Europe and the Colonisation of Black Africa, 1780s–1880s*, vol. 8, Olivier Grenouilleau (ed.) (New York: Routledge, 2004), 209–213.

4. From Here to There and Back Again

22 **"All the travelers who have roamed":** C.S. Sonnini, *Traité de l'arachide, ou, pistache de terre: Contenant la description, la culture et les usages de cette plante, avec des observations générales sur plusieurs sujets* (Paris: D. Colas, 1808), 35–36.

23 **"Peanut agriculture, which has been":** Ibid.

23 **"As long as we have known":** Ibid.

23 **Sonnini's contributions were:** Yves Péhaut summarizes the argument well in "L'arachide en Afrique occidentale," *Cahiers d'outre-mer,* 45, nos. 179–180 (1992): 387–406.

23 **In the early sixteenth century:** Ping-Ti Ho, "The Introduction of American Food Plants into China," *American Anthropologist* 57, no. 2 (1955): 191–201.

23 **Also in the sixteenth century:** Garcilaso Vega and H.V. Livermore, *Royal Commentaries of the Incas, and General History of Peru* (Austin: University of Texas Press, 1989), 501.

23 **In the seventeenth century, a botanist:** Cited in Judith A. Carney and Richard N. Rosomoff, *In the Shadow of Slavery: Africa's Botanical Legacy in the Atlantic World* (Berkeley: University of California Press, 2011), 142.

23 **"This plant is cultivated":** Sonnini, 35–36.

23 **In the 1930s:** Auguste Chevalier, "Monographie de l'arachide," in *Revue de botanique appliquée et d'agriculture coloniale,* 13e année, bulletin no. 146–147 (Octobre–novembre 1933): 689–789, 722.

24 **"an interpretation that would agree":** Ibid.

24 **after the slow accumulation of physical evidence:** In the mid-nineteenth century, a botanist had classified several other wild plants as belonging to the same family, *Arachis,* and they had all been sourced in Brazil. And in the 1880s, archaeologists discovered peanuts in ancient caves in coastal Peru. Discussed in R.O. Hammons, "Origin and Early History of the Peanut," pp. 1–20, in H.E. Pattee and C.T. Young (eds.), *Peanut Science and Technology* (Yoakum, TX: American Peanut Research and Education Society, 1982).

24 **And it took the twenty-first:** Details about the peanut's genome and origin are mostly taken from David J. Bertioli et al., "The Genome Sequences of *Arachis duranensis* and *Arachis ipaensis,* the Diploid Ancestors of Cultivated Peanut," *Nature Genetics* 48, no. 4 (2016): 438–446.

24 **one scientist said:** Interview with Peggy Ozias Akins, 14 January 2016.

24 **The conquerors were the vanguard:** Dominican missionaries arrived in Hispaniola in 1510. Hugh Thomas, *Rivers of Gold* (New York: Random House, 2003).

25 **Once there, whatever the conquerors could get their:** Christopher Columbus's note written on 6 November 1492, in Julius E. Olson and Edward Gaylord Bourne, eds., *The Northmen, Columbus and Cabot, 985–1503* (New York: Scribner's Sons, 1906).

25 **Quizqueia or Haiti:** Details from Leo Wiener, *Africa and the Discovery of America*, vol. 1 (Philadelphia, PA: Innes & Sons, 1920), 22.

25 **There, the Taíno people:** Cited in Hammons, 1–16.

25 **On the tropical coast:** Ibid.

26 **The peanut sowers:** Although the Portuguese may have pioneered the African trade, others soon followed, including Castilians and Andalusians, according to Alex Borucki, David Eltis, and David Wheat, *From the Galleons to the Highlands: Slave Trade Routes in the Spanish Americas* (Albuquerque: University of New Mexico Press, 2020), 27; Stanley B. Alpern, "The European Introduction of Crops into West Africa in Precolonial Times," *History in Africa* 19 (1992): 13–43, 26.

26 **In the early fifteenth century:** See Toby Green, *The Rise of the Trans-Atlantic Slave Trade in Western Africa, 1300–1589*, vol. 118 (Cambridge; New York: Cambridge University Press, 2012), 84–86.

26 **When one of Henry the Navigator's captains:** Robert Kerr, *A General History and Collection of Voyages and Travels. Volume II* (New York: Nova Science Publishers, 2020), 165; on the Nile, see John W. Blake, *Europeans in West Africa, 1540–1560: Documents to Illustrate the Nature and Scope of Portuguese Enterprise in West Africa, the Abortive Attempt of Castilians to Create an Empire There, and the Early English Voyages to Barbary and Guinea* (Farnham, UK: Taylor and Francis, 2017), 73–75.

27 **Soon after that:** Philip D. Curtin, *Economic Change in Precolonial Africa: Senegambia in the Era of the Slave Trade* (Madison: University of Wisconsin Press, 1975), 61.

27 **They would bring:** Green, *The Rise of the Trans-Atlantic Slave Trade in Western Africa*, 84–86.

27 **pilgrimage to Mecca:** Michael A. Gomez, *African Dominion: A New History of Empire in Early and Medieval West Africa* (Princeton, NJ: Princeton University Press, 2020), 106.

27 **On at least two occasions:** Blake, *Europeans in West Africa*, 33; D.T. Niane, "Recherches sur l'empire du Mali au moyen age," *Presence africaine* (Paris, 1975), 81.

27 **Maybe it was all they were permitted:** See George E. Brooks, *Eurafricans in Western Africa: Commerce, Social Status, Gender, and Religious Observance from the Sixteenth to the Eighteenth Century* (Athens: Ohio University Press, 2003), 108–121; Bruce L. Mouser, "Accommodation and Assimilation in the Landlord-Stranger Relationship," in *West African Culture Dynamics: Archaeological and Historical Perspectives*, B.K. Swartz and Raymond E. Dumett (eds.) (Berlin: De Gruyter, 1980).

27 **The people along the Senegambian coast:** Péhaut, "L'arachide en Afrique occidentale."

28 **In coastal Guinea:** Stanley J. Kays, *Cultivated Vegetables of the World: A Multilingual Onomasticon* (Wageningen, Netherlands: Wageningen Academic Publishers, 2011), 173–174.

28 **When French explorer:** René Caillié, *Travels Through Central Africa to Timbuctoo and Across the Great Desert to Morocco, 1824–1828* (London: Henry Colburg & Richard Bentley, 1830).

28 **"Several Foulah [Fulbe] shepherds":** Ibid., vol. 1, 177.

28 **Some ethnobotanists:** H. Jacques-Félix, "Contribution de René Caillié à l'ethnobotanique africaine au cours de ses voyages en Mauritanie et à Tombouctou (1819–1828)," *Journal d'agriculture tropicale*, 10, nos. 8, 10, 12 (1963): 464–466, 513.

29 **"I felt that I possessed energy enough":** Caillié, vol. 1, 143.

29 **On the list of species grown in:** René Tourte, *Histoire de la recherche agricole en Afrique tropicale francophone* (Rome: FAO, 2005), vol. 3, 169–178.

29 **He went disguised as a Moor:** Caillié, vol. 1, 146–152.

5. A Peanut Ruse

30 **One of the first regions:** George E. Brooks, "Peanuts and Colonialism: Consequences of the Commercialization of Peanuts in West Africa, 1830–70," *Journal of African History* 16, no. 1 (1975): 29–30.

30 **From the point of view:** John D. Hargreaves, *Prelude to the Partition of West Africa.* (London: Macmillan, 1963), 93–94, 138.

31 **The Rio Pongo:** Alfred H. Barrow, *Fifty Years in Western Africa: Being a Record of the Work of the West Indian Church on the Banks of the Rio Pongo* (London: Society for Promoting Christian Knowledge, 1900), 14–17.

31 **Although the British government:** Siân Rees, *Sweet Water and Bitter: The Ships That Stopped the Slave Trade* (Hanover: University of New Hampshire Press, 2011), 50–63.

31 **Stiles Edward Lightbourn:** Bruce L. Mouser, "Lightbourn Family of Farenya, Rio Pongo," *Mande Studies* 13 (2011): 24–26.

31 **Stiles, "an accomplished":** George E. Brooks, *American Legitimate Trade with West Africa, 1789–1914*, Boston University, 1962 (PhD dissertation), 116.

31 **where he married:** Mouser, "Lightbourn Family," 27–28.

31 **When, in 1822, a British patrol ship:** *Eighteenth Report of the Directors of the African Institution*, 1824, 161–164.

32 **By the end of that year:** Bruce Mouser, *Trade and Politics in the Nunez and Pongo Rivers, 1790–1865* (ProQuest Dissertations Publishing, 1971), 156.

32 **they thought that merchants:** Mouser, "Lightbourn Family," 50–52.

32 **And if the British ever suspected:** Bruce L. Mouser, "Accommodation and Assimilation in the Landlord-Stranger Relationship," in *West African Culture Dynamics: Archaeological and Historical Perspectives*, B.K. Swartz and Raymond E. Dumett (eds.) (Berlin: De Gruyter, 1980), 505.

32 **Since these European traders usually:** George E. Brooks, *Eurafricans in Western Africa: Commerce, Social Status, Gender, and Religious Observance from the Sixteenth to the Eighteenth Century* (Athens: Ohio University Press, 2003), 124–129.

32 **One of the biggest perpetuators:** Mouser, "Lightbourn Family," 50–52.

32 **Her name was either:** Ibid., 25–29.

32 *Nyara* **was an honorific:** Brooks, *Eurafricans in Western Africa*, 124–129.

33 **Nyara Bely's:** Mouser, "Lightbourn Family," 56.

33 **In the words of one foreigner:** "Sierra Leone. Baptism of the Lady Chief Mrs. Lightburn," *Mission Field*, Dec. 2, 1878, 583–585.

33 **Some of the most interesting sources:** See Barrow, *Fifty Years*; Henry Caswall, *The Martyr of the Pongas: Being a Memoir of the Rev. Hamble James Leacock, Leader of the West Indian Mission to Western Africa* (London: Rivingtons, 1857).

33 **"She appeared to be about 50 years":** Barrow, *Fifty Years*, 59.

33 **She had studied in England:** Mouser, "Lightbourn Family," 67.

33 **The price of coffee fell:** Ibid., 64–65.

33 **When a French naval captain:** Comte Louis-Edouard Bouët-Willaumez, *Commerce et traite des noirs aux côtes occidentales d'Afrique: 1er Janvier 1848* (Paris: Impr. Nationale, 1848), 76.

6. The Legend of Ndakaaru

34 **The people of Ndakaaru:** The villages on the Cap Vert peninsula and their reputation are discussed in Roger Pasquier, *Le Sénégal au milieu du XIXe siècle: La crise économique et sociale* (thèse de doctorat d'état, Paris IV, 1987), tome 1, 47.

34 **"Keep your slaves":** Attributed to Rousseau, a merchant from Rouen in Jean Adam, *Les plantes oléiferes de l'Afrique occidentale française. I. L'arachide, culture, produits, commerce, amélioration de la production* (Paris:

Challamel, 1908), 16. See also Roger Pasquier, "Rouen, Le Havre et la côte occidentale d'Afrique au milieu du XIXe siècle," *Annales de Normandie* 49, no. 2 (1999): 171–174.

7. The Caravan

36 **The caravan master:** Most details about the caravan journey come from David Boilat, *Esquisses sénégalaises: Physionomie du pays, peuplades, commerce, religions, passé et avenir, récits et légendes* (Paris: P. Bertrand, 1853), 166–170.

36 **Caravans led by Moors from Trarza:** See Bethwell A. Ogot (ed.), *General History of Africa: Vol. 5, Africa from the Sixteenth to the Eighteenth Century* (London: Heinemann, 1992), 321.

37 **The caravan master in this case:** Boilat, 166–170.

37 **may have been full of desirable:** James L.A. Webb Jr., *Desert Frontier: Ecological and Economic Change Along the Western Sahel, 1600–1850* (Madison: University of Wisconsin Press, 1995), 60–61.

37 **Any aristocrats or important leaders:** Isabelle Leymarie-Ortiz, "The Griots of Senegal and Change," *Africa (Roma)* 34, no. 3 (1979): 183–197; Bassirou Dieng, *L'épopée du Kajoor: Poétique et réception*, 2 tomes (thèse de doctorat d'Etat des Lettres, Université de la Sorbonne Nouvelle, Paris III, Paris, 1987), vol. 2, 639–641.

38 **In the village of Karsala:** Boilat, 169. On the role of the baadoolo, see Abdoulaye Bara Diop, *La sociéte Wolof* (Paris: Karthala, 1981), 115–116.

38 **That French merchant:** In 1841, Rousseau exported 70 tons of peanuts. In 1843, he sent 266. And by 1850, he sent an entire ship, according to Roger Pasquier, "Rouen, Le Havre et la côte occidentale d'Afrique au milieu du XIXe siècle," *Annales de Normandie* 49, no. 2 (1999), 171.

38 **And most of Senegal's peanut exports:** James Searing, *West African Slavery and Atlantic Commerce* (Cambridge: Cambridge University Press, 1993), 187; Michael D. Marcson, *European-African Interaction in the Precolonial Period: St. Louis, Senegal, 1758–1854* (ProQuest Dissertations Publishing, 1976), 256.

8. Those of the Sand

39 **what the Wolof call *joor*:** Yves Péhaut, *Les oléagineux dans les pays d'Afrique occidentale associés au marché commun: La production, le commerce et la transformation des produits* (Paris: H. Champion, 1976), two volumes, vol. 1, 33–34.

39 **so winds:** Sylvain M.X. Golbéry and William Mudford, *Travels in*

Africa, Performed by Silvester Meinrad Xavier Golberry, in the Western Parts of That Vast Continent: Containing Various Important Discoveries with a Particular Account Of . . . the Internal Government, Both Civil and Military, of the Various Kingdoms and Nations; Together with an Account of the Discovery of Extensive Gold Mines (London: Jones and Bumford, 1808). On p. 204, Golbéry talks about seeing this phenomenon on the banks of the Senegal River, but sand spouts are frequent across Senegal and are known in Wolof as *ngelaw djinné*, or the spirit's wind.

39 **The joor of Kajoor:** Auguste Chevalier, "Monographie de l'arachide," *Revue de botanique appliquée et d'agriculture coloniale* 16, no. 181 (1936): 673–837, 736. He says joor soil is the "ideal terrain for peanut agriculture."

39 **Roots will grow as slender:** Inspired by Darold Ketring et al., "Growth Physiology," in *Peanut Science and Technology*, H.E. Pattee and C.T. Young (eds.) (Yoakum, TX: American Peanut Research and Education Society, 1982).

40 **Geocarpy is practiced by only:** Leendert Pijl, *Principles of Dispersal in Higher Plants* (Berlin; New York: Springer-Verlag, 1972).

40 **"The peanut grows almost":** Cited in Péhaut, *Les oléagineux*, vol. 1, 321.

40 **By the time that:** Ibid., 259–279.

40 **The people of Kajoor were used to responding:** James Searing, *West African Slavery and Atlantic Commerce* (Cambridge: Cambridge University Press, 1993), 80–88; Lucie Colvin, *Kajor and Its Diplomatic Relations with Saint-Louis du Senegal, 1763–1861* (ProQuest Dissertations Publishing, 1972), 257–258.

9. A Middleman

42 **This was the story for Walter Taylor's:** *JME*, 1878, 247–251.

42 **The ship was brought:** On the Royal Navy's anti-slavery squadron, see Siân Rees, *Sweet Water and Bitter: The Ships That Stopped the Slave Trade* (Hanover: University of New Hampshire Press, 2011).

42 **Their true last name:** See Christopher Fyfe, *A History of Sierra Leone* (London: Oxford University Press, 1962), 170; and on donors see Suzanne Schwarz, "Reconstructing the Life Histories of Liberated Africans: Sierra Leone in the Early Nineteenth Century," *History in Africa* 39 (2012): 175–207.

43 **the biggest attraction:** Paul E. Lovejoy and Suzanne Schwarz, *Slavery, Abolition and the Transition to Colonialism in Sierra Leone* (Trenton, NJ: Africa World Press, 2014), 14.

43 **Nearly 100,000 enslaved people:** Richard Peter Anderson, *Abolition in Sierra Leone: Re-Building Lives and Identities in Nineteenth-Century West Africa* (Cambridge: Cambridge University Press, 2020), 2.

43 **These newly freed people:** Fyfe, *History of Sierra Leone*, 114–116.

43 **Adolescent and adult:** On apprenticeships and other opportunities available to those liberated, see Anderson, *Abolition in Sierra Leone*, 96–105; on other established communities, see John Peterson, *Province of Freedom: A History of Sierra Leone, 1787–1870* (Evanston, IL: Northwestern University Press, 1969), 17–44.

44 **According to the regulations:** Daniel Augustine Vonque Stephen, *A History of the Settlement of Liberated Africans in the Colony of Sierra Leone During the First Half of the 19th Century* (MA thesis, Durham University, 1962), 81.

44 **Each liberated person also:** Ibid., 77.

44 **"amphitheatre of mountains":** Descriptions of Hastings from George Thompson, *The Palm Land; Or, West Africa, Illustrated. Being a History of Missionary Labors and Travels, with Descriptions of Men and Things in Western Africa. Also, a Synopsis of All the Missionary Work on that Continent* (Cincinnati, OH: Moore, Wilstach, Keys & Company, Printers, 1859), 360–361.

44 **rocky earth:** C.J. Birchall, P. Bleeker, and C. Cusani-Visconti, *Land in Sierra Leone: A Reconnaissance Survey and Evaluation for Agriculture* (Freetown: PNUD/FAO, 1979), 100–101.

44 **They were known as Aku:** Fyfe, *History of Sierra Leone*, 170.

44 **For more than a century:** Paul Lovejoy, *Transformations in Slavery: A History of Slavery in Africa* (Cambridge: Cambridge University Press, 2000), 79, 96.

44 **The fall of the empire:** Ibid., 142.

45 **Aku people predominated:** Gibril R. Cole, *The Krio of West Africa: Islam, Culture, Creolization, and Colonialism in the Nineteenth Century* (Ohio University Press, Athens, Ohio, 2013), 93; Anderson, *Abolition in Sierra Leone*, 115–117.

45 **But some maintained:** Cole, *The Krio*, 179: "Hastings had the reputation of being the center of Egugu activities during the early nineteenth century in spite of the sustained intolerance of the European clergy."

45 **In the years just before:** Peterson, *Province of Freedom*, 251–265.

45 **The drums usually started:** Descriptions of the Egungun masquerades are compiled from Henry John Drewal, "The Arts of Egungun among Yoruba Peoples," *African Arts* 11, no. 3 (1978): 18–98; Mary

Ann Fitzgerald, Henry J. Drewal, and Moyo Okediji, "Transformation through Cloth: An Egungun Costume of the Yoruba," *African Arts* 28, no. 2 (1995): 55–57; and Anderson, *Abolition in Sierra Leone*, 220–222.

46 **"was an inhabitant":** Crowther, cited in Cole, *The Krio*, 179.
46 **But the missionaries:** Fyfe, *History of Sierra Leone*, 234; *The Church Missionary Gleaner*, 1881, 104.
46 **"He began to castigate":** Peterson, *Province*, 266.
46 **A Church Missionary Society:** Kehinde Olumuyiwa Olabimtan, *Samuel Johnson of Yoruba Land, 1846–1901: Religio-Cultural Identity in a Changing Environment and the Making of a Mission Agent* (PhD dissertation, University of KwaZulu-Natal, Pietermaritzburg, 2009), 48.
46 **What he doesn't say:** Ibid., 43–51; Anderson, *Abolition in Sierra Leone*, ch. 6.
46 **Walter Taylor said:** *JME*, 1878, 247–251.
47 **The missionaries were resilient:** Cole, *The Krio*, 73.
47 **Top students:** A.E. Toboku-Metzger, "Historical Sketch of the Sierra Leone Grammar School. 1845–1935. Delivered in the school hall on 29th March, 1935, on the occasion of the 90th Anniversary of the School" (Freetown: The Grammar School, 1935), 9.
47 **Hastings village schoolmaster:** A.B.C. Sibthorpe, *The History of Sierra Leone* (3rd ed., London, 1906; 4th ed., Frank Cass, 1970), 171.
47 **The Grammar School:** Robert W. July, *The Origins of Modern African Thought: Its Development in West Africa During the Nineteenth and Twentieth Centuries* (New York: F.A. Praeger, 1968), 130–154.
48 **"I left the institution":** *JME*, 1878, 247–251.
48 **Like so many of his social class:** Sibthorpe, *History*, 167; Jesse Page, *The Black Bishop: Samuel Adjai Crowther* (London: Simpkin, Marshall, Hamilton, Kent & Company, 1910), 33–67.
48 **He was arrested:** All the details of the book-theft ring and the trial are from: Police Office Proceedings, 13 May 1865 to 11 October 1865, SLNA, Hamilton, 19 October 1865, and Special Conference held at Fourah Bay, September 1865, CMS CA 1 O109.
49 **In 1866 or 1867:** I never found any records about when Walter Taylor arrived in Bathurst, but in 1868 he's listed as giving a contribution to the Sierra Leone Auxiliary Church Missionary Association in the Gambia.
49 **Bathurst was a new city:** Richard F. Burton, Sir, and Verney L. Cameron, *To the Gold Coast for Gold: A Personal Narrative* (London: Chatto and Windus, 1883), chapter 10; Florence Mahoney, *Stories of Senegambia* (Banjul: Govt. Printer, 1986), 43–44; James A.B. Horton, *Physical*

and *Medical Climate and Meteorology of the West Coast of Africa: With Valuable Hints to Europeans for the Preservation of Health in the Tropics* (London: Churchill,, 1867), 76–77, 234–239; on the lack of habitation: "The low, sandy island had no regular inhabitants," writes Donald R. Wright in *The World and a Very Small Place in Africa: A History of Globalization in Niumi, the Gambia*, 4th ed. (Abingdon, Oxon, and New York: Routledge, an imprint of Taylor and Francis Group, 2018), 125.

49 **Walter Taylor said he came to Bathurst:** *JME*, 1878, 247–251.

50 **The colonial government:** James Africanus Beale Horton, *West African Countries and Peoples, British and Native: And a Vindication of the African Race* (London: W.J. Johnson, 1868), 61–62; Martha Frederiks, "The Krio in the Gambia and the Concept of Inculturation," *Exchange (Leiden, Netherlands)* 31, no. 3 (2002): 219–229.

50 **"The European merchant":** D'Arcy, 9 November 1866. Gambia CSO 1/30.

10. The People Who Came from the Sea

53 **a sickness emerged:** The cholera pandemic of the 1860s started in India and spread to all corners of the globe. See Myron Echenberg, *Africa in the Time of Cholera: A History of Pandemics from 1817 to the Present*, vol. 114 (Leiden: Cambridge University Press, 2011), 45–48; Kalala J. Ngalamulume, *City Growth, Health Problems, and Colonial Government Response: Saint-Louis (Senegal), from Mid-Nineteenth Century to the First World War* (ProQuest Dissertations Publishing, 1996); Adama Aly Pam, *Fièvre jaune et choléra au Sénégal: Histoire des idées, pratiques médicales et politiques officielles entre 1816 et 1960* (thèse de troisième cycle, Université Cheikh Anta Diop de Dakar, December 2005).

53 **"Bathurst for the last month":** Patey to Kennedy, 5 June 1869, Gambia CS0 1/16.

53 **"The cadavers remained":** Quoted in Pam, *Fièvre jaune*, 32.

54 **That governor:** Governor Emile Pinet-Laprade died of cholera in August 1869. Echenberg, *Cholera*, 46.

54 **This was cholera:** Descriptions of cholera symptoms culled from Tim Radford, "Life in Time of Cholera," *The Guardian*, 3 August 2000; Echenberg, *Cholera*, 6–10.

54 **The 1868–69 epidemic:** Numbers from Echenberg, *Cholera*, 43–44.

54 **"The prospects of the River Gambia":** Patey to Earl Granville, 5 June 1869, Gambia Archives CSO 1/16.

54 **a yellow fever outbreak:** Pam, *Fièvre jaune*, 24. He notes that out of 178 infected on Gorée, 83 died.

54 **locust swarms:** *Moniteur*, 7 February, 1865.

54 **"at um xiif":** Quoted in Mamadou Diouf, *Le Kajoor au XIXe siècle: Pouvoir ceddo et conquête coloniale* (Paris: Karthala, 2014), 235.

55 **But a series of disputes:** Boubacar Barry, *Senegambia and the Atlantic Slave Trade*, trans. Ayi Kwei Armah (New York: Cambridge University Press, 1998), 138–142, 182.

55 **But most of all:** On the strategic location of Kajoor, see Diouf, *Kajoor*, 197–207; Julian W. Witherell, *The Response of the Peoples of Cayor to French Penetration, 1850–1900* (ProQuest Dissertations Publishing, 1964), 42–51.

55 **The French governor at the time:** Henri Wallon, "Notice historique sur la vie et les travaux du général Louis-Léon-César Faidherbe, grand chancelier de la légion d'honneur, membre libre de l'Académie des Inscriptions et Belles-Lettres," *Comptes rendus des séances de l'Académie des Inscriptions et Belles-Lettres, 36ᵉ année*, no. 6 (1892): 444–480; L.C. Barrows, *General Faidherbe, Maurel and Prom Company and French Expansion in Senegal* (ProQuest Dissertations Publishing, 1974).

56 **"isolate and surround Kajoor":** Cited in Lucie Colvin, *Kajor and Its Diplomatic Relations with Saint-Louis du Senegal, 1763–1861* (ProQuest Dissertations Publishing, 1972), 344.

56 **In early 1861:** Diouf, *Kajoor*, 217–223.

56 **It was a ruse:** Diouf, *Kajoor*, 213; Colvin, *Kajor and Its Diplomatic Relations*, 356.

56 **The damel title:** Mbaye Guèye, *Les transformations des sociétés wolof et sereer de l'ère de la conquête à la mise en place de l'administration coloniale: 1854–1920* (Dakar: UCAD, FLSH. Diss. thèse d'Etat, 1990), 69.

56 **In this way, the reigning Geej:** The Geej lineage was founded and came to power with Latsukaabe Ngooné Jééy Faal in 1697.

56 **"the weapons that had given him":** Guèye, *Transformations*, 96.

56 **With the election of the new damel:** Diouf, *Kajoor*, 213.

57 **The griots who sing:** Bassirou Dieng, *L'épopée du Kajoor: Poétique et réception*, 2 tomes (thèse de doctorat d'Etat des Lettres, Université de la Sorbonne Nouvelle, Paris III, Paris, 1987), tome 1, 443–446.

57 **Majojo:** For a clear outline of events, see Vincent Monteil, "Lat Dior, Damel du Kayor (1842–1886) et l'islamisation des Wolofs," *Archives de sociologie des religions* 8, no. 16 (1963): 77–104.

57 **spindly arms:** Dieng, *L'épopée*, 460. In the epic story, the Buur Siin insults Lat Joor as "this being with such thin forearms."

57 **Lat Joor was short in stature:** Assane M. Samb, *Cadior Demb: Essai sur l'histoire du Cayor* (Dakar: Nouvelles Editions Africaines, 1981), 46; Dieng, *L'épopée*, vol. 1, 579.

57 **He saw what the French:** This is suggested as part of the unrest in Diander, according to Guèye, *Transformations*, 244–262.

57 **Lat Joor had been damel:** Diouf, *Kajoor*, 227–230; Louis L.C. Faidherbe, *Le Sénégal: La France dans l'Afrique occidentale* (Paris: Hachette et cie, 1889), 268–275.

57 **In Faidherbe's own account:** Faidherbe, *Le Sénégal*, 269.

57 **The French invaded Kajoor:** Diouf, *Kajoor*, 228–235; Guèye, *Transformations*, 244–262.

58 **Lat Joor continued to wage:** Guèye, *Transformations*, 260.

58 **It took the French several more months:** Diouf, *Kajoor*, 228–235.

58 **But once the French had disrupted:** Diouf, *Kajoor*, 235–238; Guèye, *Transformations*, 244–262.

58 **An official wrote in the late 1860s:** Quoted in Diouf, *Kajoor*, 235.

11. The African Business

59 **traders and their agents:** Inspired by the notebook of deceased Gorée trader Nicolas Aubert, assessed by the local notary in 1871, ANS 4Z1 78.

59 **a merchant:** Taylor biography, *JME*, 1878, 247–251.

59 **At the free port:** George E. Brooks, *Yankee Traders, Old Coasters & African Middlemen: A History of American Legitimate Trade with West Africa in the Nineteenth Century*, vol. 11 (Brookline, MA: Boston University Press, 1970), 216.

59 **As the peanut trade expanded:** Alain Sinou, *Comptoirs et villes coloniales du Sénégal: Saint-Louis, Gorée, et Dakar* (Paris: Karthala, 1993), 82. A good synopsis of the search for new objects of trade can be found in Martin Klein, "Slaves, Gum, and Peanuts: Adaptation to the End of the Slave Trade in Senegal, 1817–48," *The William and Mary Quarterly*, Third Series, 66, no. 4 (2009): 895–914; and George E. Brooks, "Peanuts and Colonialism: Consequences of the Commercialization of Peanuts in West Africa, 1830–70," *Journal of African History* 16, no. 1 (1975).

59 **Gorée was a rock:** P.W. Bakhoum, A. Ndour, I. Niang, B. Sambou, V.B. Traore, A.T. Diaw, H. Sambou H., and M.L. Ndiaye, "Coastline Mobility of Gorée Island (Senegal), from 1942 to 2011," *Marine Science* 7, no. 1 (2017): 1–9.

59 **on which lived:** According to 1868 census information, found in Charles Becker, Victor Martin, Jean Schmitz et al., *Les premiers*

recensements au Sénégal et l'évolution démographique. Présentation de doc-
uments (Dakar: ORSTOM, Centre IRD de Bondy, 1983), 6.

59 **The island had:** Most details about life on Gorée are from Sinou, *Comptoirs.*

60 **Taylor never revealed:** Taylor, 25 March 1872, Defap.

60 **Samuel Crocker Cobb:** James Bugbee, "Memoir of Hon. Samuel Crocker Cobb," *Massachusetts Historical Society*, Feb. 1892, 318–330.

60 **Cobb's agendas:** Cobb's diaries are collection MS0101 of the Bostonian Society.

60 **These "exotic" nut wholesalers:** Andrew F. Smith, *Peanuts: The Illustrious History of the Goober Pea* (Urbana: University of Illinois Press, 2007), 16–17, 22–26; F. Roy Johnson, *The Peanut Story* (Murfreesboro, NC: Johnson Publishing Co., 1964), 42–43.

60 **The peanut had long been associated:** On the bad reputation of the peanut and Thomas Rowland's work, see Edward Mott Wooley, "Tom Rowland—Peanuts," *McClure's Magazine* (1913): 183–202.

60 **It was one of the foods they grew:** Robert L. Hall, "Africa and the American South: Culinary Connections," *Southern Quarterly: A Journal of the Arts in the South* 44, no. 2 (Winter 2007): 19–52.

61 **it caught on:** *Harper's Weekly*, v. 14, 16 July 1870.

61 **As the peanut started:** Arthur G. Peterson, "Peanuts: Prices, Production, and Foreign Trade since the Civil War," *Economic Geography* 7.1 (1931): 59–68, 66, notes "the demand for pea-nuts after the Civil War increased even faster than domestic production and imports were quite large from 1864 to 1875. Practically all of our peanut imports at this time came from Africa and during the year beginning July, 1867, our imports amounted to over 7,700,000 pounds."

61 **Rowland noted:** Wooley, "Tom Rowland—Peanuts."

61 **Cobb was one of a handful:** Brooks, *Yankee Traders*, 217.

61 **"News from Gorée":** Cobb diaries, 21 March 1870, Bostonian.

61 **Whatever the unfavorable news:** Ibid., 10 July 1870.

61 **We don't know what Hasty found:** See Simone Müller-Pohl, "By Atlantic Telegraph," *Social Research* 35.1 (2010).

62 **The following year:** Cobb diaries, 19 May 1871, Bostonian.

62 **And in January of 1872:** Cobb diaries, 25 January 1872; 20 February 1872; 17 May 1872, Bostonian.

62 **He said he accepted the proposition:** Taylor biography, *JME*, 1878, 247–251.

62 **the buildings on Gorée:** William Winwood Reade, *Savage Africa; Being the Narrative of a Tour in Equatorial, Southwestern and*

Northwestern Africa (New York: Harper & Brothers, 1864), vol. 2, 387–388; Yves Péhaut, *La doyenne des "sénégalaises" de Bordeaux: Maurel et H. Prom de 1831 à 1919* (Pessac: Presses universitaires de Bordeaux, 2014), vol. 2., 30–31.

63 **to dry out fresh:** From Norman R. Bennett and George E. Brooks Jr., *New England Merchants in Africa: A History Through Documents, 1802 to 1865* (Boston: Boston University, African Studies Center, 1965), 279–280.

63 **"Our peanuts are stowed":** Stephen H. Grant, *Peter Strickland: New London Shipmaster, Boston Merchant, First Consul to Senegal* (Washington, DC: New Academia Publishing, 2007), 34.

63 **Educated men of color:** Roger Pasquier, "Villes du Sénégal au XIXe siècle," *Revue française d'histoire d'outre-mer* 47, no. 168 (1960): 387–426, 388.

63 **Manual laborers:** Ibid.

63 **After abolition:** Cited in Denise Bouche, *Les villages de liberté en Afrique noire française 1887–1910* (Paris: Mouton, 1968), 54.

63 **The conditions:** Taylor biography, *JME*, 1878, 247–251.

63 **Their state:** Ibid.

12. Unholy Wars

64 **He had been allowed:** Mamadou Diouf, *Le Kajoor au XIXe siècle: Pouvoir ceddo et conquête coloniale* (Paris: Karthala, 2014), 238.

64 **North of Kajoor:** Details about the Madiyankobe movement come from Alfred Le Chatelier, *L'Islam dans l'Afrique occidentale* (Paris: G. Steinheil, 1899), 147–149; David Robinson, *Chiefs and Clerics: Abdul Bokar Kan and Futa Toro, 1853–1891* (Oxford: Clarendon Press, 1975), 82–84; Eunice Charles, *Precolonial Senegal: The Jolof Kingdom, 1800–1890* (Boston: African Studies Center, Boston University, 1977), 67–81.

65 **Amadu's adherents multiplied:** 17 October 1869, ANS 13 G 124.

65 **"had let himself be seduced":** *Moniteur*, 27 July 1869.

65 **In July 1869:** Mbaye Guèye, *Les transformations des sociétés wolof et sereer de l'ère de la conquête à la mise en place de l'administration coloniale: 1854–1920* (Dakar: UCAD, FLSH. Diss. thèse d'Etat, 1990), 306–309; L. Jore and Yves J. Saint-Martin, "Le colonel de cavalerie Henri-Philibert Canard (1824–1894), spahi et gouverneur du Sénégal," *Revue française d'histoire d'outre-mer* 61, no. 223, 2e trimestre (1974): 284–310, 290–296; and for descriptions of the layout of defensive settlements, see Adama Guèye, "The Impact of the Slave Trade on Cayor and

Baol: Mutations in Habitat and Land Occupancy," in *Fighting the Slave Trade: West African Strategies*, Sylviane A. Diouf (ed.) (Athens: Ohio University Press, 2003), 54–58.

65 **"As the soldiers [for the French]":** *Moniteur*, 27 July 1869.

65 **More of the combined:** Guèye, *Transformations*, 306–309; Jore and Saint-Martin, "Le colonel de cavalerie Henri-Philibert Canard," 290–296.

66 **As one observer wrote:** Quoted in Guèye, *Transformations*, 19.

66 **French reprisals soon came:** Guèye, *Transformations*, 306–309; Jore and Saint-Martin, "Le colonel de cavalerie Henri-Philibert Canard," 290–296.

66 **One French military bureaucrat:** Quoted in Diouf, *Kajoor*, 243.

66 **In France at the same time:** A.S. Kanya-Forstner, *The Conquest of the Western Sudan* (Cambridge: Cambridge University Press, 2008), 45.

66 **And after the governor died of cholera:** Guèye, *Transformations*, 311–323.

67 **"If I have authorized":** Quoted in Diouf, *Kajoor*, 242.

67 **The French insisted upon the restricted:** Treaty Between Lat Joor and France, 12 January 1871, cited in Lucie Colvin, *Kajor and Its Diplomatic Relations with Saint-Louis du Senegal, 1763–1861* (ProQuest Dissertations Publishing, 1972), 432.

13. A Word on Slavery

68 **it bears underscoring:** Claude Meillasoux, *The Anthropology of Slavery: The Womb of Iron and Gold* (Chicago: University of Chicago Press, 1991), 20–21, reminds us: "Slavery is a period in universal history which has affected all continents, sometimes simultaneously, sometimes successively."

68 **Slave labor:** See James C. Scott, *Against the Grain: A Deep History of the Earliest States* (New Haven, CT: Yale University Press, 2017), 276–319; Pamela Kyle Crossley, "Slavery in Early Modern China," *Cambridge World History of Slavery* 3 (2011): 186–214.

68 **Long before:** See Ralph A. Austen, *Trans-Saharan Africa in World History* (New York: Oxford University Press, 2010), 31–33.

69 **In general, the enslaved:** Igor Kopytoff and Suzanne Miers, eds., *Slavery in Africa: Historical and Anthropological Perspectives* (Madison: University of Wisconsin Press, 1977), 12–16; Meillasoux, *Anthropology of Slavery*, 23–40; Paul Lovejoy, *Transformations in Slavery: A History of Slavery in Africa* (Cambridge: Cambridge University Press, 2000), 1–23.

69 **"In the marketplaces,":** Laurent Bérenger-Féraud, *Les peuplades de la Sénégambie: Histoire, ethnographie, moeurs et coutumes, etc.* (Paris: Ernest Leroux, 1879), 367.

70 **On the Rio Pongo:** Mamadou Camara Lefloche, "Traditions orales, traitement occulte et domptage de l'esclave au Rio Pongo," in *Traditions orales et archives de la traite négrière*, Djibril Tamsir Niane (ed.) (Brussels: UNESCO, 2001), 34.

70 **Eighteenth-century French slave trader:** Dominique Harcourt Lamiral, *L'Affrique et le peuple affriquain considérés sous tous leurs rapports avec notre commerce & nos colonies: de l'abus des privilèges exclusifs, & notamment de celui de la Compagnie du Sénégal: Ce que c'est qu'une société se qualifiant d'Amis des Noirs* (Dessenne, 1789), 187.

14. This Black Man from Gorée

72 **Gorée's brisk crosswinds:** *Notices statistiques sur les colonies françaises,* vol. 3 (1839), 218.

72 **"Although situated in the torrid zone":** Ibid.

72 **In 1871:** Villéger, 17 October 1871, Defap.

72 **Saint Louis, Senegal, was Villéger's:** *JME,* 1869, 446.

72 **The young missionary couple:** Villéger, 17 October 1871, Defap; Jean-François Zorn, *Le grand siècle d'une mission protestante: La mission de Paris de 1822 à 1914* (Paris: Karthala, 1993), 46.

72 **Villéger wrote:** Villéger, 14 December 1871, Defap.

72 **The Protestants of France:** See Jean-François Rigoulot, "Protestants and the French Nation Under the Third Republic: Between Recognition and Assimilation," *National Identities* 11, no. 1 (2009): 45–57.

73 **Villéger said that on Gorée:** Villéger, 17 October 1871, Defap.

73 **"There are also about":** Ibid.

73 **a woman of Liberated African:** An ad in the *Sierra Leone Weekly News,* 17 April 1909, notes that Mrs. Taylor was born in the Gambia.

73 **Walter Taylor said that he had not been:** This is from Taylor himself in *JME,* 1878, 249.

73 **Nicol had been a lecturer:** Jill Farrow, *Native Agency in British West Africa: The Development of an Idea 1835–65, with Special Reference to Sierra Leone* (Dissertation, Durham University, 1974), 113. According to the Grammar School's register, Walter Taylor started there on 22 August 1859.

73 **Taylor responded to this call:** Taylor, March 1872, Defap.

73 **Taylor wrote to Villéger:** Copied in Villéger's correspondence, 14 December 1871, Defap.

74 **Taylor also shared how he converted:** Ibid.

74 **Some months later:** Taylor to Villéger, March 1872, Defap.

74 **Villéger took up his pen:** Ibid.

74 **In Sierra Leone:** David Northrup, "Becoming African: Identity Formation Among Liberated Slaves in Nineteenth-Century Sierra Leone," *Slavery & Abolition* 27, no. 1 (2006): 1–21, 8.

74 **What Sierra Leone had:** Taylor to Villéger, 25 March 1872, Defap.

74 **In the same letter Taylor:** Ibid.

74 **Villéger shared the strategy:** Villéger to Casalis, 13 April 1872, Defap.

75 **"As for the Black man from Gorée":** Ibid.

15. Lat Joor Wants His Slaves Back

76 **The newly reinstalled:** Lat Joor's correspondence and some of the responses are preserved in ANS 13G 258 and ANS 13G 259.

77 **a special stamp:** The stamp said "Lat-Dior, Damel du Cayor," but I changed the orthography for consistency.

77 **October 29, 1874:** ANS 13G 258.

77 **September 20, 1876:** ANS 13G 259.

77 **December 27, 1876:** Ibid.

78 **In 1870 or 1871:** Canard to Lat Joor, ANS 13G 306.

78 **The same year:** Villéger to M. Banzet, 16 March 1877, Defap; Also in "Lettre de M. Villéger contenant les faits d'esclavage qu'il a signalés," *L'Eglise Libre*, 27 September 1879.

78 **But in the latter half of 1871:** Ibid.

78 **What happened after is a matter:** Ibid.

79 **That version of the story was disputed:** Michaux, le conseiller d'etat, "Notes pour le ministre sur la question des captifs au Senegal," 1879, ANOM Senegal XIV/15a.

16. A Sickness with No Name

83 **In Senegambia:** Jean Adam, *Les plantes oléiferes de l'Afrique occidentale française. I. L'arachide, culture, produits, commerce, amélioration de la production* (Paris: Challamel, 1908), 40.

84 ***Dugub jaa ngiy dee:*** Momar Cisse, *Parole chantée ou psalmodiée wolof. Collecte, typologie et analyse des procédés argumentatifs de connivence associés aux fonctions discursives de satire et d'éloge* (thèse de doctorat d'Etat de linguistique, Université Cheikh Anta Diop, Dakar, 2006), vol. 1, 356–357.

84 **In some villages:** Details on peasant agriculture and how the

nawetaan fit in are from James F. Searing, *"God Alone Is King": Islam and Emancipation in Senegal: The Wolof Kingdoms of Kajoor and Bawol, 1859–1914* (Portsmouth, NH: Heinemann, 2002), 203–213; L.B. Venema, *The Wolof of Saloum: Social Structure and Rural Development in Senegal* (Wageningen: PUDOC, 1978), 103–123; Philippe David, *Les navetanes: Histoire des migrants saisonniers de l'arachide en Sénégambie des origines à nos jours* (Dakar: Les Nouvelles Éditions Africaines, 1980); Kenneth Swindell, "Serawoollies, Tillibunkas and Strange Farmers: The Development of Migrant Groundnut Farming along the Gambia River, 1848–95," *Journal of African History* 21, no. 1 (1980).

84 **On the Gambia River:** See Philip D. Curtin, *Economic Change in Precolonial Africa: Senegambia in the Era of the Slave Trade* (Madison: University of Wisconsin Press, 1975), 230–233.

85 **When the slave trade:** François Manchuelle, *Willing Migrants: Soninke Labor Diasporas, 1848–1960* (Athens: Ohio University Press: 1997), 53–59; Kenneth Swindell and Alieu Jeng, *Migrants, Credit, and Climate: the Gambian Groundnut Trade, 1834–1934* (Boston: Brill, 2006), 5–25.

85 **In the 1860s:** E. Mage, *Voyage dans le Soudan occidental (Sénégambie-Niger)* (Paris: L. Hachette et Cie, 1868), 106–110.

85 **"A vigorous captive":** Ibid., 106–110.

86 **As luck:** Swindell and Jeng, *Migrants, Credit, and Climate*, 29–33.

86 **"He [the native trader]":** Governor D'Arcy to Colonel Blackall, sent 9 November 1866, Gambia CSO 1/30.

86 **In between the wars:** Julian W. Witherell, *The Response of the Peoples of Cayor to French Penetration, 1850–1900* (ProQuest Dissertations Publishing, 1964), 62–63; Swindell and Jeng, *Migrants, Credit, and Climate*, 29–33; Laurence Marfaing, *L'évolution du commerce au Sénégal 1820–1930* (Paris: L'Harmattan, 2010), 40–42.

86 **Along the Casamance River:** Swindell and Jeng, *Migrants, Credit, and Climate*, 33–34.

86 **Plus, after the harvest:** D'Arcy, 9 November 1866, Gambia CSO 1/30.

86 **"A disease, for which I have no name":** 1 October 1867, ANS 13G 368.

87 **"It is a disease":** 24 October 1867, ANS 13G 368.

87 **He undercut the impact of his warning:** Ibid.

87 **And he was right:** Marina Diallo Cô-Trung, *La Compagnie générale des oléagineux tropicaux en Casamance de 1948 à 1962: Autopsie d'une opération de mise en valeur coloniale* (Paris: Karthala, 1998), table on pp. 152–153.

17. A Native Evangelist

88 **The director of the Paris:** Casalis, 7 June 1872, Defap.

89 **When Villéger first arrived:** *JME*, 1870, 45.

89 **His evangelical outreach:** Ibid., 253–255.

90 **From the beginning:** Jean-François Rigoulot, "Protestants and the French Nation Under the Third Republic: Between Recognition and Assimilation," *National Identities* 11, no. 1 (2009); Frédéric Hartweg, "Mission, colonisation et décolonisation: De quelques particularités du protestantisme français," *Kirchliche Zeitgeschichte* (1992): 223–239.

90 **But Taylor:** Villéger to Casalis, 12 October 1872, Defap. He says that Taylor had arrived at the beginning of the month.

90 **The population of Saint Louis:** Alain Sinou, *Comptoirs et villes coloniales du Sénégal: Saint-Louis, Gorée, et Dakar* (Paris: Karthala, 1993), 33–47, 285–288.

90 **the same housing patterns remained:** Hilary Jones, *The Métis of Senegal: Urban Life and Politics in French West Africa* (Bloomington: Indiana University Press, 2013).

90 **although some also built:** Sinou, *Comptoirs et villes*, 46, 112.

90 **"a veritable oriental palace":** Golaz, 1 April 1881, Defap.

90 **After Taylor arrived:** Villéger, 13 May 1873, Defap.

91 **"He fetches the Blacks":** Villéger, 12 October 1872, Defap.

91 **A couple of years:** Taylor, 11 February 1876, Defap.

91 **His good friend:** Villéger, 24 June 1873, Defap.

91 **Taylor was also friends:** On Sy's background and career, see Abdoul Sow, *Mamadou Racine Sy: Premier capitaine noir des tirailleurs sénégalais (1838–1902)* (Dakar: L'Harmattan, 2010).

91 **He and the committee:** Villéger, 24 June 1873, Defap.

91 **Taylor had written:** Taylor, 11 November 1875, Defap.

92 **Walter Taylor preached:** Villéger, 20 April 1876, Defap.

92 **"It must also be said":** Ibid.

92 **In 1877, Villéger:** *JME*, 1877, 54–55.

92 **many early tirailleurs:** Myron Echenberg, *Colonial Conscripts: The Tirailleurs Sénégalais in French West Africa, 1857–1960* (Portsmouth, NH: Heinemann, 1991), 7–19.

92 **During his time:** *JME*, 1877, 54–55.

93 **Following this happy event:** Taylor, 25 April 1877, Defap; *Moniteur* 1877, 67, lists a Dimé Dialo who was declared by Villéger and was liberated on 14 March 1877.

93 **Taylor wrote that Moussa's:** Ibid.

93 **across the river:** *Moniteur*, 4 July 1865, 119–121.

93 **Wolof may have been:** Taylor, 25 April 1877, Defap.

93 **this broad category:** According to documents, many of the Bambara with the mission were from Wasulu. On Wasulu, see Brian J. Peterson, "History, Memory, and the Legacy of Samori in Southern Mali, c. 1880–1898," *Journal of African History* 49, no. 2 (2008): 261–279; also Martin Klein, "Defensive Strategies: Wasulu, Masina, and the Slave Trade," in *Fighting the Slave Trade: West African Strategies*, S. Diouf (ed.) (Athens: Ohio University Press, 2003).

93 **Taylor and Villéger:** Taylor, 18 August 1877, Defap.

94 **"Come unto me":** Matthew 11:28, KJV.

94 **Here, he told the director:** Taylor, 18 August 1877, Defap.

18. Ceebu Jën

95 **Senegal's national dish:** Information about the preparation of ceebu jën and speculation about Penda Mbaye are gleaned from Aminata Sow Fall, *Un grain de vie et d'espérance* (Paris: Éditions Françoise Truffaut, 2002), 28–29, 134; Amadou Sarra Ba, *Arts culinaires et équilibré alimentaire en Sénégambie du VIIIeme au XXIÈME siècle*, Mémoire de DEA (UCAD, 2010), 69–71; Chantal Crenn, "La fabrique de l'identité culinaire nationale dans les écrits sur l'alimentation et la cuisine sénégalaises: du regard colonial à celui de Youssou N'Dour" *Food and History* 9, no. 2 (2011): 261–305; Manon Laplace, "Le tieboudiène, plat de résistance et de résilience," *Jeune Afrique*, 28 December 2020; J. Huntington, "There Is More Than One Way to Make a Ceebu Jën: Narrating African Recipes in Texts," in *Writing Through the Visual and Virtual*, R. Larrier and O.D. Alidou (eds.) (Lanham, MD: Lexington, 2015), 123–148.

96 **Taylor was then paid:** Procès-verbaux, 22 July 1878, and Villéger, 6 February 1875, Defap.

96 **But for the children:** Villéger, 6 February 1875, Defap.

96 **A species of rice:** Judith A. Carney, *Black Rice: The African Origins of Rice Cultivation in the Americas* (Cambridge: Harvard University Press, 2001), 13–25.

96 **The French army:** Myron Echenberg, *Colonial Conscripts: The Tirailleurs Sénégalais in French West Africa, 1857–1960* (Portsmouth, NH: Heinemann, 1991), 22; J. Malcolm Thompson, "Colonial Policy and the Family Life of Black Troops in French West Africa, 1817–1904," *International Journal of African Historical Studies* 23, no. 3 (1990): 423–453, 426–427.

96 **But most of Taylor's friends:** Monique Chastanet, "Couscous 'à la

sahélienne' (Sénégal, Mali, Mauritanie)," in *Couscous, boulgour et po-*
lenta. Transformer et consommer les céréales dans le monde, Hélène Fran-
conie, Monique Chastanet, and François Sigaut (eds.) (Paris: Karthala,
2010), 149–187, traces millet-based couscous across the Western Sahel;
René Tourte, *Histoire de la recherche agricole en Afrique tropicale franco-*
phone (Rome: FAO, 2005), vol. 1, 69–71.

96 **"The specialties of the Senegalese people":** David Boilat, *Esquisses*
sénégalaises: physionomie du pays, peuplades, commerce, religions, passé et
avenir, récits et légendes (Paris: P. Bertrand, 1853), 300.

97 **The transformation of millet stalks:** James Searing, *West African*
Slavery and Atlantic Commerce (Cambridge: Cambridge University
Press, 1993), 121–127.

97 **"Using the mortar and pestle is grueling":** François-Pierre Ricard,
Dr., *Le Sénégal: Étude intime* (Paris: Challamel aîné, 1865), 180.

98 *Kur kandang*: Momar Cisse, *Parole chantée ou psalmodiée wolof. Col-*
lecte, typologie et analyse des procédés argumentatifs de connivence associés
aux fonctions discursives de satire et d'éloge (thèse de doctorat d'Etat de
linguistique, Université Cheikh Anta Diop, Dakar, 2006), vol. 1, 189.

98 **This had always been the work:** R. Rousseau, "Le Sénégal d'autre-
fois. Étude sur le Oualo," *Bulletin du comité d'études historiques et scien-*
tifiques de l'Afrique occidentale française, vol. 12 (1929), 173.

98 **an enterprising pileuse:** Searing, *West African Slavery*, 127.

98 **In November 1871:** *Moniteur*, 1872, 103.

98 **Most of the millet that:** Searing, *West African Slavery*, 188–189.

98 **Savvy farmers knew they should rotate crops:** Ricard, *Le Sénégal*,
168.

99 **In some places:** The beginnings of this problem were seen in the
Gambia as early as the 1850s, according to Kenneth Swindell and
Alieu Jeng, *Migrants, Credit, and Climate: the Gambian Groundnut Trade,*
1834–1934 (Boston: Brill, 2006), 21–22.

99 **"The natives of these territories":** Comte Louis-Edouard Bouët-
Willaumez, *Commerce et traite des noirs aux côtes occidentales d'Afrique:*
1er Janvier 1848 (Paris: Impr. Nationale, 1848), 54.

99 **From the 1840s:** Roger Pasquier, "Un aspect de l'histoire des villes
du Sénégal: Les problèmes de ravitaillement au XIXe siècle," in *Con-*
tributions à l'histoire du Senegal, Jean Boulegue (ed.) (Paris: Cahiers du
CRA, 1987), 210.

99 **This was helped along:** Thompson, "Colonial Policy and the Family
Life," 427.

99 **"If the Blacks simply eat the millet":** Cited in L.C. Barrows, *General*

Faidherbe, Maurel and Prom Company and French Expansion in Senegal (ProQuest Dissertations Publishing, 1974), 618.

19. A Steamboat on Land

100 **Kajoor had two main doors:** Georges Savonnet, "Une ville neuve du Sénégal: Thiès," *Cahiers d'outre-mer* no. 33 - 9e année (January–March 1956): 70–93, 70–73; Roger Pasquier, *Le Sénégal au milieu du XIXe siècle: La crise économique et sociale* (Thèse de doctorat d'état, Paris IV, 1987), vol. 1, 60.

100 **The Seereer groups:** Seereer resistance in this area is long and storied. See Robert Kerr, *A General History and Collection of Voyages and Travels. Volume II* (New York: Nova Science Publishers, 2020), 238–239; David Boilat, *Esquisses sénégalaises: physionomie du pays, peuplades, commerce, religions, passé et avenir, récits et légendes* (Paris: P. Bertrand, 1853), 59–60; Ousseynou Faye, "Mythe et histoire dans la vie de Kaañ Fay du Cangin (Sénégal)," *Cahiers d'études africaines* 34, no. 136 (1994): 616–617.

101 **When the French started:** Mbaye Guèye, *Les transformations des sociétés wolof et sereer de l'ère de la conquête à la mise en place de l'administration coloniale: 1854–1920* (Dakar: UCAD, FLSH. Diss. thèse d'Etat, 1990), 24-25.

101 **As the port of Rufisque:** "Notice sur les Sérères," *Moniteur*, 4 July 1865, 123–124.

101 **In April of 1872:** 17 April 1872, ANS 13G 306.

101 **In the 1870s:** See ANS 13G 309; Antoine-Alfred Marche, *Trois voyages dans l'Afrique occidentale* (Paris: Librairie Hachette et compagnie, 1879), 32–39.

102 **This sense of lawlessness:** On Brière and colonial ambitions, see Germaine Ganier, "Lat Dyor et le chemin de fer de l'arachide, 1876–1886," *Bulletin de l'IFAN* XXVII, nos. 1–2 (1965): 223–281; Francine N'diaye, "La colonie du Sénégal au temps de Brière de l'Isle 1876–1881," *Bulletin De L'IFAN* XXX, no. 2 (1968): 463–512; John Hargreaves, *Prelude to the Partition of West Africa* (London: Macmillan, 1963), 253–254; Paul E. Pheffer, *Railroads and Aspects of Social Change in Senegal* (ProQuest Dissertations Publishing, 1975), 42–54.

102 **The official who conducted:** Walter Report, quoted in Pheffer, *Railroads*, 75.

102 **"In consideration of the friendship":** Brière to LJ, 16 January 1877, ANS 13G 259.

103 **he was an equine collector:** In Assane M. Samb, *Cadior Demb: Essai*

sur l'histoire du Cayor (Dakar: Nouvelles Éditions Africaines, 1981), 55, he lists some of the damel's other horses.

103 **He wrote back:** cited in Vincent Monteil, "Lat Dior, Damel du Kayor (1842–1886) et l'islamisation des Wolofs," *Archives de sociologie des religions* 8, no. 16 (1963): 97.

20. The Ebbs and Flows of My Courage

104 **When Walter Taylor first joined:** Taylor, 10 February 1877, Defap.

104 **Elizabeth and Walter Jr.:** Villéger, May 1873, Defap.

104 **She did speak Bambara:** Taylor's correspondence often mentions his wife's language skills.

104 **"She seems like a very good woman":** Villéger, 13 May 1873, Defap.

105 **A few years later:** Taylor, 6 November 1877, Defap.

105 **The mission in Saint Louis:** The battle between Villéger and the teacher, Louis Rémond, was carried out in years of correspondence. Jean-François Zorn, *Le grand siècle d'une mission protestante: La mission de Paris de 1822 à 1914* (Paris: Karthala, 1993), makes a brief reference to it (p. 46), but it was much larger and longer than that.

105 **"neuralgic pains":** Taylor, 10 July 1875, Defap.

105 **He wrote to the director to describe:** Taylor, 11 March 1875, Defap.

106 **The schoolteacher was fired:** Procès-verbaux, 2 June 1875, Defap.

106 **A new helper:** Villéger, on 21 November 1876, writes that she has arrived. Defap.

106 **Salimata was about twelve years old:** Céline Badiane-Labrune, "La Société des Missions Évangéliques de Paris en Casamance (Sénégal) 1863–1867," *Histoire et missions chrétiennes* 1 (2008): 125–152, 144–147.

106 **Salimata wanted:** Villéger, 21 November 1876, Defap.

107 **Casalis pushed back:** Director's register, 4 January 1877, Defap.

107 **About six months later:** Villéger, 7 April 1877, Defap.

107 **For one, the house:** Taylor, 22 October 1878, Defap.

107 **Taylor was paid much less:** On pay: Procès-verbaux, 22 July 1878. Villéger, 6 February 1875, Defap. For Sally Margaret and Samuel's births: A notice of her birth appears in SLNA, Births, 2nd Eastern District, Waterloo, 30 March 1872 to 24 July 1875; and a letter from Taylor on 11 January 1877 (Defap) mentions the birth of Samuel the previous December.

108 **It was the schoolteacher:** Taylor, 6 November 1877, Defap.

108 **"I have the right to demand":** Ibid.

108 **this young man "told the natives":** Ibid.

108 **According to Taylor's telling of it:** Ibid.

108 **In May 1877:** Taylor, 19 May 1877, Defap.
108 **Salimata, who also grew up:** Taylor, 18 August 1877, Defap. He says that Salimata is a Bambara girl and that the Bambara members are always happy to see her.
108 **He wrote to Director Casalis:** Taylor, 18 August 1877, Defap.
109 **At the end of that year:** Taylor, 22 November 1877, and 19 December 1877, Defap.
109 **The board did not accept:** Procès-verbaux, 7 January 1878, Defap.
109 **The French missionary:** Villéger's letter tending his resignation seems to be missing from the correspondence, but the committee discussed it on 2 July 1877, according to the Procès-verbaux, Defap.
109 **Between Taylor and Villéger:** Procès-verbaux, 7 January 1878, Defap.
109 **At the beginning of 1878:** Director's register, 18 January 1878, Defap.

21. Saxayaay
113 **The time it takes:** Jean Adam, *Les plantes oléiferes de l'Afrique occidentale française. I. L'arachide, culture, produits, commerce, amélioration de la production* (Paris: Challamel, 1908), 60–61.
113 **One agronomist:** Ibid.
113 **When that happens:** Ibid.
113 **Even after all of this effort:** Auguste Chevalier, "Monographie de l'arachide (Suite)," *Revue de botanique appliquée et d'agriculture coloniale* 14, no. 156 (1934): 565–632, 566.

22. Springtime in Paris
115 **Walter Taylor prepared:** Villéger, 7 February 1878, Defap.
115 **The Paris Evangelical Missionary Society's journal:** *JME*, 1878, 105.
115 **The Maison des Missions:** Details from Jean-François Zorn, *Le grand siècle d'une mission protestante: La mission de Paris de 1822 à 1914* (Paris: Karthala, 1993), 613.
116 **It was not yet spring:** Procès-verbaux, 25 February 1878, Defap. They say they received a letter that Taylor left on February 23 and that he should arrive in Paris on the 10th or 12th of March.
116 **They were impressed by his:** Procès-verbaux, 18 March 1878, Defap.
116 **Taylor mentions at some point having:** Taylor, 6 May 1879, Defap.
116 **Throughout the 1870s:** On the Fisk Jubilee Singers' European tours, see Kira Thurman, "Singing the Civilizing Mission in the Land of Bach, Beethoven, and Brahms: The Fisk Jubilee Singers in Nineteenth-Century Germany," *Journal of World History* 27, no. 3 (2016): 443–471.

116 **Taylor gave his first big speech:** *JME*, 1878, 165–172.
117 **After this speech:** *JME*, 1878, 172.
118 **In Senegal, the buzz about:** *Moniteur*, 1878, 77.
118 **The Catholic establishments:** From Catalogue officiel. Tome 3, *Exposition universelle internationale de 1878 à Paris*, publié par le commissariat, 365.
118 **Maybe he visited:** Hippolyte-Albert Gautier and Adrien Desprez, *Les curiosités de l'exposition de 1878, guide du voyageur* (Paris: C. Delagrave, 1878), 32, 83–85, 121–122, 200.
118 **Maybe, like so many others:** Robert Belot and Daniel Bermond, *Bartholdi* (Paris: Perrin, 2004), 329.
119 **And perhaps he went to see:** July 1878. *L'exposition universelle de 1878 illustrée, publication internationale autorisée par la Commission.* Jules Brunfaut ed. 661.
119 **He may have even gotten to take a ride:** S.L. Kotar and J.E. Gessler, *Ballooning: A History, 1782–1900* (Jefferson, NC: McFarland, 2011), 260.
119 **One July evening:** *JME*, 1878, 241.
119 **Temple de l'Oratoire:** Roger Braun, "Histoire de L'Eglise de l'Oratoire Saint Honoré ou du Louvre," Based on a talk given on 22 April 1932 to the Société d'Histoire et d'Archéologie des 1er et 2e arrondissements de Paris and later published in 1936 in *Bulletin du Centre de Paris*, https://oratoiredulouvre.fr/documents/eglise-oratoire-saint-honore-louvre (accessed 14 September 2021).
119 **It started at:** *JME*, 1878, 241.
119 **He picked up the thread:** Ibid., 245.
120 **Just after Mr. Taylor's departure:** Villéger, 21 March 1878, Defap.
120 **The committee members:** Procès-verbaux, 22 July 1878, Defap.

23. Reports from the Rivers
121 **According to interested accounts, Nyara:** See "Sierra Leone. Baptism of the Lady Chief Mrs. Lightburn," *Mission Field*, 2 December 1878, 583.
121 **when she was over:** No one knows her age exactly, but Alfred H. Barrow in *Fifty Years in Western Africa: Being a Record of the Work of the West Indian Church on the Banks of the Rio Pongo* says she was "upwards of 80" in 1878 (London: Society for Promoting Christian Knowledge, 1900), 118.
121 **Once converted:** "Sierra Leone. The Rio Pongo Mission. Important Conversion. An Episcopal Tour," *Mission Field*, 2 June 1879, 273–279.

121 **The missionary who converted:** *Mission Field*, 1878, 583–585.

121 **the region had gone from being:** Boubacar Barry, *Senegambia and the Atlantic Slave Trade*, trans. Ayi Kwei Armah (New York: Cambridge University Press, 1998), 243–262.

122 **In 1869, on another corner of the continent:** On the Suez Canal, see Zachary Karabell, *Parting the Desert: The Creation of the Suez Canal* (New York: Knopf, 2003).

122 **The canal shaved off some:** Yves Péhaut, *Les oléagineux dans les pays d'Afrique occidentale associés au marché commun: La production, le commerce et la transformation des produits* (Paris: H. Champion, 1976), two volumes, 345.

122 **Those products, coupled:** Ibid., 342–345; Also, on petroleum, Octave Teissier, *Histoire du commerce de Marseille pendant vingt ans (1855–1874)* (Paris: Librairie Guillaumin, 1878), 272.

122 **In 1880, the Marseille buyers:** Numbers from Laurence Marfaing, *L'évolution du commerce au Sénégal 1820–1930* (Paris: L'Harmattan, 2010), 94.

122 **Once peanuts from West Africa:** Jean Adam, *Les plantes oléiferes de l'Afrique occidentale française. I. L'arachide, culture, produits, commerce, amélioration de la production* (Paris: Challamel, 1908), 84–85; Auguste Chevalier, "Monographie de l'arachide," in *Revue de botanique appliquée et d'agriculture coloniale*, 13e année, bulletin nos. 146–147 (Octobre–novembre 1933): 622–623, n156.

123 **The peanuts from Kajoor:** Louis L.C. Faidherbe, *Le Sénégal: La France dans L'Afrique occidentale* (Paris: Hachette et cie, 1889), 105.

123 **"an excellent cooking oil":** Péhaut, *Oléagineux*, 352.

123 **Farther down the coast:** Ibid., table on p. 342.

123 **Merchants were increasingly calling it:** Ibid., 346–347.

123 **Or it could have been:** Yves Péhaut, *La doyenne des "sénégalaises" de Bordeaux: Maurel et H. Prom de 1831 à 1919* (Pessac: Presses Universitaires de Bordeaux, 2014), vol. 2, 77, on Edouard Sorano in Casamance.

124 **Most often these bad peanuts:** Adam, *Les plantes*, 143–145; also *Journal de jurisprudence commerciale et maritime*, 1867, 234.

124 **For a long time:** Bernard Moitt, *Peanut Production and Social Change in the Dakar Hinterland: Kajoor and Bawol, 1840–1940* (ProQuest Dissertations Publishing, 1985), 172–173; also Péhaut, *Doyenne*, vol. 2, 60.

124 **As the prices went down:** Péhaut, *Oléagineux*, 342–345.

124 **In the early 1880s:** Péhaut, *Doyenne*, vol. 2, 60, 79.

124 **In the Casamance:** Péhaut, *Doyenne*, vol. 2, 80.

124 **Smart merchants recognized:** Péhaut, *Doyenne*, vol. 2, 148–149.

124 **On the Rio Nunez:** Commandant at Benty to Governor, 24 March 1882, ANS 7G 16.

124 **Many farmers resisted:** Kenneth Swindell and Alieu Jeng, *Migrants, Credit, and Climate: The Gambian Groundnut Trade, 1834–1934* (Boston: Brill, 2006), 34.

125 **"The 1881 harvest":** Emile Maurel, quoted in Péhaut, *Doyenne*, vol. 2, 79.

125 **Usually, the traders on certain rivers:** Christian Roche, *Histoire de la Casamance: Conquête et résistance, 1850–1920*, vol. 15 (Paris: Karthala, 1985), 122.

125 **In other years:** Swindell and Jeng, *Migrants, Credit, and Climate*, 36–37.

125 **Nyara Bely breathed:** Although Barrow writes, in *Fifty Years in Western Africa*, p. 118–119, that she died in 1879, the *Mission Field* reported that she died in 1880, on p. 322.

126 **On the Rio Pongo that she left:** Odile Goerg, *Commerce et colonisation en Guinée (1850–1913)* (Paris: L'Harmattan, 1986), 85–86.

126 **By the 1880s, farmers were:** Bulletin agricole, commercial et politique, Rio Nunez, 31 December 1883, ANS 7G 10.

24. A New Appeal

127 **When Walter Taylor left France:** Taylor, 7 September 1878, Defap.

127 **In that city:** *JME*, 1878, 296–297.

127 **The ship sailed down the coastline:** Taylor, 9 August 1878, Defap.

127 **From Lisbon:** On the Canary Current, Salif Diop, Jean-Paul Barusseau, and Cyr Descamps, eds., *The Land/Ocean Interactions in the Coastal Zone of West and Central Africa* (New York: Springer, 2014), 3–4.

128 **Taylor arrived in Dakar:** Taylor, 7 September 1878, Defap.

128 **The committee in Paris took:** Procès-verbaux, 9 October 1878, Defap.

128 **Casalis wrote right away:** Director's register, 19 October 1878, Defap.

128 **He said that this work:** Taylor, 6 November 1878, Defap.

129 **In the end:** Procès-verbaux, 9 December 1878, Defap.

129 **he would soon form:** *Asile*, 1879.

129 **But Taylor wrote:** Taylor, 7 September 1878, Defap.

129 **Not long after his return:** Taylor letter to subscribers, 22 October 1878, Defap.

130 **In October:** Taylor, 7 October 1878, Defap.

130 **"On the day of the baptism":** Taylor to director, 22 October 1878, Defap.

130 **pastor's robes:** A letter mentions that Taylor prefers to preach in

robes, although the new generation is more secular in appearance. Taylor, 6 November 1878, Defap.

130 **"After the sermon, and":** Taylor to director, 22 October 1878, Defap.

25. The Fifteen Captives of Ndiack Ndiaye

131 **In 1878, the court in Saint Louis:** Ndiack Ndiaye dossier appears in ANOM, Sénégal XIV/15C. All information about his case, the origin of the enslaved people, and debates about the outcome are from that file.

133 **All people born in Gorée and Saint Louis:** The interplay between French subjects and French citizens played a big role in many policy decisions. See Catherine Coquery-Vidrovitch, "Nationalité et citoyenneté en Afrique occidentale français: Originaires et citoyens dans le Sénégal colonial," *Journal of African History* 42, no. 2 (2001): 285–305.

133 **When it concerned the enslaved:** The unequal application of the free-soil principle is covered by Mamadou Badji, "L'abolition de l'esclavage au Sénégal: Entre plasticité du droit colonial et respect de l'Etat de droit," *Droit et cultures. Revue internationale interdisciplinaire* 52 (2006): 239–274.

134 **"Article 5":** Cited in Victor Schœlcher, *L'esclavage au Sénégal en 1880* (Paris: Librairie centrale des publications populaires, 1880), 8–9.

134 **A close reading of a letter:** 26 June 1879, ANOM Senegal XIV/15c.

135 **What the administrators:** The practice of purchasing the liberty of an enslaved person is covered well in François Renault, "L'abolition de l'esclavage au Sénégal: L'attitude de l'administration française (1848–1905)," *Revue française d'histoire d'outre-mer* 58, no. 210 (1971): 20–30, 52.

135 **The French colonial military:** Myron Echenberg, *Colonial Conscripts: The Tirailleurs Sénégalais in French West Africa, 1857–1960* (Portsmouth, NH: Heinemann, 1991), 7–18.

136 **One reason:** Elements of Bou-el-Mogdad's biography are from David Robinson, *Paths of Accommodation: Muslim Societies and French Colonial Authorities in Sénégal and Mauritania, 1880–1920* (Athens: Ohio University Press, 2000), 83–85; Tamba Eadric M'bayo, *Muslim Interpreters in Colonial Senegal, 1850–1920* (New York: Lexington Books, 2016), 39–46.

137 **The governor wrote to the minister:** 8 December 1878, ANOM Senegal XIV/15c.

137 **That year, yellow fever had already broken. . . . "Would Kajoor":** Ibid. 1 August 1878.

138 **The territory defined as French land:** Renault, "L'abolition," 14–15.

138 **The slaveholding population was worried:** 4 January 1879 (situation politique) ANS 13G 309.

138 **In the end:** Renault, "L'abolition," 13.

26. The Future of France

139 **France in the 1870s:** A.S. Kanya-Forstner, *The Conquest of the Western Sudan* (Cambridge: Cambridge University Press, 2008), 60.

139 **In early 1878, a French explorer:** Paul Soleillet and Gabriel Gravier, *Voyage à Ségou, 1878–1879* (Paris: Challamel aîné, 1887), 11–13.

139 **he marveled at what he saw:** See Paul Soleillet, *Les voyages et découvertes de Paul Soleillet dans le Sahara et dans le Soudan, en vue d'un projet d'un chemin de fer transsaharien. Raconté par lui-même, rédigés sur ses mémoires, notes et carnets de voyage et sténographié sur ses conversations par Jules Gros. Préf. Par E. Levasseur* (France: M. Dreyfous, 1881), 145.

140 **Once he arrived:** Ibid.

140 **He also met:** Soleillet and Gravier, *Voyage à Ségou*, 23–24.

140 **And so Soleillet set off:** Ibid., 1–8.

140 **A few years before this trip:** Paul Soleillet, *Exploration du Sahara central: Avenir de la France en Afrique* (Paris: Challamel aîné, 1876), 48.

140 **A train connecting Algiers to Senegal:** Ibid., 53.

140 **"When the idea first arose":** Ibid., 48–49.

141 **Soleillet sailed up:** Soleillet and Gravier, *Voyage à Ségou*, 26–36.

141 **The Joliba:** Mungo Park, *Travels in the Interior Districts of Africa: Performed Under the African Association, in the Years 1795, 1796, and 1797*, 3rd ed. (London: printed by W. Bulmer and Co., for the author; and sold by G. and W. Nicol, 1799), vol. 1, 194–195.

141 **Awaiting more funds:** Soleillet and Gravier, *Voyage à Ségou*, 455–456.

141 **Walter Taylor said:** Taylor, 7 February 1880, Defap.

141 **Soleillet addressed the administrative council:** *Moniteur du Sénégal*, 8 April 1879.

141 **In France, railroad boosters:** See Paul E. Pheffer, *Railroads and Aspects of Social Change in Senegal* (ProQuest Dissertations Publishing, 1975), 23–51.

141 **In September of 1879:** On the treaty intermediary Bou-el-Mogdad, see Germaine Ganier, "Lat Dyor et le chemin de fer de l'arachide, 1876–1886," *Bulletin de l'IFAN* XXVII, nos. 1–2 (1965): 228; I imagine the landscape during his journey using details from Mbaye Guèye, *Les transformations des sociétés wolof et sereer de l'ère de la conquête à la mise en place de l'administration coloniale: 1854–1920* (Dakar: UCAD,

FLSH. Diss. thèse d'Etat, 1990), 19, who describes the topography of the region. And details about Lat Joor's compound come from ANS 1G 48 and, for description of the tata, Dupré, *La campagne du Cayor en 1883* (French Edition), FeniXX réédition numérique (Kindle Edition).

142 **the diplomat persuaded Lat Joor:** The treaty and addendum in their entirety appear in the appendices of Ganier, "Lat Dyor," 261–264.

142 **"You must understand":** ANOM Senegal IV/98A, Lat Joor to Governor, 17 September 1879.

142 **Lat Joor's change of heart:** See Mamadou Diouf, *Le Kajoor au XIXe siècle: Pouvoir ceddo et conquête coloniale* (Paris: Karthala, 2014), 257–270; James F. Searing, *"God Alone Is King": Islam and Emancipation in Senegal: The Wolof Kingdoms of Kajoor and Bawol, 1859–1914* (Portsmouth, NH: Heinemann, 2002), 48–57.

142 **Over the years:** The relationship between Lat Joor and Demba Waar Sall is storied in the oral tradition. See Assane M. Samb, *Cadior Demb: Essai sur l'histoire du Cayor* (Dakar: Nouvelles Éditions Africaines, 1981); Bassirou Dieng, *L'épopée du Kajoor: Poétique et réception*, 2 tomes (thèse de doctorat d'Etat des Lettres, Université de la Sorbonne Nouvelle, Paris III, Paris, 1987).

143 **One of the clerics said:** Omar Niang, quoted in Searing, *"God Alone,"* 50.

143 **a *jaami-buur*:** See Abdoulaye Bara Diop, *La sociéte wolof* (Paris: Karthala, 1981), 115–120.

143 **Even at the time:** "Mission Valière dans le Cayor," 9 August 1879, ANS 1G 48.

143 **In June of 1879:** 22 June 1879, ANS 13G 260.

144 **On its face:** "Mission Valière dans le Cayor," 9 August 1879, ANS 1G 48.

144 **"The people of Kajoor":** Ibid.

144 **Ibra Fatim:** Ibid.

145 **"Those who are inciting":** Ibid.

145 **who was still just a teenager:** Ganier, "Lat Dyor," 249, says he was 24 in 1885, making him just 18 in 1879.

145 **"What did Ibra want":** "Mission Valière dans le Cayor," 9 August 1879, ANS 1G 48.

27. A Word on Freedom

147 **The 1848 French proclamation:** Mbaye Guèye, *Les transformations des sociétés wolof et sereer de l'ère de la conquête à la mise en place de*

l'administration coloniale: 1854–1920 (Dakar: UCAD, FLSH. Diss. thèse d'Etat, 1990), 644–645.

148 **the dispensary in Saint Louis:** 9 November 1849, on prostitution, ANOM Senegal XI/4C.

148 **Other newly freed people:** Alain Sinou, *Comptoirs et villes coloniales du Sénégal: Saint-Louis, Gorée, et Dakar* (Paris: Karthala, 1993), 114.

148 **"The new freedmen do exactly":** Cited in Denise Bouche, *Les villages de liberté en Afrique noire française 1887–1910* (Paris: Mouton, 1968), 54.

148 **Later, as one century turned to the next:** Ibid., 79–89.

148 **On the Rio Pongo:** See Mamadou Camara Lefloche, "Traditions orales, traitement occulte et domptage de l'esclave au Rio Pongo," in *Traditions orales et archives de la traite négrière*, Djibril Tamsir Niane (ed.) (Brussels: UNESCO, 2001).

148 **"any runaway":** Ibid., 39.

148 **Underneath an old:** Ibid.

149 **In another village:** Personal interview with Daouda Camara, Region of Dagana, February 2019.

149 **Across the region:** On options for the formerly enslaved, see Bernard Moitt, "Slavery and Emancipation in Senegal's Basin: The Nineteenth and Twentieth Centuries," *International Journal of African Historical Studies* 22, no. 1 (1989): 41–49.

28. The Civilizing Mission

151 **Samba Coumba was among:** Taylor, 22 October 1878, Defap.

151 **A month after Samba Coumba's baptism:** Taylor, 22 November 1878, Defap.

151 **including Illou Seck:** Taylor, 6 January 1879, 22 January 1880, and 7 February 1880, Defap. Both letters mention Samba Coumba's evangelization activities.

152 **Taylor often talked about the hidden effects:** See *Asile*, 1880–1881.

152 **"We must instruct them carefully":** Taylor to Schulz, 7 March 1879, Defap.

152 **When some members had trouble:** Taylor, 22 November 1878, Defap.

152 **When a few others had difficulty:** Taylor, 22 September 1879, Defap.

152 **In a short amount of time:** Taylor to Director, 7 March 1879, Defap.

152 **"In a little while":** Ibid.

152 **Writing to contributors:** *Asile*, 1879–1880.

152 **On the days that Taylor:** Details about the classes comes from *Asile*, 1880–1881.

153 **Taylor recounted an interaction:** *Asile*, 1880–1881.

153 **"I then arranged for a fire"**: Ibid.

153 **Many colonial officials:** See Mbaye Guèye, *Les transformations des sociétés wolof et sereer de l'ère de la conquête à la mise en place de l'administration coloniale: 1854–1920* (Dakar: UCAD, FLSH. Diss. thèse d'Etat, 1990), 509; François Renault, "L'abolition de l'esclavage au Sénégal: L'attitude de l'administration française (1848–1905)," *Revue française d'histoire d'outre-mer* 58, no. 210 (1971): 34.

153 **Gaspard Devès, was known to speak in not-so-flattering:** See, Devès to Governor, 3 April 1882, Defap.

154 **"The first converts were just like":** Taylor to Schulz, 7 March 1879, Defap.

154 **"One of them recently refrained":** Taylor, 22 April 1879, Defap.

154 **Model subjects also needed:** Taylor, 22 January 1880, Defap.

154 **Taylor bragged about officiating:** Taylor, 22 September 1879, Defap.

154 **Marriage not only helped people:** See Hilary Jones, *The Métis of Senegal: Urban Life and Politics in French West Africa* (Bloomington: Indiana University Press, 2013), ch. 3.

155 **when he read about the war the British:** Taylor, 22 November 1879, Defap.

155 **Some hints may come:** See Robert W. July, *The Origins of Modern African Thought: Its Development in West Africa During the Nineteenth and Twentieth Centuries* (New York: F.A. Praeger, 1968), 130–154.

155 **Nicol had:** Ibid., 143.

156 **Not long after coming back:** Taylor, 7 October 1878, Defap.

156 **his trade empire:** See David Robinson, *Paths of Accommodation: Muslim Societies and French Colonial Authorities in Sénégal and Mauritania, 1880–1920* (Athens: Ohio University Press, 2000), 110; Jones, *Métis du Sénégal*, 57–58; François Manchuelle, "Métis et colons: La famille Devès et l'émergence politique des Africains au Sénégal, 1881–1897," *Cahiers d'études africaines* 24, no. 96 (1984): 477–504.

156 **Devès's deputy mayor:** Crespin's name occasionally shows up on lists for various special collections for the Senegal mission.

156 **Crespin had spent years as a merchant:** See Nigel Browne-Davies, "Jewish Merchants in Sierra Leone, 1831–1934," *Journal of Sierra Leone Studies* 6, no. 2 (October 2017): 3–110; July, *Modern African Thought*, 243.

157 **Crespin and Taylor also belonged:** Jones, *Métis du Senegal*, 111.

157 **"good French workers":** Ibid., 110–112.

157 **Devès was a powerful and generous ally:** Taylor, 6 December 1878, 13 February 1879, Defap.

157 **especially since his own family's record:** See Robinson, *Paths*, 108–116.

157 **On at least one occasion in 1880:** Taylor, 7 February 1880, Defap.

157 **Devès was opposed by the colonial establishment:** Gaspard Devès's marriage to Madeleine Tamba worked for him electorally in Guet Ndar, according to Jones, *Métis du Senegal*, 141.

157 **Soon after joining:** Taylor, 22 April 1879, Defap.

29. A Stain That Must Be Washed

159 **It was the first of March in 1880:** Most details from this chapter come from Victor Schœlcher, *L'esclavage au Sénégal en 1880* (Paris: Librairie centrale des publications populaires, 1880).

159 **he had finally been recognized:** Anne Girollet, *Victor Schœlcher, républicain et franc-maçon* (Saint-Pierre-de-l'Isle: Éditions maçonniques de France, 2018), 79.

159 **the audience interrupted:** Schœlcher, *L'esclavage au Sénégal*, 12.

159 **"In 1876":** Ibid., 18.

160 **When his father:** See Ernest Legouvé, *Soixante ans de souvenirs* (Paris: J. Hetzel, 1888), 93–116.

160 **When noted American abolitionist:** Theodore Stanton, "Frederick Douglass on Toussaint L'Ouverture and Victor Schœlcher," vol. 17 (Chicago: Open Court Pub. Co., 1903).

161 **Mr. Schœlcher said:** Schœlcher, *L'esclavage au Sénégal en 1880*, 93.

161 **One of the letters:** 12 September 1879, *L'Eglise Libre*.

161 **about six months before Mr. Schœlcher's display:** Ibid.

161 **Soon, another letter:** 26 September 1879, *L'Eglise Libre*.

30. A Delicate Business

165 **Taylor would get the full details:** Director's register, 2 March 1880, Defap.

165 **Jauréguiberry, who was a member:** For details about his biography, see Jauréguiberry's obituary, *JME*, 1887, 401–402.

165 **During that same year:** See Victor Schœlcher, *L'esclavage au Sénégal en 1880* (Paris: Librairie centrale des publications populaires, 1880), 8–9.

165 **Jauréguiberry defended the policy:** Ibid., 29–45; quotation: p. 37.

166 **"It's very unfortunate":** Director's register, 2 March 1880, Defap.

166 **Taylor wrote back:** Taylor, 22 March 1880, Defap.

166 **he was pleased with one aspect:** Director's register, 2 March 1880, Defap.

166 **No one on the Paris committee:** Procès-verbaux, 15 March 1880, Defap.

166 **When Villéger's detailed letters:** Taylor, 22 October 1879, Defap.
166 **fourth child:** Taylor, 6 December 1879, Defap.
167 **But as the controversy picked up:** Ibid. Taylor mentions Villéger's having written to the evangelist Mademba Guèye.
167 **He wrote in even stronger terms:** Ibid.
167 **Even as Jauréguiberry:** See ANOM Senegal XIV/15d and N'diaye, "La colonie du Sénégal au temps de Brière de l'Isle."
167 **A couple of months:** Brière to Minister, 8 June 1880, ANOM Senegal XIV/15d.
167 **"I have given you these details":** Ibid.
168 **In March, he wrote to the director:** Taylor, 22 March 1880, Defap.
168 **In a letter several months later:** Taylor, 23 August 1880, Defap.
168 **Taylor cited:** Taylor, 22 March 1880, Defap.
168 **In the days and maybe even months:** This is suggested by Golaz in early 1881. See Golaz, 9 March 1881, Defap.
169 **his political ally:** Taylor, 23 August and 22 September 1880, Defap.
169 **In October, after a month of suffering:** Taylor, 7 October 1880, Defap.
169 **After Taylor's ordination:** Taylor, 7 September 1878, Defap.
169 **Marzolff may not have been:** Procès-verbaux, 9 October 1878, and Director's register, October 1878, Defap.
169 **It was for the best, since:** See Kalala J. Ngalamulume, *City Growth, Health Problems, and Colonial Government Response: Saint-Louis (Senegal), from Mid-Nineteenth Century to the First World War* (ProQuest Dissertations Publishing, 1996), 201–204.
169 **The committee agreed:** Procès-verbaux, 22 July 1878, Defap.
170 **In September 1879:** Taylor, 22 September 1879, Defap.
170 **And in January 1880:** Taylor, 22 January 1880, Defap.
170 **Soon, a candidate emerged:** Director's register, 17 January 1880 and 4 October 1880, Defap.

31. You Will Find Only Jackals and Hyenas
171 **Just as Governor Brière de l'Isle:** See ANOM Senegal IV/98A and Senegal XII/53B.
171 **Following the tension:** Mbaye Guèye, *Les transformations des sociétés wolof et sereer de l'ère de la conquête à la mise en place de l'administration coloniale: 1854–1920* (Dakar: UCAD, FLSH. Diss. thèse d'Etat, 1990), 370.
171 **Lat Joor did move:** He says he has moved near Soguère in a letter to the governor on 4 March 1880, ANS 13G 259.
171 **the young man as his heir apparent:** Samba Lawbé is referred to as the "petit damel" in some colonial documents in ANS 1D 40.

172 **The treaty on the railroad:** Mamadou Diouf, *Le Kajoor au XIXe siècle: Pouvoir ceddo et conquête coloniale* (Paris: Karthala, 2014), 269.

172 **Lat Joor was himself:** 22 April 1881, ANS 13G 261.

172 **The formal letter about the railroad:** 27 April 1881, ANOM, Senegal IV/98A.

172 **Just a couple of weeks into:** Brière de l'Isle to Minister, May 1881, ANOM Senegal IV/98A.

173 **Instead, the governor:** Governor to Lat Joor, 28 April 1881, ANOM Senegal IV/98A.

173 **But the man who had brokered:** Bou-el-Mogdad died in October of 1880. See *Moniteur*, 1880, 244.

173 **When Lat Joor had received word:** 14 November 1880, ANS 13G 260.

173 **Brière had said:** Quoted in David Robinson, *Paths of Accommodation: Muslim Societies and French Colonial Authorities in Sénégal and Mauritania, 1880–1920* (Athens: Ohio University Press, 2000), 83.

173 **The new qadi:** Ibid., 83.

173 **The new qadi's visit:** Reported in letter from Samba Lawbé to the Governor, 21 May 1881, in ANOM Senegal IV/98A.

173 **The governor soon wrote:** Ibid., 11 May 1881.

174 **Samba Lawbé's next letter:** Ibid., 29 May 1881.

32. A Colleague and a Partner

175 **Georges Golaz thought the house:** All details pulled from Golaz, 22 February 1881, excerpted in *Asile*, 1880–1881; and Golaz letter to Casalis, 9 March 1881, Defap.

175 **From the speeches Golaz made:** *JME*, 1880, 425–427.

176 **Before leaving for Senegal:** *JME*, 1881, 84–85.

177 **First one night, then two:** Golaz, 9 March 1881, Defap.

177 **"When a poor slave":** Ibid.

177 **having grown up in a tidy Swiss town:** Golaz was born and grew up in Chaux-de-Fonds, Switzerland. "Neuchatel," 7 October 1880, *Feuille d'avis de Neuchatel*, 4.

177 **Saint Louis was an assault:** Descriptions derived from Golaz's letters on the city. Golaz, 1 April 1881, Defap.

177 **The Golaz couple's trip to Senegal:** Taken from Golaz's account, written on 22 February 1881 and excerpted in *JME*, 1881, 137–149.

179 **The Golazes settled quickly:** Golaz, 1 April 1881, Defap.

179 **Georges Golaz soon proved himself:** Golaz, 9 March 1881 and 1 April 1881, Defap.

179 **Golaz also undertook:** Golaz, 9 March 1881, Defap.

180 **Every couple of letters, Golaz would rant:** Golaz, 18 February 1881, Defap.

180 **In 1879, he decided:** Taylor, 7 March 1879, Defap.

180 **Taylor would finally get authorization:** On 18 June 1881, *Moniteur*, 146, a notice of a concession given to M. Taylor, measuring 8 hectares 6 ares.

181 **When Golaz arrived:** Golaz, 9 March 1881, Defap.

33. Since the Invention of the Peanut

182 **"This railroad will become":** *Moniteur*, 1879, Supplement, 56.

182 **the governor when he assured:** Ibid., p. 5.

182 **"Nothing is simpler":** Jean Marie Antoine de Lanessan, *Les plantes utiles des colonies françaises* (France: Imprimerie nationale, 1886), 103.

183 **Doctor Laurent Bérenger-Féraud:** Laurent Bérenger-Féraud, *Les peuplades de la Sénégambie: Histoire, ethnographie, moeurs et coutumes, etc.* (Paris: Ernest Leroux, 1879), 357.

183 **In 1880, a colonial official:** *Moniteur*, 1880, Supplement, 12–13.

184 **Émile Maurel:** Cited in Yves Péhaut, *La doyenne des "sénégalaises" de Bordeaux: Maurel et H. Prom de 1831 à 1919* (Pessac: Presses Universitaires de Bordeaux, 2014), vol. 1, 140.

184 **"The use of this machine":** Cited in Yves Péhaut, *Les oléagineux dans les pays d'Afrique occidentale associés au marché commun: La production, le commerce et la transformation des produits* (Paris: H. Champion, 1976), 381.

184 **And the Conseil General:** *Moniteur*, 1880, Supplement, 12–13.

34. Special Seeds

185 **In March 1881:** Golaz, 9 March 1881, Defap.

185 **Taylor wrote the committee:** Taylor, 22 June 1881, Defap.

185 **The committee members did not:** Procès-verbaux, 18 July 1881, Defap.

186 **the English liners:** Golaz, 6 August 1881, Defap.

186 **"a gnawing canker":** John Gamgee, *Yellow Fever: A Nautical Disease* (New York: D. Appleton and Company, 1879), preface.

186 **"special seeds":** J.C. Faget, *Mémoires et lettres sur la fièvre jaune et la fièvre paludéenne* (Nouvelle Orléans: Impr. du Propagateur Catholique, 1864), viii.

186 **The beginnings of the disease:** See https://www.cdc.gov/yelowfever /symptoms/index.html (accessed 17 July 2021); Henry D. Schmidt,

The Pathology and Treatment of Yellow Fever (Chicago: Chicago Medical Press Association, 1881).

186 **"The common mischievous":** See John B.C. Gazzo, *Yellow Fever Facts, as to Its Nature, Prevention and Treatment* (MF Dunn & Bro., printers, 1878), 9.

186 **In 1881, a Cuban doctor:** See Kalala Ngalamulume, "Keeping the City Totally Clean: Yellow Fever and the Politics of Prevention in Colonial Saint-Louis-du-Sénégal, 1850–1914," *Journal of African History* 45 (2004): 183–202, 188.

186 **Public health officials:** Ibid.

186 **The conventional wisdom:** See Gazzo, *Yellow Fever Facts*, 22–23; John M. Keating and Memphis Howard Association, *A History of the Yellow Fever: The Yellow Fever Epidemic of 1878, in Memphis, Tenn.* (Printed for the Howard Association, Memphis, TN, 1879), 21.

187 **Many cities also tried:** See J. A. Carrigan, "Yellow Fever in New Orleans, 1853: Abstractions and Realities," *Journal of Southern History* 25, no. 3 (1959): 339–355; Manoel da Gama Lobo, *The Swamps and the Yellow Fever, with Medium, Minimum and Maximum Thermometric, Barometric and Hygrometric [Observations] and Direction of Winds of the City of Rio De Janeiro During 26 Years* (New York, 1881).

187 **For treatment:** Keating, *A History of the Yellow Fever.*

187 **Golaz reacted:** Taylor, 23 August 1881, Defap.

187 **"Our poor governor":** Golaz, 6 August 1881, Defap.

187 **But he had other concerns:** Taylor, 23 August 1881, Defap.

188 **While long-suffering schoolteacher:** Ibid.

188 **In the day of my trouble:** Authorized King James version.

188 **They were both buried by nightfall:** Taylor, 23 August 1881, Defap. Also, Laurent Bérenger-Féraud, *Traité théorique & clinique de la fièvre jaune* (Paris: O. Doin, 1890), 904.

188 **A week later:** Taylor, 26 August 1881, Defap.

188 **Taylor was shattered:** Taylor excerpts Golaz's letter in his own. Taylor, 23 August 1881, Defap.

189 **It had been a deadly summer:** Kalala J. Ngalamulume, *City Growth, Health Problems, and Colonial Government Response: Saint-Louis (Senegal), from Mid-Nineteenth Century to the First World War* (ProQuest Dissertations Publishing, 1996), 213. Adama Aly Pam, *Fièvre jaune et choléra au Sénégal: Histoire des idées, pratiques médicales et politiques officielles entre 1816 et 1960* (thèse de troisième cycle, Université Cheikh Anta Diop de Dakar, December 2005), citing Pulvenis on p. 23.

189 **The bells:** Golaz relates the tradition of ringing the bells when some-one died when the epidemic first flared at the beginning of the year. Golaz, 9 March 1881, Defap.

189 **In December:** Taylor, 20 December 1881, Defap.

189 **The new village project:** *Aisle*, 1881–1882.

35. Interregnums

190 **Throughout the personnel changes:** ANS 13G 261.

190 **In early 1882, Lat Joor had:** Cited in Germaine Ganier, "Lat Dyor et le chemin de fer de l'arachide, 1876–1886," *Bulletin de l'IFAN* XXVII, nos. 1–2 (1965): 267.

190 **That governor:** Colonel Canard. See L. Jore and Yves J. Saint-Martin, "Le colonel de cavalerie Henri-Philibert Canard (1824–1894), spahi et gouverneur du Sénégal," *Revue française d'histoire d'outre-mer* 61, no. 223, 2e trimestre (1974).

191 **The governor was concerned:** Ganier, "Lat Dyor," 229–230.

191 **The minister:** Cited in Ganier, "Lat Dyor," 267.

191 **In a letter a couple of months:** Jauréguiberry to Governor, 2 May 1882, ANOM Senegal XIV/15e.

191 **The commerce, though, was already suffering:** Especially in the re-gions of Diander—a region of Kajoor that had been annexed two de-cades before, and in the port of Rufisque, where many peanuts from Kajoor found their way onto steamers bound for Bordeaux and Mar-seille. See ANS 13G 309.

191 **March 4, 1882:** Ibid.

192 **October 20, 1882:** Ibid.

192 **the railroad project itself had:** French Parliament finally authorized the spending in June 1882 with an initial estimated cost of 17,680,000 francs, according to Paul E. Pheffer, *Railroads and Aspects of Social Change in Senegal* (ProQuest Dissertations Publishing, 1975), 94–95.

192 **"For as long as I live":** Lat Joor, 25 July 1882, ANS 13G 261..

192 **Spies infiltrated:** See ANS 1D 40, which has several intelligence re-ports from secret informants.

192 **After the harvest:** Report, 9 November 1882, ANS 1D 40.

192 **"Lat Joor is only trying":** Undated document by the Thiès comman-dant titled "Renseignements sur les intentions de Lat Joor" in ANS 1D 40.

192 **And another report:** 18 October 1882 in ANS 1D 40.

193 **The French already knew of Lat Joor's:** 13 September 1882, ANS 1D 40.

193 **news came that Lat Joor:** Letter from governor to minister, 1 August 1882, ANS 13G 261.

193 **The governor sent a flurry:** See Mamadou Diouf, *Le Kajoor au XIXe siècle: Pouvoir ceddo et conquête coloniale* (Paris: Karthala, 2014), 272; and a report from 8 September 1882 in ANS 13G 261.

193 **Lat Joor also had his ways:** See note from 19 October 1882 in ANS 1D 40 and quotation from 4 November 1882 in ANOM Senegal IV/98A.

193 **The first railroad construction:** Alexis Bois, *Sénégal et Soudan: Travaux publics et chemins de fer* (Paris: Challamel aîné, 1886), 34–35.

193 **Lat Joor saw it as a provocation:** See letter to governor 17 November 1882 in ANOM Senegal IV/98A.

194 **In one neighborhood of Saint Louis:** Report, 1 August 1882 in ANS 13G 261.

194 **Reinforcements were requested:** See Ganier, "Lat Dyor," 233; Rapport des operation dans le Kajoor de la colonne commande par M. le Colonel Wendling, in ANS 1D 40; Instructions from Governor to Colonel Wendling, ANOM Senegal IV/98B.

36. The Propagation of French Culture?

195 **"You are all aware":** See *Asile*, 1881–1882.

195 **Most colonial schools:** See Kelly M. Duke Bryant, *Education as Politics: Colonial Schooling and Political Debate in Senegal, 1850s–1914* (Madison: University of Wisconsin Press, 2015), 12–20.

196 **Some Muslim parents:** Taylor, 6 May 1882, Defap.

196 **Muslim parents:** See *JME*, 1885, 390.

196 **In mid-1882:** Taylor, 7 August 1882, Defap. For context, see Martin A. Klein, *Slavery and Colonial Rule in French West Africa* (Cambridge: Cambridge University Press, 1998), 75, on children confided to habitants or administrative services.

196 **His tense relations:** See *JME*, 1883, 123.

197 **But the same problem:** Taylor, 7 August 1882, Defap.

197 **Into the breach:** Taylor, 7 February 1882, Defap.

197 **Taylor described his schedule:** Taylor, 7 August 1882, Defap.

197 **"Twenty boys!":** Ibid.

197 **Earlier in the year:** Klein, *Slavery and Colonial Rule*, 75.

197 **some members of the committee:** Procès-verbaux, 12 March 1883, Defap.

198 **Taylor even asked:** Taylor, 7 February 1882, Defap.

198 **Taylor wrote some months later:** Taylor, 6 May 1882, Defap.

198 **He explained:** Ibid., and Taylor, 7 August 1882, Defap.

198 **"In such a state of affairs":** *JME*, 1883, 127.

198 **Taylor summarized the different:** Ibid., 127–128.

199 **All that Taylor:** Ibid.

199 **The "native question":** Taylor, 7 August 1882, Defap.

200 **"to guarantee the continuation":** Ibid.

200 **It seems illogical:** quoted in Denise Bouche, *Les villages de liberté en Afrique noire française 1887–1910* (Paris: Mouton, 1968), 79–80.

200 **A memo from the minister:** Ibid.

200 **And in January 1883:** *L'Afrique Explorée et Civilisée*, 16–17.

200 **Taylor announced:** *Asile*, 1882–1883.

201 **Bethesda:** See Gospel of John, chapter five.

37. The Damel

205 **In the nineteenth century:** This chapter blends the version in Assane M. Samb, *Cadior Demb: Essai sur l'histoire du Cayor* (Dakar: Nouvelles Editions Africaines, 1981), with the Bassirou Dieng, *L'épopée du Kajoor: Poétique et réception*, 2 tomes (thèse de doctorat d'Etat des Lettres, Université de la Sorbonne Nouvelle, Paris III, Paris, 1987).

38. Bethesda

208 **"on either side":** Benjamin Escande, *Souvenirs intimes: Extraits de son journal et de sa correspondance* (Genève, Switzerland: Jeheber, 1898), 74; he describes the landscape and provides an estimate for how long the trip takes at full gallop, and writes descriptions of the village.

208 **an hour of walking:** *Asile*, 1883–1884, mentions that the Khor Bridge community is an hour away.

208 **Colonial officials were glad:** *Asile*, 1882–1883.

208 **Taylor also constructed a little hut:** Ibid.

208 **In 1884, a young lady:** Details about Coumba's wedding in Jaques, 28 February 1884, Defap.

209 **Most of the inhabitants:** *Asile*, 1883–1884.

209 **"I had to go and demarcate":** Ibid.

209 **The population of Bethesda would swell and then:** As early as 1886, Taylor, in *Asile*, said it was difficult to place more people on the land. Similar reflections occur in many annual reports. See also Hilary Jones, "Fugitive Slaves and Christian Evangelism in French West Africa: A Protestant Mission in Late Nineteenth-Century Senegal," *Slavery & Abolition* 38, no. 1 (2017): 76–94.

209 **masquerade groups called** *komo* **societies:** See Un Bambara de Saint-Louis, "La colonie Bambara de Ndioloffen et de Khor à Saint-Louis," *Notes Africaines*, no. 40 (October 1948): 18–20.

210 **"covered with a number":** Ibid.

210 **"a cap featuring an animal's":** Ibid.

210 **One woman:** *JME*, 1886, 439.

210 **And, saddest of all:** Ibid.

39. Poor Lat Joor

211 **The military offensive:** ANOM Senegal IV/98B.

211 **"Poor Lat-Joor":** Taylor, 7 March 1883, Defap.

211 **taking with him:** Dupré, *La campagne du Cayor en 1883* (French Edition), FeniXX réédition numérique (Kindle Edition).

211 **The French rounded up:** Germaine Ganier, "Lat Dyor et le chemin de fer de l'arachide, 1876–1886," *Bulletin de l'IFAN* XXVII, nos. 1–2 (1965): 236.

211 **As the military spread out:** ANOM Senegal IV/98B.

212 **After all, the instructions from the governor:** Ibid., 22 December 1882.

212 **Some notables:** 11 January 1883, ANS 1D 40.

212 **A certain Captain Dupré:** Dupré, *La campagne.*

213 **"Today, good, short and interesting stopover":** Ibid.; and in Wendling's report, ANS 1 D 40.

213 **When Dupré reached Lat Joor's:** Ibid.

213 **a young man called Samba Yaya:** 23 December 1882, ANS 13G 261.

213 **In February of 1883:** Taylor, 7 March 1883, Defap.

214 **Taylor wondered, like many others:** Ibid.

40. Go East!

215 **Walter Taylor again took up his pen:** 22 February, *Asile*, 1882–1883.

215 **that did not seem to be the case:** Taylor, 22 January 1880, Defap.

215 **"it would be dangerous":** Ibid.

215 **"Sometimes, to thwart the vigilance":** 22 February in *Asile*, 1882–1883.

216 **The colonial administration would:** François Renault, "L'abolition de l'esclavage au Sénégal: L'attitude de l'administration française (1848–1905)," *Revue française d'histoire d'outre-mer* 58, no. 210 (1971): 37.

216 **Taylor informed his readers:** 22 February in *Asile*, 1882–1883.

216 **"I will never forget all the setbacks":** Ibid.

216 **a representative of Trarza's emir:** ANOM Senegal XIV/16.

216 **Taylor told them about a tirailleur:** 22 February, *Asile,* 1882–1883.

217 **In fact, the events happening:** A.S. Kanya-Forstner, *The Conquest of the Western Sudan* (Cambridge: Cambridge University Press, 2008), 87–94.

217 **On placing the first brick:** Borgnis-Desbordes's speech of 5 February 1883, reprinted in *Moniteur,* 20 March 1883.

218 **Speeches like this:** See Daniel Laqua, "The Tensions of Internationalism: Transnational Anti-Slavery in the 1880s and 1890s," *International History Review* 33, no. 4 (2011): 705–726; Stig Förster et al., *Bismarck, Europe, and Africa: The Berlin Africa Conference 1884-1885 and the Onset of Partition* (New York: Oxford University Press, 1988); Alice Conklin, "Colonialism and Human Rights, A Contradiction in Terms? The Case of France and West Africa, 1895–1914," *American Historical Review* 103, no. 2 (April 1998): 419–442.

218 **Taylor, though, saw Borgnis-Desbordes's:** *JME,* 1883, 170–171.

218 **And, in this way, he underscored:** Ibid.

219 **Two years after the death:** *JME,* 1883, 454; on Morin's biography, in *JME,* 1885, 261, Morin mentions that his grandfather was Adolphe Monod. Jean-François Zorn, *Le grand siècle d'une mission protestante: La mission de Paris de 1822 à 1914* (Paris: Karthala, 1993), 738.

219 **Casalis had retired:** *JME,* 1882, 81–83.

219 **Jaques wrote a personal letter:** Jaques, January 1884, Defap.

219 **"He is so well known":** Ibid.

219 **The committee hoped:** *JME,* 1884, 11 and 109.

219 **The place Taylor and Jaques decided upon:** Boubacar Barry, *Senegambia and the Atlantic Slave Trade,* trans. Ayi Kwei Armah (New York: Cambridge University Press, 1998), 182–183.

219 **Ndaté Yalla, whose:** David Boilat, *Esquisses sénégalaises: Physionomie du pays, peuplades, commerce, religions, passé et avenir, récits et légendes* (Paris: P. Bertrand, 1853), 292–294.

220 **Taylor had been interested:** Taylor writes about meeting Sidya in 1873, in his 22 January 1884, Defap; on Sidya's biography, see Yves J. Saint-Martin, "Une source de l'histoire coloniale du Sénégal: Les rapports de situation politique (1874–1891)," *Revue française d'histoire d'outre-mer* 52, no. 187 (1965): 153–224, 192–202.

220 **As some still slept away:** Taylor, 22 January 1884, Defap.

220 **But he wasn't much impressed:** Ibid.

220 **"When we arrived in 'Kerbala,' ":** Ibid.

221 **"Some days earlier":** Ibid.

221 **This area was part of a larger:** Omar Sy, "Dynamiques environne-

mentales actuelles dans le Galodjina et politiques d'aménagement de l'espace dans le nord-ouest du Sénégal." Conference paper. *Changements socio-environnementaux et dynamiques rurales en Afrique de l'ouest*, July 2016, Paris, France.

221 **the region had been placed under:** Renault, "L'abolition," 37.

221 **The Bambara who lived in Kerbala:** Procès-verbaux, 18 October 1882, ANS 13G 111.

222 **Jaques's impressions on the subject:** Jaques, January 1884, Defap.

222 **"When I was telling the governor":** Ibid.

222 **By the end of 1884, Jaques:** *JME*, 1884, 47.

222 **Jaques would himself soon enjoy:** "Échos et nouvelles," 15 June 1885, *La Femme: Journal bi-mensuel*; *JME*, 1885, 328–332.

41. The Dawn of a New Era

223 **On the morning of July 27, 1883:** *Moniteur*, 1883, 163–166.

223 **The first handful of railroad:** Alexis Bois, *Sénégal et Soudan: Travaux publics et chemins de fer* (Paris: Challamel aîné, 1886), 34–37; Paul E. Pheffer, *Railroads and Aspects of Social Change in Senegal* (ProQuest Dissertations Publishing, 1975), 127, on Italian workers. And *Bulletin de la société de géographie commerciale de Bordeaux*, 8 June 1883, 464.

223 **"In a few moments":** *Moniteur*, 1883, 163–166.

224 **Officials boarded this vehicle:** Ibid.

224 **All of this ceremony:** Bois, *Sénégal et Soudan*, 34–37.

224 **"July 27":** *Moniteur*, 1883, 163–166.

224 **After Lat Joor fled:** Dupré, *La campagne du Cayor*.

225 **Lat-Joor:** In Bassirou Dieng, *L'épopée du Kajoor: Poétique et réception*, 2 tomes (thèse de doctorat d'Etat des Lettres, Université de la Sorbonne Nouvelle, Paris III, Paris, 1987), vol. 1, 502–504.

225 **Even if those leaders:** See Mamadou Diouf, *Le Kajoor au XIXe siècle: Pouvoir ceddo et conquête coloniale* (Paris: Karthala, 2014), 272.

225 **But Albury Njaay:** Mbaye Guèye, *Les transformations des sociétés wolof et sereer de l'ère de la conquête à la mise en place de l'administration coloniale: 1854–1920* (Dakar: UCAD, FLSH. Diss. thèse d'Etat, 1990), 386-407; Eunice Charles, *Precolonial Senegal: The Jolof Kingdom, 1800–1890* (Boston: African Studies Center, Boston University, 1977), 82–84, 106–110.

225 **Albury suffered:** Charles, *Precolonial Senegal*, 108–112.

226 **Lat Joor, former damel of Kajoor:** Charles, *Precolonial Senegal*, 110–112. Guèye, *Transformations*, 400; Claudine Gerresch, "Le livre de métrique Mubayyin al-Iškâl du Cadi Madiakhaté Kala," *Bulletin de l'IFAN* 36 (1974): 714–832, 759.

226 **Amary Ngooné Faal:** Diouf, *Kajoor*, 274–275.

226 **merchants in the coastal cities:** 11 May 1883, ANS 1D 40.

227 **At the beginning of May 1883:** Guèye, *Transformations*, 384.

227 **the French administration:** Diouf, *Kajoor*, 276.

227 **Samba Lawbé and his entourage:** Possibly Hyacinthe Devès? Undated letter in ANS 1Z 12.

227 **In the governor's political situation report:** Governor to Minister, 24 September 1883, ANOM Senegal IV/98C.

227 **According to one historian:** Yves Péhaut, *La doyenne des "sénégalaises" de Bordeaux: Maurel et H. Prom de 1831 à 1919* (Pessac: Presses Universitaires de Bordeaux, 2014), vol. 2, 42.

227 **Senegal exported:** Jean Adam, *Les plantes oléiferes de l'Afrique occidentale française. I. L'arachide, culture, produits, commerce, amélioration de la production* (Paris: Challamel, 1908), 118.

227 **The brand-new damel:** 23 September 1883, ANOM Senegal IV/98C.

228 **The terms of that treaty:** Reproduced in Germaine Ganier, "Lat Dyor et le chemin de fer de l'arachide, 1876–1886," *Bulletin de l'IFAN* XXVII, nos. 1–2 (1965): 276–277.

228 **Part of the Dakar-to-Rufisque section:** Paul E. Pheffer, *Railroads and Aspects of Social Change in Senegal* (ProQuest Dissertations Publishing, 1975), 102.

228 **Smaller and less congratulatory:** Ibid., 102–104; Bois, *Sénégal et Soudan*, 37–39.

228 **One tricky section of the line:** ANOM Senegal XII/53B, multiple documents on attacks and attempted derailments.

229 **Reports followed about:** Pheffer, *Railroads*, 125–128; 18 January 1885, ANS O 35.

229 **Still, the construction continued:** ANOM Senegal XII/53B.

229 **Finally, on May 12, 1885:** Pheffer, *Railroads*, 103, 112–113.

229 **Would train company officials:** 10 April 1885, ANS O 35.

229 **all of the speeches:** Documents on inauguration of 6 July 1885, ANS O 35.

230 **Just as his uncle had:** 2 September 1884, ANOM Senegal IV/98C.

42. We Have Already Proven That the Negro Is Capable

231 **In early 1885:** Taylor, 26 September 1885, Defap.

231 **"I only got up when I was told":** Ibid.

231 **"At the sight of the coast":** Ibid.

232 **Notice of Taylor's arrival would appear:** "General News," 11 April 1885, *Sierra Leone Weekly News* (hereafter *SLWN*).

232 **The most meaningful moment:** Taylor, 2 June 1885, and 26 September 1885, Defap.

232 **He would attend:** *SLWN*, 10 October 1885.

232 **guest preach:** Taylor, 2 June 1885, and August 1885, Defap. Taylor translated an article from *the Methodist Herald* about his guest preaching at a church.

232 **make inquiries about enrolling:** Walter and Samuel Taylor's names appear on the Grammar School's registers in early 1886 (students 1261 and 1262), which suggests that Taylor made arrangements for them while there in 1885. He also mentions making a visit to the school in a letter on 27 January 1886, and mentions the school fee issue on 28 January 1886, Defap.

232 **Taylor also got a chance:** Taylor, 27 January 1886, Defap.

232 **"It is true that we are far":** Taylor, 26 September 1885, Defap.

233 **That was how early Sierra Leonean:** See July, *Modern African Thought*, 143.

233 **Taylor's Bordeaux collaborators:** *Asile*, 1882–1883.

233 **The following year:** *Asile*, 1883–1884.

233 **one Moussa Tarawaré:** *Moniteur*, 1883, 154.

234 **Moussa was also impressing:** *Asile*, 1884–1885.

234 **Could they soon become like Sierra Leoneans?:** Taylor, 26 September 1885, Defap.

234 **"Thus, we must anticipate":** Ibid.

43. Lost and Found (Ephemera)
237 **September 27, 1886:** List from ANOM Senegal XII/53C.

44. Why Have the Peanuts Degenerated?
239 **Between Christmas:** "La nuit de Noël," *Le Reveil du Sénégal*, 3 January 1886.

239 **a columnist from:** Ibid.

239 **As the Dakar–Saint Louis:** Paul E. Pheffer, *Railroads and Aspects of Social Change in Senegal* (ProQuest Dissertations Publishing, 1975), 168.

239 **Merchants came:** Quoted in Pheffer, *Railroad*, 207.

240 **In Thiès, where the train:** Pheffer, *Railroad*, 178.

240 **Just over a month:** "Pourquoi les arachides de la Sénégambie ont dégénéré," *Le Réveil du Sénégal*, 30 August 1885.

240 **"People who have":** Ibid.

240 **In another article:** *Le Réveil du Sénégal*, 26 July 1885.

240 **"It is necessary":** Ibid.

240 **Farmers in Pondicherry:** Jean Adam, *Les plantes oléiferes de l'Afrique occidentale française. I. L'arachide, culture, produits, commerce, amélioration de la production* (Paris: Challamel, 1908), 116.

241 **Indian peanuts were of lower quality:** Ibid., 87.

241 **The overall price:** Bernard Moitt, *Peanut Production and Social Change in the Dakar Hinterland: Kajoor and Bawol, 1840–1940* (ProQuest Dissertations Publishing, 1985), 172–173.

241 **One observer:** Benjamin Escande, *Souvenirs intimes: Extraits de son journal et de sa correspondance* (Genève, Switzerland: Jeheber, 1898), 53.

241 **when merchants complained:** 12 March 1886, ANS 2B 75.

45. Kerbala

242 **During the rainy season:** See Jean-Yves Gac and Alioune Kane, "Le fleuve Sénégal: I. Bilan hydrologique et flux continentaux de matières particulaires à l'embouchure," *Sciences Géologiques, bulletins et mémoires* 39, no. 1 (1986): 99–130, 116–117.

242 **Jaques experienced:** *JME*, 1885, 447.

242 **"After solidifying":** Ibid.

242 **Soon after arriving:** *JME*, 1885, 267–268.

242 **Morin, who had been called:** *JME*, 1885, 274.

242 **His acquaintances in Dagana:** Jaques, 25 May 1885, Defap.

243 **"The ways of God":** *JME*, 1885, 217 (reportedly for 4 June letter).

243 **As the rains ended:** *JME*, 1886, 28–29.

243 **several structures:** See *JME*, 1887, 389.

243 **Jaques had requested:** Jaques, June 1886, Defap; *JME*, 1886, 28.

243 **A Decauville rail system:** Jaques, 24 November 1885, Defap.

243 **From all the justifications that Jaques:** *JME*, 1886, 64.

244 **By mid-February of 1886:** *JME*, 1886, 133–134, 304.

244 **For one, he discovered:** *JME*, 1887, 356–357.

245 **He discovered that the area:** On different reasons for Fulbe emigration, see John H. Hanson, "Islam, Migration and the Political Economy of Meaning: Fergo Nioro from the Senegal River Valley, 1862–1890," *Journal of African History* 35, no. 1 (1994): 37–60.

245 **Their grievances were many:** See François Renault, "L'abolition de l'esclavage au Sénégal: L'attitude de l'administration française (1848–1905)," *Revue française d'histoire d'outre-mer* 58, no. 210 (1971): 38–43.

246 **Jaques said in June 1886:** *JME*, 1886, 305.

246 **In 1884, when Jaques and Taylor:** Jaques, January 1884, Defap.
246 **Even after all this emigration:** Manetche report from Dagana, ANS K 18.

46. On the Run

247 **When the train had been completed:** Mamadou Diouf, *Le Kajoor au XIXe siècle: Pouvoir ceddo et conquête coloniale* (Paris: Karthala, 2014), 277–279.

248 **Samba Lawbé said he refused:** Joseph du Sorbiers de la Tourrasse, *Au pays des Woloffs: Souvenirs d'un traitant du Sénégal* (Paris: Alfred Mame et fils, Editeurs, 1897), 103–104.

248 **The French merchant:** Ibid., 106.

248 **he established a new policy:** Ibid., 108; See also Diouf, *Kajoor*, 277–279; Mbaye Guèye, *Les transformations des sociétés wolof et sereer de l'ère de la conquête à la mise en place de l'administration coloniale: 1854–1920* (Dakar: UCAD, FLSH. Diss. thèse d'Etat, 1990), 407.

248 **The trains ran once a day:** Early schedules in the *Moniteur* say 6:30 but other reports (Faidherbe, Escande) say 6:00 a.m.

248 **building up to:** A notice in the *Moniteur* on 6 May 1884 noted that the train was to run at speeds of 25 km/hour between Dakar and Thiaroye and 23 km/hour between Sebikotane and Pout.

249 **264 kilometers:** Alexis Bois, *Sénégal et Soudan: Travaux publics et chemins de fer* (Paris: Challamel aîné, 1886), 3.

249 **so passengers would spend:** Descriptions inspired from Benjamin Escande, *Souvenirs intimes: Extraits de son journal et de sa correspondance* (Genève, Switzerland: Jeheber, 1898), 63–65.

249 **The train had ticket prices to meet:** Paul E. Pheffer, *Railroads and Aspects of Social Change in Senegal* (ProQuest Dissertations Publishing, 1975), 193.

249 **a family arrived at the Tivaouane:** Details of this incident drawn from: Lt. Commandant in Thiès to the Director of Political Affairs, 12 September 1886, ANS K 12; and Interim Governor Henard to the Minister, ANOM Senegal I/75.

250 **So he dashed off a response:** Ibid.

250 **The interim governor wrote:** ANOM Senegal I/75.

250 **What happened after:** Details drawn from de la Tourrasse, *Au pays des Woloffs*, 109–113; Diouf, *Kajoor*, 279–280; Julian W. Witherell, *The Response of the Peoples of Cayor to French Penetration, 1850–1900* (ProQuest Dissertations Publishing, 1964), 122–123; Guèye, *Transformations*, 408–409; correspondence and report, ANS1D 48.

251 **According to de la Tourrasse:** de la Tourrasse, *Au pays des Woloffs*, 113.

251 **The whole colony was in shock:** Letter from the governor to the admiral, 8 October 1886, ANOM Senegal IV/99A.

251 **When he wrote to Paris:** Rapport politique de 12 October 1886, ANOM Senegal I/76A.

251 **And was the point of:** "Exécution de Samba Lawbé, damel du Cayor," 10 October 1886, *Le Réveil du Sénégal.*

252 **the governor attempted:** 28 November 1886, ANOM Senegal I/76a.

252 **Passing on the train:** Jaques, 14 October 1886, Defap.

252 **Strickland penned a cable:** 14 October 1886, *Despatches from the US consuls in Gorée-Dakar.*

47. Your Civilization Has Not Dazzled Him

254 **Moussa Tarawaré:** *Asile,* 1885–1886.

254 **Taylor wrote to his collaborators:** *JME,* 1886, 29–30.

254 **"a duly Frenchified":** Ibid.

254 **The young man:** *Asile,* 1885–1886.

254 **he would help Taylor out:** Ibid.

255 **"Your civilization has not dazzled him":** *JME,* 1886, 30.

48. This Land of My Ancestors

256 **Sometime in 1885:** Mbaye Guèye, *Les transformations des sociétés wolof et sereer de l'ère de la conquête à la mise en place de l'administration coloniale: 1854–1920* (Dakar: UCAD, FLSH. Diss. thèse d'Etat, 1990), 400.

256 **He reassured the governor:** 11 October 1886, ANS 1D 48.

256 **Lat Joor said:** Ibid.

256 **The former damel:** See letter 15 October and 18 October 1886, ANS 1D 48.

257 **The editorial board of *Le Réveil*:** "La situation," 17 October 1886, *Le Réveil du Sénégal.*

257 **Officials in Saint Louis:** Report 15 October 1886, ANOM Senegal I/76a.

257 **What if, they wondered:** Paul E. Pheffer, *Railroads and Aspects of Social Change in Senegal* (ProQuest Dissertations Publishing, 1975), 133–134; Mamadou Diouf, *Le Kajoor au XIXe siècle: Pouvoir ceddo et conquête coloniale* (Paris: Karthala, 2014), 280–282; and Mbaye Guèye, *Les transformations des sociétés wolof et sereer de l'ère de la conquête à la mise en place de l'administration coloniale: 1854–1920* (Dakar: UCAD, FLSH. Diss. thèse d'Etat, 1990), 410–412.

258 **The last section:** ANOM Senegal IV/99A.

258 **"Upon the reading of this":** Situation politique, 14 November 1886, ANOM Senegal I/76a.

258 **"to prevent looting":** Ibid.

258 **But even as the French received:** Rapport Vallois, 27 October 1886, ANS 1D 48.

259 **In the epic poems:** Bassirou Dieng, *L'épopée du Kajoor: Poétique et réception*, 2 tomes (thèse de doctorat d'Etat des Lettres, Université de la Sorbonne Nouvelle, Paris III, Paris, 1987), vol. 1, 510.

259 **"The enemy was totally defeated":** Rapport Vallois, 27 October 1886, ANS 1D 48.

259 **A telegram came from the mayor:** 27 October 1886, ANS 1D 48.

259 **For months, *Le Réveil*:** 13 November 1886, ANOM Senegal I/76a.

259 **The American consul:** 4 November 1886, *Despatches from the US consuls in Gorée-Dakar.*

260 **"Here in Kajoor":** Assane M. Samb, *Cadior Demb: Essai sur l'histoire du Cayor* (Dakar: Nouvelles Éditions Africaines, 1981), 59.

49. A Peanut Fable

263 **Contrary to the epic poems:** On storytelling, see the introduction of Lilyan Kesteloot and Bassirou Dieng, *Contes et mythes du Sénégal* (Dakar: IFAN/Enda-éditions, 2000).

264 ***A long time ago*:** Collected by Ndiaga Thiam, published in Kesteloot and Mbodj, *Contes et mythes wolof* (Dakar: Nouvelle Editions Africaines/IFAN/Enda-éditions, 2006), 205–209.

50. One of the Most Delicate Questions

266 **The Confederation had:** Quoted in Germaine Ganier, "Lat Dyor et le chemin de fer de l'arachide, 1876–1886," *Bulletin de l'IFAN* XXVII, nos. 1–2 (1965): 255.

266 **but there was a French official:** Julian W. Witherell, *The Response of the Peoples of Cayor to French Penetration, 1850–1900* (ProQuest Dissertations Publishing, 1964), 126.

267 **Some of the semi-nomadic Fulbe:** Ibid, 130.

267 **Lat Joor's cousin and sometime ally:** Eunice Charles, *Precolonial Senegal: The Jolof Kingdom, 1800–1890* (Boston: African Studies Center, Boston University, 1977), 129–131.

267 **For those who stayed:** Bernard Moitt, *Peanut Production and Social Change in the Dakar Hinterland: Kajoor and Bawol, 1840–1940* (ProQuest Dissertations Publishing, 1985), 169.

267 **The head tax was one incentive:** See James F. Searing, *"God Alone Is King": Islam and Emancipation in Senegal: The Wolof Kingdoms of Kajoor and Bawol, 1859–1914* (Portsmouth, NH: Heinemann, 2002), 197–204.

267 **Reports from French officials:** See situation reports in ANS 2G series.

267 **January 1895:** ANS 2G 1-106.

267 **July 1897:** ANS_2G 1-110.

268 **May 1898:** ANS_2G 1-97.

268 **Even though the peanut export increases weren't linear:** Yves Péhaut, *Les oléagineux dans les pays d'Afrique occidentale associés au marché commun: La production, le commerce et la transformation des produits* (Paris: H. Champion, 1976), two volumes, 459.

268 **In the peanut-growing regions:** Searing, *"God Alone,"* 154–156.

268 **In 1893, another treaty:** Poulet report in Paul E. Lovejoy and Alexander Sydney Kanya-Forstner, eds., *Slavery and Its Abolition in French West Africa: The Official Reports of G. Poulet, E. Roume, and G. Deherme* (African Studies Program, University of Wisconsin-Madison, 1994), 32; Searing, *"God Alone,"* 153.

268 **A note in 1895 from the:** ANOM Senegal XIV/17.

268 **He underscored:** Ibid.

269 **In 1899, the director of native affairs:** Deherme report in Lovejoy et al., *Slavery and Its Abolition in French West Africa*, 141.

269 **A legal traffic in slaves:** Bernard Moitt, "Slavery and Emancipation in Senegal's Basin: The Nineteenth and Twentieth Centuries," *International Journal of African Historical Studies* 22, no. 1 (1989): 38.

269 **And the colonial administration:** François Renault, "L'abolition de l'esclavage au Sénégal: L'attitude de l'administration française (1848–1905)," *Revue française d'histoire d'outre-mer* 58, no. 210 (1971): 73–74.

269 **could claim land:** Anyone could acquire land in this way. See Dennis Galvan, *The State Must Be Our Master of Fire: How Peasants Craft Culturally Sustainable Development in Senegal* (Berkeley: University of California Press, 2004), 151; also Mohamed Mbodj, *Un exemple d'économie coloniale, le Sine-Saloum (Sénégal) de 1887 à 1940: Cultures arachidières et mutations sociales* (Thèse de 3e Cycle, Histoire, Université de Paris VII, 1978), 47.

270 **The colonial administration:** Denise Bouche, *Les villages de liberté en Afrique noire française 1887–1910* (Paris: Mouton, 1968), 146–153.

270 **"captives of the whites":** Andrew F. Clark, "Freedom Villages in the Upper Senegal Valley, 1887–1910: A Reassessment," *Slavery & Abolition* 16, no. 3 (1995): 311–330, 320.

270 **At the turn of the century:** Moitt, "Slavery and Emancipation," 44-45; Marie Rodet, "Escaping Slavery and Building Diasporic Communities in French Soudan and Senegal, Ca. 1880–1940," *International Journal of African Historical Studies* 48, no. 2 (2015): 363–386.

270 **Sharecropping and similar types of labor schemes have been a common:** T.J. Byres, *Sharecropping and Sharecroppers* (London: Taylor and Francis, London, 2005; 1983), 2–29.

270 **In Senegal, the nawetaans would:** Philippe David, *Les navetanes: Histoire des migrants saisonniers de l'arachide en Sénégambie des origines à nos jours* (Dakar: Les Nouvelles Éditions Africaines, 1980), 171–196.

271 **a French administrator in the northern town of Podor:** Quoted in Moitt, *Peanut Production*, 248.

51. A Child from the Dark Continent

272 **LATEST NEWS:** *JME*, 1888, 160.

272 **By 1888, much had changed:** Procès-verbaux, 9 April 1888, Defap.

272 **Jaques had quit:** Procès-verbaux, 1 December 1886 and 7 March 1887, Defap.

273 **Morin's immediate family:** Ibid.

273 **while Morin went upriver:** Taylor, 11 June 1886, Defap.

273 **to stop using the Anglican liturgy:** Taylor, 19 January 1887, Defap.

273 **Another incident:** Taylor, 22 November 1887, Defap.

273 **Morin discussed his "unfortunate words":** Morin, 4 June 1888, Defap.

273 **"Was I wrong":** Ibid.

274 **Taylor soon started writing:** Taylor, 22 November 1887 and 6 December 1887, Defap.

274 **Sally Margaret:** Taylor's daughter went to a school near Montauban. Taylor, 16 November 1888, Defap.

274 **Marguerite went despite:** Morin, 7 March 1888, Defap.

274 **Taylor himself spent eight months:** Taylor sent letters from or mentioned stops in: Geneva, Lausanne Rothau, Carcelles, Lausanne, Chaux-de-Fonds, Montbéliard, Lyon, Annonay, Tournon, Nîmes, Mulhouse, Montauban.

274 **The only check on his constant:** *JME*, 1888, 368.

274 **Taylor complained about the cold:** Taylor, 17 July 1888, Defap.

274 **since Morin's wife:** Ibid.

274 **the director pleaded with Morin:** Boegner to Morin, 5 July 1888, Defap.

275 **In advance of Taylor's visit to one Swiss town:** "Conférence mis-
sionaire," 2 September 1888, *L'Impartial.*

275 **The paper didn't review his speech:** 18 September 1888, *L'Impartial.*

275 **when he spoke during the missionary society's:** *JME*, 1888, 202–208.

275 **"that one seeks in Africa":** Ibid., 207.

275 **"While the missions postpone":** Ibid.

276 **compare his discourse with the speeches:** On Lavigerie and the
state of anti-slavery movements, see Daniel Laqua, "The Tensions of
Internationalism: Transnational Anti-Slavery in the 1880s and 1890s,"
International History Review 33, no. 4 (2011): 705–726.

52. Emaciated Lands

277 **Even as more people:** Bernard Moitt, *Peanut Production and Social
Change in the Dakar Hinterland: Kajoor and Bawol, 1840–1940* (ProQuest
Dissertations Publishing, 1985), 172–173.

277 **Émile Maurel:** Letter from Maurel to Lucien Enfantin, 26 March 1897,
ANS R3; See also Christophe Bonneuil, *Mettre en ordre et discipliner les
tropiques: Les sciences du végétal dans l'empire français, 1870–1940* (PhD
dissertation, Université de Paris-Diderot – Paris VII, 1997), chapter 6,
for a discussion of the approaches of Enfantin and other colonial
agronomists.

277 **The members of Senegal's Conseil General:** Conseil General Deliberations, 1895, 6–14, 268–272.

277 **to test out new cash crops:** Lucien Enfantin, "Les cultures du Sénégal et l'organisation agricole de l'AOF," *Bulletin de la Société nationale
d'acclimatation de France* 47 (1900): 350–371.

277 **In his letter of instructions:** Letter from Maurel to Lucien Enfantin,
26 March 1897, ANS R3.

278 **The initial results of Enfantin's experiments:** Enfantin, "Les cultures du Sénégal," 365.

278 **The new governor-general of French West Africa:** See Conseil General Deliberations, 1897, 12.

278 **other studies in the years after:** Henri Courtet, *Étude sur le Sénégal:
Productions, agriculture, commerce, géologie, ethnographie. Événements
depuis 1884* (Paris: A. Challamel, 1903), 9–10.

278 **Another agronomist objected:** Ibid.

278 **Years of research then ensued:** Jean Adam, *Les plantes oléiferes de
l'Afrique occidentale française. I. L'arachide, culture, produits, commerce,
amélioration de la production* (Paris: Challamel, 1908), 169–173.

279 **A merchant's experiment:** René Tourte, *Histoire de la recherche agricole en Afrique tropicale francophone* (Rome: FAO, 2005), v. 4, 234.

279 **At around the same time:** See Yves Péhaut, *La doyenne des "sénégal-aises" de Bordeaux: Maurel et H. Prom de 1831 à 1919* (Pessac: Presses Universitaires de Bordeaux, 2014), v. 2, 308–309; Bruijning in *Journal d'agriculture tropicale*, Nov. 1902, 348; Yves Péhaut, *Les oléagineux dans les pays d'Afrique occidentale associés au marché commun: La production, le commerce et la transformation des produits* (Paris: H. Champion, 1976), two volumes, 509.

279 **By the early 1900s:** On the Dakar–Bamako train, see Paul E. Pheffer, *Railroads and Aspects of Social Change in Senegal* (ProQuest Dissertations Publishing, 1975), 231–273.

279 **"Since the creation":** Émile Roubaud, "La lutte contre les insectes attaquant les arachides," *Bulletin des matières grasses*, 1920, 77.

279 **"emaciated lands":** Phrase from P. Pélissier, *Les paysans du Sénégal: Les civilisations agraires du Cayor à la Casamance* (Saint-Yrieix [Haute-Vienne], Fabrègue, 1968), 66.

279 **so worn out:** Péhaut, *Oléagineux*, 467–468.

53. Drink My Cup to the Dregs

280 **In late 1890, the Paris Evangelical Missionary Society's director, Alfred Boegner:** *JME*, 1891, 162.

280 **The twenty-two baptized members stood:** Ibid., 169.

280 **"Saved and rescued physically":** Ibid., 163.

280 **esteemed that although it had been a good strategy:** Ibid.

281 **This was added:** Rapport présenté par la commission des affaires du Sénégal, 1889, Defap.

281 **He wrote:** Procès-verbaux, 2 February 1891, Defap.

281 **Maybe Walter Taylor saw the writing on the wall:** Taylor to director, 14 January 1891, Defap

281 **Although this was exactly:** Procès-verbaux, 2 March 1891, 3 April 1891, 6 April 1891, Defap.

281 **At one of the committee's meetings:** 2 March 1891, Defap.

281 **A couple of months later:** Procès-verbaux, 4 May 1891, Defap.

282 **Taylor was devastated:** Brandt, 15 July 1891, Defap.

282 **"A serious investigation":** Taylor, 8 July 1891, Defap.

282 **A week later:** Taylor, 16 July 1891, Defap.

282 **"cerebral congestion":** G.C. Roman, "Cerebral Congestion: A Vanished Disease," *Archives of Neurology (Chicago)* 44, no. 4 (1987): 444–448.

282 **"During my wife's absence":** Taylor, 16 July 1891, Defap.

282 **Bromide of potassium:** See Susan Lamb, "(Not) a Bromide Story: Myth-Busting Bromide of Potassium to Create a Case Study of Change and Continuity in Nineteenth-Century Medicine," *Pharmacy in History* 60, no. 4 (2018): 108–123.

282 **"After each illness":** Taylor, 16 July 1891, Defap.

283 **Whatever the truth:** Procès-verbaux, 1 June 1891, 6 November 1891, 9 November 1891, Defap.

283 **Walter Taylor and his family:** Taylor, 6 November 1891, 12 December 1891, Defap.

283 **In the weeks leading up to:** Brandt, 16 November 1891, Defap.

283 **domes as tall as cathedrals:** Description gleaned from the report of M. Maine, ingenieur en chef du services des douanes, in *Le mois colonial et maritime*, 1904, 315.

54. The Crushing Supremacy of the Peanut

285 **At the dawn of the new century:** See *Colonial Culture in France Since the Revolution*, edited by Pascal Blanchard et al. (Bloomington: Indiana University Press, 2013), chapter 3; Alexander C.T. Geppert, *Fleeting Cities: Imperial Expositions in Fin-De-Siècle Europe* (New York: Palgrave Macmillan, 2010), chapter 3.

285 **For the occasion:** See *L'Exposition universelle de 1900. Les colonies françaises. Le Sénégal: Organisation politique, administration, finances, travaux publics* (Paris: A. Challamel, 1900), 393–394.

285 **Merchants regularly extended credit:** Jean Adam, *Les plantes oléiferes de l'Afrique occidentale française. I. L'arachide, culture, produits, commerce, amélioration de la production* (Paris: Challamel, 1908), 105–109; Fouquet (in Joseph Fouquet, *La traite des arachides dans le pays de Kaolack et ses conséquences économiques, sociales et juridiques*, vol. 8 [Saint-Louis, Sénégal: Centre IFAN, 1958]) mentions one case of 100 percent interest in Saalum on pp. 64–65.

286 **The peanuts they bought:** See Adam, *Les plantes*, 57.

286 **The economic imperatives of the market:** Yves Henry, "Étude et avant projet d'amélioration de la culture de l'arachide," in ANS 1R 351.

286 **This was all the more tragic considering:** René Tourte, *Histoire de la recherche agricole en Afrique tropicale francophone* (Rome: FAO, 2005), vol. 4, 235.

286 **Whereas early merchants and colonial officials:** Auguste Chevalier, "L'agriculture dans nos colonies," *Bulletin de la société nationale d'acclimatation de France* (1912): 527–539.

287 **By the 1930s:** From Auguste Chevalier, "Monographie de l'arachide," *Revue de botanique appliquée et d'agriculture coloniale* no. 156, 606–610.

288 **The poor harvests and dropping oil ratios:** P. Pélissier, *Les paysans du Sénégal: Les civilisations agraires du Cayor à la Casamance* (Saint-Yrieix [Haute-Vienne], Fabrègue, 1968), 154.

288 **Already in the years between the great wars:** V. Faye, *Le travail agricole rural en milieux Wolofs et Sérères du Sénégal de 1819 à 1960* (PhD dissertation, 2016), 12.

55. What Remained

289 **Back in Freetown:** "January 1898," G3 A1 O, CMS Microfilm Reel 242.

289 **At some point:** Ibid.

289 **Walter Taylor was set to be ordained:** Ibid.

290 **The school committee:** Ibid.

290 **The last piece of correspondence:** Taylor, 6 August 1896, Defap.

290 **Eventually, in 1900, a missionary:** Moreau, Rapport sur Kerbala, 26 May 1900, Defap.

290 **For his part:** Taylor, 6 August 1896, Defap.

290 **There are, however, two letters from another Taylor:** Samuel Taylor, 18 August 1899 and 25 September 1899, Defap.

291 **printed a glowing obituary about:** *JME*, 1899, 418–419.

291 **fold ten years later in 1909:** *Asile,* Last report.

291 **"This circumstance":** Ibid.

291 **Some years earlier:** *Asile,* 1905–1906.

292 **"One day he got up":** Personal interview with Lamine Diankha, 2016. Cited from Jori Lewis, "Slaves of History," *Aeon,* 18 May 2015, https://aeon.co/essays/how-descendants-of-african-slaves-are-stigmatised-for-life.

Index

References to images are in *italic*.

About the Author

Jori Lewis is an award-winning journalist who writes about the environment and agriculture. Her reports have appeared in *Discover* magazine, *Pacific Standard*, and the *Virginia Quarterly Reviews*, among others. Jori Lewis splits her time between Illinois and Dakar, Senegal, and *Slaves for Peanuts* is her first book.

Publishing in the Public Interest

Thank you for reading this book published by The New Press. The New Press is a nonprofit, public interest publisher. New Press books and authors play a crucial role in sparking conversations about the key political and social issues of our day.

We hope you enjoyed this book and that you will stay in touch with The New Press. Here are a few ways to stay up to date with our books, events, and the issues we cover:

- Sign up at www.thenewpress.com/subscribe to receive updates on New Press authors and issues and to be notified about local events
- www.facebook.com/newpressbooks
- www.twitter.com/thenewpress
- www.instagram.com/thenewpress

Please consider buying New Press books for yourself; for friends and family; or to donate to schools, libraries, community centers, prison libraries, and other organizations involved with the issues our authors write about.

The New Press is a 501(c)(3) nonprofit organization. You can also support our work with a tax-deductible gift by visiting www.thenewpress.com/donate.